D1234270

The Fair Sex

The Fair Sex

*White Women and Racial Patriarchy
in the Early American Republic*

Pauline Schloesser

NEW YORK UNIVERSITY PRESS
New York and London

For Bette and Lee Schloesser,
and Toby and George Gleitman

NEW YORK UNIVERSITY PRESS
New York and London

Library of Congress Cataloging-in-Publication Data
Schloesser, Pauline E.
The fair sex : white women and racial patriarchy in the early American Republic /
Pauline Schloesser.
p. cm.
Includes bibliographical references (p.   ) and index.
ISBN 0–8147–9763–6 (cloth : alk. paper)
1. Sex role—Political aspects—United States—History—18th Century. 2. Women in
politics—United States—History—18th Century. 3. United States—Politics and
government—1775–1783. 4. United States—Politics and government—1783–1809.
5. United States—Race relations—Political aspects—History—18th Century.
6. Warren, Mercy Otis, 1728–1814. 7. Adams, Abigail, 1744–1818. 8. Murray,
Judith Sargeant, 1751–1820. 9. Political culture—United States—History—18th
Century. 10. Patriarchy—United States—History—18th Century.   I. Title.
HQ1075.5,U6 S39 2001
305.42'0973'09033—dc21   2001004049

An earlier version of chapter 4 appeared as "Lamenting the Loss of a Woman-centered Polity: Mercy Otis Warren's Critique of the U.S. Constitution," *Southeastern
Political Review* (September 1998): 545–70, and is reprinted here by permission.

Excerpts are reprinted by permission of the publisher from *Adams Family Correspondence*, vols. 1–4, edited by L. H. Butterfield and Marc Friedlander et al., and
vols. 5–6, edited by Richard Ryerson, Joanna Revelas, Celeste Walker, Gregg Lint,
and Humphrey Costello, Cambridge, MA: Harvard University Press, Copyright ©
1963, 1973, 1993 by the Massachusetts Historical Society.

Excerpts are reprinted by permission of the publisher from *The Adams-Jefferson Let-
ters: The Complete Correspondence between Thomas Jefferson and Abigail and John
Adams*, edited by Lester J. Cappon. Copyright © 1959 by the University of North
Carolina Press, renewed 1987 by Stanley B. Cappon.

New York University Press books are printed on acid-free paper,
and their binding materials are chosen for strength and durability.

Manufactured in the United States of America

10 9 8 7 6 5 4 3 2 1

Contents

Preface

I feel most colored when I am thrown up against a sharp white background. . . . Sometimes it is the other way around. A white person is set down in our midst. . . .

—Zora Neale Hurston, "How It Feels to Be Colored Me" (1928)

The Fair Sex: White Women and Racial Patriarchy in the Early American Republic stems from my dissertation, *A Feminist Interpretation of the American Founding* (1994). In my dissertation, I applied Carole Pateman's theory of modern patriarchy from *The Sexual Contract* to the historical case of the American founding. I viewed the American founding as the establishment of a modern patriarchy and focused on the political thought of three white women in that context.

After completing my dissertation, I accepted a position at a predominantly black, open-admissions university. As I began to prepare my dissertation for publication, my whole world view was being challenged. I taught four classes a semester to mostly first-generation college students. Most of my students worked, and many had children or other relatives for whom to care. I was the only white person in a department dominated by African American and African men, and less than 1 percent of my students were European American. I was also a Midwestern Yankee teaching in Houston, which was the Deep South to me.

There were culture wars in my own classrooms like I had never before experienced. I was idealistic. I wanted to give my students at Texas Southern University the same education that my Harvard-, Yale-, Berkeley-, and Wisconsin-educated professors had given me. I expected that if I put up the requirements and held firm to the standards, students would of course jump to meet them—the bright ones, anyway. The others would learn in time, if I held fast to my vision. It didn't work, and I was called a "missionary" by a colleague, and an "ice queen" by some students. I was arrogant and ignorant, and I had to change.

I was forced to begin to see things differently. Suddenly, it meant something to be "white." My sense of manners and virtues reflected a white, Anglo-Saxon, northern heritage, and generations of white privileges and inculcated northern European rationality. To make a long story shorter, I came to understand that the ethics, manners, and standards of excellence that I took for granted were mainly specific to the culture in which I was raised, and not universally valued in all contexts and circumstances.

Initially, my upper-level students did not revel in the abstract principles of political philosophy, nor did my freshmen take pleasure in knowing the rules of American political processes. Similarly, I was never successful at teaching a feminist theory course that wasn't very much grounded in the economics of everyday life. "Deconstruction" and post-structural theories were out of the question. Most of my students were in school to get a degree that would lead to a stable job, or that would at least keep them off the streets.

The black community at Texas Southern definitely had other cultural priorities than the ones I had brought to them. Knowledge and forms of expression were rooted in cultural memory and myth, of an African homeland, the experience of enslavement, black pride, frustration and anger, as well as an underlying hope of things better yet to come, in this world or the next. Ideas of the right, good, excellent, and beautiful reflected the priorities of cultural survival, which included visions of both cultural autonomy and multicultural inclusion. In the classroom, authenticity was more important than neutral objectivity, passion more welcome than detached reason, and understanding and care more important than erudition.

My new, situated understanding was transformative. For the first time, I experienced what it was like to be viewed as *white*. My students assumed, for example, that I was "rich" and "Republican." In previous teaching experiences at white universities in the Midwest, students saw me as "liberal," and they never let me forget that I was a woman. Early on, and for several years, I felt as though any resistance I got from students resulted from my *whiteness* rather than my femininity or my feminism. Of course, I now have a more complex view of the interrelatedness of race and gender, but those early impressions were the most formative.

Based on this new awareness of my own race and ethnicity, I was able to conduct my classes differently, and much more effectively. In a nutshell, I learned to make the most of diversity and its complexities. There were differences between my "minority" students and myself, differences between black and Hispanic students, differences between African and African American students, and within those categories, more differences: African Americans from the North and from the South, Baptists, Catholics, and Muslims; Africans from several countries, and then within those countries, religious differences. All of these differences affected the way students received me as a teacher, the material I was teaching, and whether and to what degree they would participate in class discussions, or accept the diversity within the classroom.

My students and I were able to transcend race and ethnic fears in the classroom one day at a time, through greater sensitivity. Awareness of and appreciation of differences led to conscious negotiations, compromises, and agreements. Attending to diversity with a sense of warmth and humor took a lot of effort, and the results were positive. Students became more cohesive and cooperative as a group, and there was a general air of excitement, stimulation, and mutual respect for one another. Students were more attentive in class, had more fun, and were more willing to take on new ideas that seemed foreign or irrelevant to them.

Teaching took on entirely new meanings. At its best, teaching political theory, for example, was anything but an empty ritual of exposing undergraduates to the "great Western canon." Western rationality in its grandest achievements and most gruesome brutality provided vital information for Africans and African Americans alike. To maintain an authentic connection in the classroom I was forced to interrogate social contract theory and American history, and to expose the culturally specific beliefs about God, human beings, justice, beauty, goodness, and racial and sexual differences that founded the political system we now have.

A complex understanding of this system provided vital information for my students' struggles to compete as individuals in a polity that had been designed without the consent of their ancestors, many of whom had lived in this country during the colonial period. A more complex understanding of the founding of our nation was also vital for my foreign national students. A few of my students from Nigeria and Ethiopia, for example, will return to their homelands, degree in hand, to lead the struggles for democracy and development. I now know that for them, ideas of the social contract and government by consent are radical, and the struggle for a rational polity and just development, literally a matter of life and death. And yet, their peoples and their cultures suffered in many ways by Western republicanism and democracy. Thus, teaching American politics and political theory was no longer an exercise of Western arrogance or empty ritual of transmitting "Tradition." Deconstruction was now a form of political activism to reveal the dehumanizing and violent side of Western republicanism. It was a practice necessary to avoid the schizophrenic experience of clinging to the mythology of Western republicanism (that everybody benefits; it takes no prisoners) while witnessing every day the struggles of its victims.

Obviously, a "feminist" analysis of the American founding was no longer sufficient. My concern with gender and patriarchy became eclipsed by issues of race, ethnicity, and class. A view of myself as oppressed by gender through family, work, and social life was now supplemented by a view of my life as quite privileged by race and class. I knew that I needed critical racial theory as well as critical feminist theory to adequately describe the intersectionality of race, class, and gender hierarchy.

In addition to the insights gained through teaching experiences, I must also credit the Republican Party for throwing into light their own cultural priorities when they came to dominate the U.S. House of Representatives in 1994. Newt Gingrich and Dick Armey had published their *Contract with America*, and William Bennet was writing books reminiscing about the devaluing of American culture and the virtues of the American Founders. The *Contract with America* called for sweeping changes such as the abolishment of the U.S. Department of Education, an end to welfare rights, and a serious diminution of affirmative action. Newt Gingrich argued that American "renewal" necessitated a return to the "one continuous civilization" of the "English-speaking" colonists. Our primary task toward that end, he claimed, was "teaching Americans about America and teaching immigrants how to become Americans." These conservative elites also tended to be anti-abortion, heralding the traditional roles of white women in domesticity as wives and mothers.

The pieces began to fall into place. I realized that the combatants against feminism and multiculturalism were now finding support among the ideas of the Founding Fathers. Hence, the roots for racism, sexism, and Anglo-American ethnocentrism must have existed with them. I went back to the archives and libraries, scouring the evidence that others had interpreted, looking at cultural contests to define American morals and values among the founding generation. The language they used was republicanism; they spoke about the common good, the good of the republic, and the virtues necessary to uphold this common good, and those vices which must be avoided to prevent chaos. It was the virtues associated with the Republic that held the key. American republican virtues were based on English cultural norms, adapted for the American project to build a new and better nation.

A renewed search followed two lines of inquiry. Primary and secondary sources on slavery, race, and ethnicity had to be examined in addition to those on women and gender in the early American Republic. A theory of the intersectionality of white supremacy and patriarchy had to be constructed, and as a result, the three women of my study are here viewed for the first time as white and Anglophilic, as well as gendered subjects. Mercy Warren, Abigail Adams, and Judith Sargent Murray are viewed as the "fair sex," rather than just "the sex." What follows is thus a theory of racial patriarchy in the United States, and a study of three members of the fair sex in that context.

Acknowledgments

I would like to acknowledge and thank the many persons who provided support that enabled me to complete the book. Joan Hoff believed in my project from the start, and stood behind me for ten years. Carole Pateman read my early work on patriarchy and the American founding and gave her encouragement. Sheila Skemp graciously shared her paper on Judith Sargent Murray and the Mississippi frontier, and alerted me of the existence of the Murray letters. Mark Kann and Patrick James both read the entire manuscript and offered helpful suggestions. Patrick James also generously served as a mentor for the past six years.

I had several important discussions on race and history with Kairn Klieman, whom I would also like to thank for warm friendship and consistent support. My dear college friend Lisamichelle Davis read the manuscript carefully, and hosted me for a weekend to clarify points in the theory of racial patriarchy. She made very helpful editorial comments. Katrina Price diligently read and commented on the page proofs.

I would like to express my gratitude to faculty and students at Texas Southern University who invited me into their community. Had I not had interactions with hundreds of students and faculty who openly shared their ideas and experiences, I would not have gained several insights that helped me analyze race in the early Republic. Two of my students, Yohannes Tsehai and Edna Johnson, deserve special mention for helping with some of the library research. I would also like to thank former president James Douglass, Dr. Gayla Thompson, and Dean Joseph Jones who graciously facilitated the reduction of my teaching load during the spring of 1999.

An earlier version of my chapter on Mercy Warren appeared as an article entitled "Lamenting the Loss of a Woman-Centered Polity: Mercy Otis Warren's Critique of the U.S. Constitution" in *Southeastern Political Review* (September 1998): 545–70. I thank Dr. George Cox at *Southeastern Political Review* for granting permission to reprint some of that material here. I would also like to thank the Massachusetts Historical Society for granting permission to quote from the Mercy Otis Warren Papers, the University of North Carolina Press for permission to quote from the *Adams-Jefferson Letters*, and Harvard University Press for permission to quote from the *Adams Family Correspondence*.

Several librarians also provided important assistance. Marcia Pankake, the American and English literature librarian from the University of Minnesota, helped me trace the phrase "fair sex" in English literature. Yvonne Schoffer, bibliographer and English librarian at the University of Wisconsin Memorial Library, secured the Judith Sargent Murray papers on microfiche for my research, and helped me access newspaper and magazine writings of the early national period. Richard Dickerson, the political science and history librarian at the University of Houston, provided assistance with citations via e-mail. Additionally, Gary Schroeder, computer systems manager at Texas Southern University, cheerfully took care of any technical problems I encountered.

I would like to thank many persons who generously provided accommodations in their homes to support my writing during winter and summer breaks: my parents, Bette and Lee Schloesser, and friends Mary Hillstrom and Olaf Meding, of New Glarus, Wisconsin, and Ursula Spilger, of Cloudcroft, New Mexico.

I would like to acknowledge and thank my editors at New York University Press: Stephen Magro, Jamison Stoltz, and Despina Papazoglou Gimbel. Stephen made an early offer on the manuscript with very little to go on. Jamison did the electronic editing, and Despina diligently oversaw the copy editing. I would also like to thank the anonymous reviewers for The *William and Mary Quarterly* who offered critiques of an earlier version of my fair sex thesis.

I owe a great debt of gratitude to Bette Schloesser, who generously supported me financially during my unpaid leave of absence from Texas Southern University during the spring of 2000. Lastly, I want to thank Dan Gleitman for redefining the role of husband and supporting me in every way. Dan, you're the best.

1

Race, Gender, and Woman Citizenship in the American Founding

White supremacy and patriarchy have always been part of American politics and culture. If we want to get beyond them in the twenty-first century, we must go back and understand their roots in the founding of the United States.

Scholarly debates on the American founding have only recently begun to put gender and race at the center of analysis. The field of American political thought, established and dominated by white male historians and political theorists, has centered on republicanism since the 1960s. With some notable exceptions, few works in the field have analyzed the construction of race and/or gender hierarchy in the founding period.[1] Most works in American political thought are still carrying out the task set forth in the 1960s, of interpreting concepts of republicanism in discourses among Anglo-American men. To that end, scholars have analyzed the founding generation's use of theoretical concepts such as virtue, liberty, political obligation, representation, and the public good without examining how they shaped race or gender relations in the American polity.[2]

During the mid-1970s, historians of women, made up mainly of white women, began to analyze the relationship between gender and republicanism in the Revolutionary era. Their works have ranged from criticisms of the founding for its patriarchal features, to a celebration of American republicanism for incorporating women into the polity as "republican mothers."[3] These works have suggested different answers to the question of whether and in what way we can consider "women" of the early Republic "citizens." In general, their focus has been on white women, and almost none have considered how the issue of woman citizenship had everything to do with racial identity.

What I am calling the "patriarchal" thesis holds that no women, white, or nonwhite, were considered citizens before the advent of woman suffrage, and may not be full citizens even today. The patriarchal thesis for the early Republic was put forth by Joan Hoff-Wilson in her 1976 article "The Illusion of Change: Women and the American Revolution." She argued that there was really no change in white women's legal status as a result of the Revolution; in fact, with respect to some rights, women actually lost power from their colonial status as monarchical subjects. Hoff had basically given evidence to suggest that the founders furthered the inequality of women in addition to excluding them from the rights of citizenship. Her 1991 book, *Law, Gender and Injustice*, showed that throughout American history, women had always been granted rights later than men, "too little, too late" to grant equality or equity with white males.

Hoff's studies of women's legal status confirmed Carole Pateman's analysis of modern patriarchy in *The Sexual Contract*.[4] In *The Sexual Contract*, Pateman demonstrated that patriarchy was intrinsic to Western republicanism through the gendering of spheres, and through the exclusion of women from the category of the rational human being capable of self-government. The "marriage contract" deemed wives subordinate to husbands, and simultaneously disqualified them for citizenship. Wives were viewed as *femes coverts* under the doctrine of coverture, and were thus subject to the rule of their husbands.

Subjective evidence from women's letters and diaries, however, suggested a more complex story of lived experiences. Linda Kerber and Mary Beth Norton had separately examined such subjective evidence and articulated an alternative to the patriarchal view. Kerber's *Women of the Republic* and Norton's *Liberty's Daughters* offered "difference" theses: that U.S. women were granted a gendered citizenship, as "republican" wives and mothers. Despite white women's inferior legal status, they had enjoyed a new uplifted and politicized role as wives and mothers who would exemplify the virtues so necessary for republicanism to children and husbands.

White women were valorized for exemplifying selflessness and the commitment to prioritize public interest over private gain. The issue of direct representation was minimized, on the grounds that women were not as a whole contending for it, and besides, women's voices were heard within the dynamics of family politics, which would then be translated to the public sphere through husbands, and later, sons. Hence, comparing white women with white men in terms of rights missed their different but equitable memberships in the polity. Proponents of the republican motherhood/republican womanhood thesis demonstrated that white women were indeed valorized for their efforts to model virtue and help maintain the Republic through their domestic roles.

Whether or not republican gender ideology mediated or undermined the development of modern patriarchy remains unclear. One major problem stems from a vagueness regarding the term "citizen." The traditional definition of a citizen is one who rules and is ruled in turn. In the republican motherhood thesis, it is not clear what a "citizen" is if that person does not have the legal rights normally accorded a legal citizen. If the proponents of republican motherhood mean to suggest that women had a share in ruling, through their roles as wives and mothers, their evidence is shaky at best. If they mean to redefine citizenship to mean something like inclusion without equal rights, then the concept is so distorted the question becomes meaningless. At the very least, such a redefinition begs further questions.

For example, what power or currency is granted by designating white women "citizens" as opposed to noncitizen members of the United States? What are the implications of viewing women as included in rather than excluded from the group citizens? Who remains outside the theoretical category of the citizen if white women are no longer there? One possibility seems to be that compared to unnamed others in the United States, who also lacked equal rights with white men, white women fared better. Since the concept of the woman "citizen" is cultural rather than legal for republican motherhood theorists, the burden remains on them to demonstrate in what ways women had the opportunity to rule rather than simply to be ruled, or alternatively, to explain on what basis they should be included in contrast to others who would be excluded.

The argument for woman citizenship in the early Republic has rested on white women's exemplary virtues, exercised through their roles as mothers and wives. As mothers, their political role was to rear patriotic and virtuous children. As wives, they were to reform and domesticate husbands. But this argument has not addressed the issue of family patriarchy: whether women experienced equal dignity in marriages or whether they were more or less subordinated.

Nancy Cott's recent book on marriage and the nation does not alleviate this ambiguity. Cott uses the term "citizen" at times to refer to the legal definition, which excludes women, and at other times to refer to the cultural, gendered definition offered by republican motherhood theorists. She suggests that the monarchical view of marriage, in which husbands govern, was "transformed" during the revolutionary era, toward a more contractual, egalitarian arrangement. Marriage became idealized as a "symmetrical union," characterized by mutual protection, economic advantage, and common interest. This view would seem to suggest that during the Revolution, the popular view of marriage was antipatriarchal. Later, in the post-revolutionary era, Cott notes that marriage became more hierarchical. Without examining the significance of this retrogression or the cyclical nature of wartime radicalism and postwar conservatism, Cott echoes the republican motherhood historians; she asserts the importance of women's virtues and manners for the maintenance of republicanism, but fails to address the inconsistency between a concept of woman citizenship that suggests equality in ruling power, and the restoration of family patriarchy, which does not.[5]

My aim in this book is to peer beyond the veneer of republicanism, to regard the larger cycle of wartime radicalism and postwar conservatism, and to scrutinize women's virtues for norms of racial, ethnic, sexual, and class hierarchies. Toward this end, a more fruitful and expedient question is whether and how white women became *modern subjects*, as white men generally did in the American Enlightenment and the movement for national independence.

Jurgen Habermas's distinction between "communicative" and "instrumental" rationality is useful to clarify this point. Communicative rationality is possible when persons are viewed as equals in a discursive situation, such that the validity of truth claims can be determined by the force of the better argument. In contrast, instrumental rationality takes place in a "distorted" situation, which precludes the intersubjective determination of normative claims. This distortion may result from a failure of intersubjective recognition, where one party is viewed as having authority over another, such that he fails to justify what he considers "right" to others, and will not listen to others justify their normative claims to him. In other words, ends are predetermined or coerced by one or more of the parties, and others are not allowed to debate or question those ends.[6]

In their more celebratory strains, republican motherhood proponents have suggested that white women enjoyed either an increase of power or equality with respect to white men. Kerber has argued that republican

motherhood ideology was an advancement for white women that successfully blended the domestic and public spheres, giving women a kind of political agency or voice that was new and different from the silencing and
exclusion they had experienced as colonial helpmeets. Kerber has also
noted that republican motherhood ideology was useful to justify education and political sensibility for women. Mary Beth Norton went further,
stating that in the post-revolutionary period, women were recognized as
different but "equal." Society "had at last formally recognized women's
work as valuable." The sphere of domesticity was no longer denigrated,
nor subordinated to the masculine sphere.[7]

Upon close inspection, however, most of the evidence presented by
the republican womanhood/motherhood proponents does not suggest
that women enjoyed discursive equality or communicative action in
their families. Indeed, Kerber's conclusion seems to suggest that instrumental rationality was operative. Women were seen to have a political
"function." They were "restrained" and "deferential" "subjects" while
their husbands were moving away from deference toward equal citizenship. For example, women's political voices were sharply curtailed in
the pervasive understanding that they were not supposed to tell their
male relatives for whom to vote.[8] In their subjection, wives were putatively represented by husbands in the public sphere, but as Kerber has
argued, custom dictated that men's "representation" of women need
not be based on their wives' consent or political opinions.

Jan Lewis's research also suggests that white women were viewed in
functional terms. She has emphasized women's indirect roles in republican politics as "republican wives" who were viewed as the reformers of
wayward suitors and husbands. In her view, this early formulation of a
feminine political role was not feminist, nor did it reflect a view of women
as "citizens." Rather, republicanism demanded virtue of women because
Americans recognized that women were intimately connected to *men.*
Women were to serve an instrumental purpose for social ends largely determined by men.[9]

Since women in the Anglo-American community appeared not to
have been situated as discursive equals in communicative rationality,
the argument for woman citizenship based on the claim that the domestic and public spheres were equally valued cannot hold. If republican
ideology rationalized women's exclusion and inequality, then again, the
designation "woman citizen" becomes meaningless, and the question
of women's "advancement" remains unclear.

To move beyond these problems with the republican motherhood thesis, I have focused on how power relations were shaped through communicative and instrumental rationality in the early Republic. In particular, I have been interested in whether gender ideology encouraged or discouraged the recognition of women as rational subjects with an equal status to make normative claims. Central to this question is the consideration of gender ideology in its race and class dimensions, and its power to limit and empower certain categories of women.

A few literate and privileged white women did seem to have rational and open-ended discussions with their husbands and other men. Some were extremely well-read, eloquent, and active modern subjects. Even these women had to be guarded, however, and could always be limited by others with the chastisement that they had stepped beyond the proper bounds of femininity. As we shall see, white women were rarely encouraged, and most often actively *discouraged* from considering themselves citizens of the polity, or equals in the republican family.

And yet, the proponents of republican motherhood are correct in their assessment that white women did appear to enjoy a new kind of subjectivity and elevated status in the early Republic. This elevation makes sense only when viewing white women with other noncitizens. As Mary Kelley has argued, the development of universal white female literacy and hundreds of female reading societies certainly fostered white women's empowerment.[10] Their empowered senses of self were also reflected in the founders' decision to "count" each of them as whole persons for representation purposes, in contrast to the enslaved, who were counted as three-fifths. As Jan Lewis has noted, James Wilson's suggested language in the U.S. Constitution is indicative of white women's positioning.[11] Representation in the lower house was to be:

> in proportion to the whole number of white & other free Citizens & inhabitants of every age sex & condition including those bound to servitude for a term of years and three fifths of all other persons not comprehended in the foregoing description, except Indians not paying taxes, in each state.

"Other" free citizens obviously referred to nonwhite men, while "inhabitants of every age sex and condition" referred to nonenslaved men, women, and children, including indentured servants, who lacked the full rights of those deemed "citizens."

In this work, I am mainly concerned with the race and class foundations that made white women's modern subjectivity possible, for this subjectivity was very much rooted in the positioning of children or nonwhites as the subordinate "others" of white middling women. The cultural privileges of women's moral authority were delimited by age, class, and especially, race. Only *white* women of property-owning classes enjoyed moral authority in republican discourses.

Still, race has remained marginalized from the discussion of women's status in the early Republic. The gender problematic continues to be *theoretically* isolated from the problem of race. In the 1980s and 1990s, the debate in U.S. women's history focused on the "woman citizenship" question, with the understanding that white women were the focus. The question whether white women were citizens remained dominant despite Jacqueline Jones's writings on slave women and her criticisms that the paradigm of republican motherhood failed to understand its own race and class boundaries. To go beyond a simplistic acknowledgment that the "republican mother" was white, I offer an analysis of the "intersectionality" of race and gender in the founding period, which describes how race was constructed through discourses on white femininity.[12]

In late eighteenth century republican discourses, women were not referred to as "republican mothers"; they were called "ladies," and just as frequently, the "fair sex" or "the sex" for short. This fact is important. The phrase "fair sex" reveals exactly that which the historian's trope "republican mother" makes obscure. The phrase "fair sex" can be traced to earlier conceptions of women's political role in England and Europe. In Chapter 3, I show that the term "fair sex" was one of difference and exclusion, not equity and inclusion, as the trope "republican motherhood" appears to be. In the late eighteenth century, "fair" was a reference to light skin tone, and "sex" was a reference to females. "Fair sex" was a category that in the first instance distinguished those with light complexions from those with dark complexions, and females from males. "Fair sex" meant, essentially, "white woman" or "white women."

The term "fair sex" helps makes sense of Carroll Smith-Rosenberg's postmodern analysis of American identity in "Dis-covering the Subject of the 'Great Constitutional Discussion.'" Smith-Rosenberg made an important contribution by turning the question of American citizenship to one of subjectivity and identity. She demonstrated that the center of

American identity was white, male, and property owning, but white women too gained their subjectivity through race, class, and yes, republican ideology that valorized wives and mothers.[13]

Understanding how American identities were shaped through the negation of brown, black, indentured, enslaved, barbaric, or savage "others" was key to my own development of a theory of racial patriarchy. Fair sex ideology supported the development of racial patriarchy by giving white women a sense of subjectivity in a world that legally subjected them to white men. In other words, though fair sex discourses positioned women instrumentally to support the subjectivity and agency of white men, the ideology also granted white women subjectivity and agency by positioning nonwhite persons and children instrumentally to them.

A close inspection of primary sources reveals that the virtues associated with or prescribed for white females during, and especially, after, the Revolution were much broader and more specific than the emphasis of public over private interest. The virtues contained a gender system that defined the norms for white womanhood, and effectively barred white women from participation as equals in political discussions. Because discourses on the fair sex took *white* women as their object, they were already bound by race and class. Articles on the fair sex or the "ladies" were directed at white women from the property-owning classes, not women of color, enslaved, or indentured women. Many authors presumed that the readers had servants. Discourses on the fair sex articulated an ethics for white women, affixing virtues like industry, frugality, domesticity, delicacy, modesty, subservience, and literacy to national survival and cultural superiority, through white femininity. The ascribed virtues and vices of the fair sex created "women" and "ladies" as categories through a system of ethics that was bound by race and class.

If race and class were structured through language simultaneously through the utterance "fair sex," then the linguistic and cultural system that housed it could not have been only about patriarchy and class. Its racial dimensions also shaped gender. Thus, the question of woman citizenship has been conceived too narrowly. The question is not simply whether and in what ways "patriarchy" limited or excluded women, but rather how discourses on gender and race facilitated the development of white women as modern subjects through a structure of racial patriarchy. That inquiry must also consider the forces that prevented the development of black patriarchy in the early Republic.

Secondary literature on race, ethnicity, and slavery are relevant to the gender question, just as literature on the gender question is relevant to understanding race and ethnicity. Works by Winthrop Jordan, Kathleen Brown, and Gary Nash are particularly helpful for understanding the historical development of race relations that gave meaning to the word "fair" in the fair sex duo.[14]

Two works in critical race theory have been essential to this book. Charles Mills's book *The Racial Contract*, designed after Pateman's *The Sexual Contract*, provided an important argument about the development of white supremacy within modern social contract theory and liberalism. His criteria for what constitutes consent to the "racial contract" is applied in my own analysis of racial patriarchy. Paul Gilroy's *The Black Atlantic* offered a penetrating theoretical account of the brutality of modern rationality, through which slavery and racism became internal to the history of Western civilization. Gilroy's analysis of modernity from the slaves' point of view helped me to shift my sights away from the question of an altered citizenship toward the question of white women as modern subjects. Together, these works helped me identify white supremacist values in the subjects of my analysis, and to see the struggles that Warren, Adams, and Murray faced as they tried to insert themselves as rational equals in discursive situations. Specifically, *The Black Atlantic* and *The Racial Contract* enabled me to see how white women were implicated in the brutality of instrumentalist rationality toward nonwhites as much as white men of the United States were. White women reconciled slavery and racism with beliefs in Enlightenment rationality, the universal "human being," and confident assertions that the "common good" could be determined without the discursive participation of most of the population, even as they themselves struggled to be heard and treated as rational beings.[15]

Historians will find no surprising new evidence here. What is offered is an examination of familiar evidence through a new lens. That new lens is the theory of racial patriarchy, and its supporting ideology, the ideology of the fair sex. This lens provides a different view of the events and ideas that supported slavery and enforced domesticity for white women. It is through this lens that the political thought and participation of Mercy Warren, Abigail Adams, and Judith Sargent Murray are analyzed. Vestiges of these eighteenth-century ideas remain with us today in American society and politics, having outlived the specific institutions and practices they once justified.

Chapter 2 outlines a rudimentary theory of racial patriarchy. It shows how American republicanism was based on hierarchies that were conceived through the articulation of differences. The theory is based on evidence that differences in race and sex were the foundations for dominance that were made material through institutions and practices. It also poses questions concerning the relative positioning of individuals with specific racial, ethnic, and class considerations within racial patriarchy.

In Chapter 3, I argue that ordinary and notable persons of the early Republic "signed on" or acquiesced to racial patriarchy through an ideology of the fair sex. Virtues and vices of fair sex discourses encoded ethnic, racial, class, and gender norms, and as such provided a way for ordinary people to sign on to the racial and sexual contracts simultaneously. Fair sex ideology is viewed as a key facilitator for the development of racial patriarchy in the United States. Fair sex ideology provided a linguistic context for the definition of white women's roles in the early Republic and a means by which American nationalism was defined through race and gender norms.

Chapters 4, 5, and 6 focus on three white women intellectuals who lived through the Revolutionary and early national periods: Mercy Otis Warren (1728–1814), Abigail Smith Adams (1744–1818), and Judith Sargent Murray (1751–1820). They were the three great female *political intellectuals* of the period. Unlike Sarah Wentworth, who wrote fiction and poetry, and Phillis Wheatley, whose deeply encoded poetry still requires serious analysis, Warren, Adams, and Murray made direct arguments in political debates during the Revolutionary and founding eras.

Warren, Adams, and Murray all lived in the state of Massachusetts, and all of them were married to prominent men, two of whom were distinguished through political leadership, and the third through religious leadership. Chapters 4 through 6 attempt to place each woman in the historical context of national and state politics, as well as the theoretical context of racial patriarchy. Warren, Adams, and Murray are viewed as white women in a nation and culture that was coming out of radicalism and attempting to define itself through "civilized" hierarchies.

My analyses of them are informed by Jacqueline Jones's penetrating observation that white women were "so awkwardly suspended between their racial prerogatives on the one hand and gender and class liabilities on the other."[16] I place Warren, Adams, and Murray on the tight rope between racial privilege and gender oppression, and look keenly for every dip of their balance rods. I am deeply interested in the nature of their "suspension." I examine each woman's political thought and agency with respect to racial privileges and racial ideology. I examine their stances on racial hierarchy in light of their protests against gender hierarchy. I consider how they may have suffered class liabilities as women, and how they may have enjoyed class privileges on account of race. I also examine how each woman's acceptance or rejection of modern gender hierarchy related to her acceptance or rejection of racial hierarchy.

Chapter 7 concludes the book by summarizing the patterns of resistance to and complicity with the norms of fair sex ideology and modern patriarchy. I offer an explanation for the three women's common pattern of feminist resistance followed by conservative retreat, noting that all eventually accepted the norms of racial patriarchy. In the Epilogue, I discuss some of the applications and implications of my theory for interpreting contemporary American politics, and I offer suggestions for further research.

2

Toward a Theory of
Racial Patriarchy

How, then, could we devise one of those useful falsehoods . . . ,
one noble falsehood that would, in the best case, persuade even
the rulers, but if that's not possible, then the others in the city?

All of you in the city are brothers, we'll say, but the god who
made you mixed some gold into those who are adequately
equipped to rule, because they are most valuable. He put silver in
those who are auxiliaries and iron and bronze in the farmers and
other craftsmen.

—Plato, *The Republic*

[T]he northern colonies . . . are well settled, not as the common
people of *England* foolishly imagine, with a compound mongrel
mixture of *English, Indian, and Negro,* but with freeborn *British
white subjects,* whose loyalty has never yet been suspected.

—James Otis III, "Rights of the British Colonists
Asserted and Proved"

Republics, ancient and modern, are built on hierarchy. In
Plato's *Republic,* Socrates concedes to his followers that to implement his
scheme of republicanism, a "noble falsehood" will have to be told to persuade all members of society to accept their prescribed roles within the hierarchy that undergirds his ideal state. In this "myth of the metals," hierarchy is naturalized metaphorically through the value of metals; gold, silver, bronze, and iron all represent the more and less valuable versions of
human nature. In Plato's view, the myth that one's metal comes from God
and one's birthing from the Earth is "noble" precisely because it is told to
promote what he considers to be in the common interest. The myth must
be told because the "truth" is both inaccessible and unpalatable to the

masses: Human nature is profoundly unequal, and justice requires that the most valuable persons rule over those who are less valuable.[1]

Modern republicanism is also based on an underlying belief in natural hierarchy. And the founders of the American Republic also employed a mythology. The contours of the natural hierarchy and its supporting mythology were different than those of Plato's Republic. In the American founders' version, the natural hierarchy of humanity was based on differences in race, culture, class, and gender, which were seen to be indicative of political value or worth. I call this hierarchy "racial patriarchy." Its supporting mythologies come from stories, not of birth, but of nature, in theories of the social compact.

According to my theory of racial patriarchy, the development of white male supremacy and economic classes in the United States occurred through the articulation of race, class, and gender *differences*. These articulated differences were translated into institutional arrangements, which resulted in or were reflective of relations of dominance and subordination. Since it is not possible to establish institutions apart from discursive participation, I do not attempt to argue unidirectional causality. Instead, I suggest that ideas and institutions coexisted and were reflexive of one another.

The theory also raises questions about the relative positioning of white women compared to other groups in the hierarchy, including white men, nonwhite men, and nonwhite women. The definition of racial patriarchy is fundamentally derived from critical race and gender theories, especially those that have deconstructed social contract theory. In particular, I have borrowed heavily from and sought to unify work done by Carole Pateman and Charles Mills, who have separately identified the sexual and racial contracts within Enlightenment social contract theories.

The chapter is divided into three sections. The first provides a working definition of racial patriarchy, in which I review the theories of the sexual and racial contracts and the main political thinkers associated with the ideas that supported them. I emphasize the continuity of European and American thought on race and gender and expose the reconciliation of hierarchy and brutality with ideas of equality and universalism in Enlightenment thought on both sides of the Atlantic. The question of primacy with respect to the ordering of race and gender hierarchies is raised and left indeterminate, in recognition of the need to answer such a question in the context of specific thinkers and individual practices.

In the next section, I examine the institutions and practices through which racial patriarchy was established and maintained in the early

American Republic. This section reviews work done by historians on the law of coverture and its effect in shaping white and nonwhite women's lives; the institution of slavery and policies of gradual emancipation, especially as they related to black families; the meaning of domesticity and the intact family unit in white and nonwhite families; patterns and rights of property ownership and paid labor; military service and compensation; patriotic celebrations; the franchise; and educational and religious privileges and practices. I conclude with a few brief remarks about how these institutions and practices established hierarchies. I also emphasize the nondeterministic nature of the theory, as well as the limits of its use as a tool to interpret lived experience, which will always remain infinitely more complex than any theory could predict or capture.

Defining Racial Patriarchy

Racial patriarchy is a pecking order among persons that came into being in the early national period of U.S. history. It differs from "patriarchy," in that it takes into account race *as well as* gender as organizing principles. It developed through ideas, institutions, and social practices. In terms of ideas, racial patriarchy developed from a convergence of human agreements on white supremacy and male supremacy that privileged white males, especially those with property, above everyone else. This convergence can be represented in political theory terms as the sexual and racial contracts embedded within social contract theory. Enlightenment social contract theories represent the modern noble lie. Because they ostensibly begin with principles of universal equality, liberty, and natural rights, while masking implied social hierarchies and cultural contests, they tell falsehoods deemed necessary for a specific order. They are cultural myths that operated in their own day and to some extent in our own day to persuade persons to accept their prescribed places in the hierarchy of American Republicanism.

"Modern Patriarchy" and the Sexual Contract

Gender hierarchy was preserved through theories of natural sexual difference that lay beneath different versions of social contract theory. In *The Sexual Contract*, Carole Pateman demonstrates how social contract theories contained a hidden "sexual contract."[2] The sexual contract was essentially an agreement among men on sexual hierarchy based on sexual difference. This difference would be used to exclude women from citizenship and keep them subordinate within families. The social contract theories of Locke, Rousseau, and Kant all incorporated women into republicanism through marriage. Only men were allowed to become signatories to the social contract that created a formal political society and, subsequently, a government of their choosing. Women were incorporated as wives, "represented" by their husbands, who stood as patriarchal heads of households.

Although the social contract theorists all employed the concept of a universal human nature, which appeared to suggest a radical equality in natural rights, Pateman and other feminist theorists have shown that their conceptions of natural rights were not truly universal. None of them envisioned women as equal citizens in their schemes of republican government. Women were viewed to be less rational and more emotional, more lascivious than men, or simply the weaker sex, more appropriately ruled by husbands. The sexual contract was thus an agreement of differential gender roles based on a concept of natural sexual differences. Women's difference and inferiority justified male rule in the family. In turn, men's patriarchal authority in the family justified the male right to create compacts of civil society and government without the presence of women. Modern patriarchy is the term that Pateman coined to describe the gendered separation of spheres into public and private in social contract theory.

There are many works by feminist political theorists that have uncovered gender construction in the canons of Western political thinkers and thus will not be reviewed here.[3] Pateman's contribution is particularly relevant because she showed the duplicity of social contract thinkers with respect to gender. Women were considered both as equals, in the universal "human nature," *and* as unequals, in comments on natural female weakness and inferiority.

Terrell Carver has also shown the dualism inherent in generalizations about humanity and mankind. "Mankind" and "humanity" have been used to demarcate a boundary between human beings, on one hand, and social animals, supernatural entities, and unthinking matter, on the other. In this respect, they seemed to be inclusive: Women were part of mankind and humanity. But the category mankind has also meant, quite specifically, "man" as opposed to "woman." Carver's analysis suggested that the dualism served a purpose; by appearing to be general, the category avoided raising issues that might be awkward, but by arguing the specifics where absolutely necessary, it ensured interpretations that reinforced masculine superiority in theory and male superiority in practice. The placeholder "mankind" disguised oppression by "simultaneously promising and denying equality in theory, as well as in practice," and permitted exceptions that were already in practice or possible, such as female rulers, or widows as heads of households, or in the colonial context, single women property owners and voters.[4]

Most of the major social contract theorists of the seventeenth and eighteenth centuries viewed women as equally rational individuals who can make agreements and negotiate with others, particularly in their decision to marry. But within marriage, women are demoted to "natural" inferiority and subjected to the direction of their husbands.[5] For Hobbes, Locke, Rousseau, and Kant, "nature" figures as the incontrovertible grounding of sexual difference as metals figure as the incontrovertible grounding of class differences in Plato's *Republic*. Femaleness disqualifies all women from political participation in the public sphere, or as participants in the social compact through suffrage rights. *The Sexual Contract* thus exposed the noble lie of universal natural rights, and the equality that such universality implies, as a way of masking the gender *inequality* built into the system, which was also taken to be "natural."

The American revolutionary thinkers adopted theories of gender articulated by these and other English and European thinkers, whose ideas have been shown to relegate women to inferior status. James Otis raised the issue of gender in his famous 1764 pamphlet "The Rights of the British Colonists, Asserted and Proved," quoted above. His comments on the issue of women and consent to government have been repeatedly misinterpreted as evidence that Otis was a feminist thinker. But close inspection reveals that this was not the case. In the pamphlet he made a natural rights argument that the British government was violating the representation rights of the colonists, denying the natural right of all to consent to the government that bound them. In the process, he addressed the question of the universal, "Whether every man and woman were not then equal?"—and thus had "a natural and equitable right to be consulted in the choice of a new King or in the formation of a new original compact or government."

Otis was responding to the "opposers of contract" who considered the issue of women's consent one of the ridiculous consequences of a social compact theory and universal natural rights. His answer was that women would not have to consent because the compact was not an "arbitrary" one based solely on human agreement, but rather on the "solid foundation" of the "unchangeable will of God, the author of nature, whose laws never vary." Otis actually answers the question of women's consent much as Locke had done for the Royalists when fighting the Crown, in the Glorious Revolution in England a century earlier. That all men were born in a state of perfect liberty and equality did not in any way alter the natural difference and hierarchy of the sexes. The Creator of the Universe

> made it necessary that from *Adam* and *Eve* to these degenerate days the different sexes should sweetly attract each other, form societies of *single* families, of which *larger* bodies and communities are as naturally, mechanically, and necessarily combined as the dew of heaven and the soft distilling rains is collected by the all-enlivening heat of the sun. *Government* is therefore most evidently founded *on the necessities of our nature.* It is by no means an *arbitrary* thing depending merely on *compact* or *human will* for its existence.[6]

Government was not based on human agreements alone, but on God's will. God created gender difference since the days of "Adam and Eve," and social compact theory, contrary to its opponents, did not suggest that *everyone* be involved in the formation of government. For Otis, women are not even equal individuals outside of marriage. Natural gender differences make the sexes attract one another, and form families, communities, and finally government. For Otis as well as Locke, women were incorporated into political society through marriage, not as signatories to the social contract.

During the Revolutionary War, the question of women's natural rights as signatories to the social compact came up again, as several historians have noted. In 1776, John Adams was hit on two sides, as his wife and a colleague both questioned the exclusion of women from the franchise. In late March, before independence had been declared, Abigail Adams began to see a contradiction between the law of coverture and revolutionary republican principles. Coverture denied rights to women, yet still required their political obligation.

Because it made the relationship of husband and wife analogous to that of king and subject, it made men "tyrants" in their homes. Thus Abigail pleaded with her husband to "remember the ladies" when he drafted the new state constitution. If they were not given "voice and representation," she argued, the ladies would "foment a rebellion" of their own.

The anxious response of John Adams to his wife's challenge is well known. John ridiculed her for behaving like the Negroes, apprentices, Indians, and children, who had found freedom during the War in the "loosened bands of government." "Depend upon it," he wrote:

> we know better than to repeal our Masculine systems. Altho they are in full Force, you know they are little more than Theory. We dare not exert our Power in its full Latitude. We are obliged to go fair, and softly, and in Practice you know We are the subjects. We have only the Name of Masters, and rather than give up this, which would compleatly subject Us to the Despotism of the Peticoat, I hope General Washington and all our brave Heroes would fight. I am sure every good Politician would plot, as long as he would against Despotism, Empire, Monarchy, Aristocracy, or Ochlocracy.[7]

John Adams's suggestion that husbands were but nominal masters over wives was controverted by his letter to James Sullivan on the same issue. In May of the same year, Sullivan had written his now famous letter to John Adams, asking on what grounds women could be denied the opportunity to consent to the government that bound them. Shouldn't every individual of the community consent expressly to every Act of Legislation? Adams responded to him that it would be "dangerous" to open up such a controversy. If any change in voter qualifications were enacted, new claims would arise, and there would be no end to it.

> Women will demand a Vote. Lads from 12 to 21 will think their Rights not enough attended to, and every Man, who has not a Farthing will demand an equal Voice with any other in all Acts of State. It tends to confound and destroy all Distinctions, and prostrate all Ranks, to one common Levell.

John Adams was a firm believer in ranks and levels—old over young, rich over poor, virtuous over wicked, master over slave, native-born Anglo-American over foreigner, white over Negro and Indian, and man over woman.[8] Only white American-born men with property and education were equipped with the rationality and judgment necessary for political deliberation; therefore only they needed to be consulted for the formation of a government that would bind all.

Thus, when Jefferson wrote in the *Declaration of Independence* that "all men are created equal," the psychological denial had already been laid for him to assert it without discussion of the contradictions between the universal placeholder in "the rights of man," and its specific boundaries that excluded women and slaves. The "rights of man" incorporated the dualism of man as *human being* and man as *masculine*, simultaneously including and excluding the nonmasculine and "sub-human."

In his private correspondence, Jefferson romanticized women as the tender, sympathetic sex, in opposition to the competitive male citizen. He discouraged politically minded women from engaging in political discussions, suggesting they refrain from "wrinkling their foreheads" about politics. In 1788, during the campaign to ratify the Constitution in the states, Jefferson began to express anxieties about the threat of women in the public sphere. In Paris, he witnessed first-hand women who spoke and roamed freely in society and government, and decidedly rejected these privileges for his own countrywomen. His correspondences with women such as Angelica Schuyler Church and Anne Willing Bingham in 1788 show a definite distaste for women who even inquired about politics. In the same year he warned George Washington that the woman question must be handled if the nation was to succeed. Commenting on French society, he wrote:

> In my opinion a kind of influence, which none of their plans of reform take into account, will elude them all; I mean the influence of women in the government. The manners of the nation will allow them to visit, alone, all person in office, to solicit the affairs of the husband, family, or friends, and their solicitations bid defiance to laws and regulations. This obstacle may seem less to those who, like our countrymen, are in the precious habit of considering Right, as the barrier against all solicitation. Nor can such an one, without the evidence of his own eyes, believe in the desperate state to which things are reduced in this country from the omnipotence of an influence which, fortunately for the happiness of the sex itself, does not endeavour to extend itself in our country beyond the domestic line.[9]

Jefferson, like Adams, viewed the presence of women as an "omnipotent" influence that corrupted law and rationality in the public realm. Compared to the French, the American fair sex seemed more respectful of authority, more civilized. Whether Jefferson was issuing a warning or expressing relief, it is clear that in this period he preferred the political passivity of those without the franchise, especially women.

Following the publication of Mary Wollstonecraft's *Vindication of the Rights of Woman* (1792), male and female sympathizers in the United States also contended that women ought to be included in the theoretical category of the rational human being, and argued for women's equal natural rights. They were met by conservatives, some of whom devised a distinct concept of human nature for women, with a corresponding set of "rights."

As Rosemarie Zaggari has demonstrated, Americans who preferred to keep the state male turned to the more conservative Scottish Enlightenment thinkers such as David Hume, Thomas Reid, Lord Kames, and Francis Hutcheson for support. Conservative American writers of both sexes articulated a set of women's rights to include, for example, the choice of a husband, the right to share in the instruction of children, the "rights" to promote industry, frugality, and economy, to be "neat and decent" in their persons and families, and to "delight," "civilize," and "ameliorate mankind." Both liberal and conservative Enlightenment theorists justified the exclusion of women from political power. The liberal theory of Locke, Otis, and Jefferson offered no real conception of woman citizenship, and the Scottish theorists appear to have offered a gendered, instrumental conception clearly based on women's duties. The differential conceptions of men's and women's rights seem to support claims by Joan Hoff and Ruth Bloch that virtue and sacrifice became feminized just as men were becoming self-interested citizens and individuals.[10] They allowed men individual privileges and personal autonomy while conferring duties and domesticity to women, and thereby facilitated the establishment of separate spheres in the post-revolutionary period.

White Supremacy, Slavery, and the Racial Contract

Following Pateman's gender analysis of the social contract, Charles W. Mills argued that social contract theory also incorporates a "racial contract." The racial contract is a political system of white supremacy that also lies within social contract and other republican theories. It is essentially an agreement among whites on white supremacy which provides the foundation for a white polity and white economic dominance. It is an agreement that assumes entitlement to and acceptance of deferential privileges.

White supremacy is created and maintained by what Mills calls an "epistemology of ignorance" and deception. Moral and cognitive dissonance are marked by a denial of inconsistencies between egalitarian ideals and slavery, or other racially discriminatory practices; the denial of uncomfortable truths; and a refusal to validate nonwhite intellect, rationality, or creative genius. It is a tacit agreement among those who consider themselves full persons to categorize the remaining subset of humans as "nonwhite" and of a different and inferior moral status. They are considered subpersons and then relegated to a subordinate civil standing in the white-controlled polity.

The racial contract also invokes a "moral geography" separating white, civilized from dark, barbarian space and land. This geography is theoretically similar to but physically different from the public/private geography separating white men and white women. As the sexual contract exists to differentiate and privilege males with respect to females, the racial contract exists to differentiate and privilege whites with respect to nonwhites. According to Mills, "all whites are beneficiaries of the Contract, though some whites are not signatories to it."[11]

Mills has argued that all the major social contract theorists viewed nonwhite humans as inferior either by culture or by nature. Because Mills's ideas, and critical racial theory, are newer and perhaps less familiar, I will reiterate them here. In the myth of the social contract, the "state of nature" figures as a demarcating ground between white civilization and nonwhite savagery. For example, for Locke, uncultivated land is considered "wild woods" and "wasteland." White industrial European culture is valorized by his statement that God gave the world "to the use of the Industrious and the Rational." Presumably, he viewed native Americans who labored the land as neither "industrious" nor "rational." White persons are taken to exhibit their superior rationality by appropriating uncultivated land and adding value to it. Thus, the appropriation of Native lands in America is viewed as perfectly just and legitimate, in keeping with God's intentions. By extension, he argues, Africa is another uncultivated wasteland occupied only by those of inferior rational capacities.[12]

Additional evidence that Locke did not consider Africans full human beings endowed with equal rationality may be found in his personal investment in the Royal Africa Company, which traded slaves, as well as in the constitution of the Carolina colony, which he wrote and which made provisions for the institution of slavery.[13]

Even Rousseau, who seems to criticize European civilization and glorify nature and nature's man through his imagery of the "noble savage," denigrates non-Europeans as less moral, uncivilized beings. In defining the beginnings of civilization through technological developments of agriculture and metallurgy, he erroneously or selectively credits Europe as "the earliest to be civilized," or at least the culture "more continuously and better civilized than other parts of the world," leaving aside arguments that suggest that European civilization began in Egypt.[14] As Mills points out, Europeans encountered the Aztec and Incan empires 200 years before Rousseau's writing, and both of these were highly developed civilizations using agriculture and metallurgy. Second, to the extent that Rousseau glorifies the "noble savage," and precivilized nature, he holds that one must attain language and rationality, and participate in republican politics to become fully human.

Kant was also a signatory to the racial contract. He wrote explicitly on the "different races of mankind," and attributed talent, rationality, and morality to whites exclusively. According to Mills, in Kant's hierarchy of human nature, the whites occupied the superior position, followed by the "yellow," the "black," and the "red." The absolute limits of skin color show his "universal" claims on human nature to be limited to the population of white males; reason as God's gift to all men to "think for themselves" and education as a means for anyone to attain knowledge turn out to be particularistic claims applicable only to white males.[15] Because the state of nature represents a demarcation between savage and civilized humanity, and because nonwhites are identified with savage nature, the racial contract is a "hidden operator" in theories of the social contract.

Neither did Scottish philosophers challenge racial hierarchy. As Winthrop Jordan noted, David Hume was a proponent of the biological inferiority of blacks. In his view, Negroes were incapable of arts, science, rationality, and civilization. The best they could do was mimic, "like a parrot, who speaks a few plain words clearly"; only those of white, Anglo, or European descent could produce works of genius and talent. Adam Smith also suggested that Africans were uncivilized, noting their "barbarous" amusements of music and dance.[16]

Many of the American revolutionary thinkers and founders expressed ideas of white supremacy and took part as signatories to the racial contract. When James Otis first employed social contract theory to argue against taxation without representation, he noted the contradiction between universal natural rights and the institution of slavery. He criticized Locke's support of slavery: "Slavery is so vile and miserable an estate of man and so directly opposite to the generous temper and courage of our nation that 'tis hard to be conceived that an *Englishman*, much less a *gentleman*, should plead for it."

Indeed, several of Otis's statements would seem to imply that black men would naturally be party to the original compact: "The colonists are by the law of nature freeborn, as indeed all men are white or black." But his claim that blacks are "men" is used to denounce slavery and the slave trade, not necessarily to suggest that blacks be considered equal, or deserving equal representation rights with white men.

> Can any logical inference in favor of slavery be drawn from a flat nose, a long or a short face? Nothing better can be said in favor of a trade that is the most shocking violation of the law of nature, has direct tendency to diminish the idea of the inestimable value of liberty, and makes every dealer in it a tyrant, from the director of an African company to the petty chapman in needles and pins on the unhappy coast.

Slavery threatened to reduce Europe and America to "the ignorance and barbarity of the darkest ages."[17]

Other statements reveal a deep ambiguity on whether Otis considered nonwhite males as equal members of the Anglo-American body politic. The Native Americans figure as members of a subdued foreign nation. Otis argues that the representation rights of the British colonists are deserved because the colonists' forefathers had "worn away" their lives "in war with the savages." They thought they were earning a sure inheritance for their posterity; it was unjust to deprive them or theirs of their charter privileges. Both white and black men are "good, loyal, and useful subjects" of King George III. But Otis supports his argument by claiming that the colonists were not a "compound mongrel mixture of English, Indian, and Negro," but "freeborn *British white* subjects," the "noble discoverers and settlers of a new world."[18] Such statements suggest that Otis's claim of white purity may have represented an act to become signatory to racism in order to win representation rights in the British parliament.

Some Americans found the inconsistencies of their egalitarian natural rights philosophy and the legality of slavery awkward.[19] Many of the members of the Philadelphia convention, including slaveholders, openly acknowledged that slavery was a source of corruption inconsistent with the principles of the Revolution. Nearly all of the virtues that Americans professed were contradicted by the tyrannical rule of the slave master. The capture of Africans for slavery was often done by charging them with false crimes. Removing them from their native lands obstructed "the natural course of civilization and improvement" in Africa.[20] It corrupted reason, industry, political obligation, sympathy, and marital chastity.

Thomas Jefferson was most explicit in his analysis of slavery and the vices it engendered in both master and slave. The slave system promoted "a perpetual exercise of the most boisterous passions" resulting in "the most unremitting despotism." We now know through DNA evidence that Jefferson was likely referring to his own unrestrained passions with his slave Sally Hemings.[21] Additionally, few slave masters were seen to labor, and the normal benefits that flowed from honest industry were denied the slave. The denial of material prosperity to the slave laborer made it reasonable for him to steal, since "the man in whose favour no laws exist probably feels himself less bound to respect those made in favour of others." May not the enslaved man, Jefferson argued, "as justifiably take a little from one who has taken all from him?"[22]

Slavery also corrupted the virtues of benevolence and marital chastity. The free often ignored the plight of slave women, separated from their children and "spoiled" by "the hideous groans of men with the clanking of chains" at midnight.[23]

These inconsistencies stimulated debates on human nature and race, in which Anglo-American writers devised ideologies of white supremacy, and here is where Mills's point about moral cognitive distortion may apply. If humanness was the essential quality by which one was endowed with natural rights, the question of who belonged in that category was now a matter of controversy. Slaves and other anti-slavery advocates were quick to argue the biblical point that all were descended from a common ancestor, so that the Negro *was* endowed with rational human nature. Their opponents pointed to physical and cultural differences to buttress their claim that the Negro was of a different species than the fair-skinned person of European ancestry.

Winthrop Jordan has suggested that David Hume's proclamation of white supremacy, first published in 1748, may have been influential in American political thought:

> I am apt to suspect the negroes, and in general all the other species of men (for there are four or five different kinds) to be naturally inferior to the whites. There never was a civilized nation of any other complexion than *white*; nor even any individual eminent either in action or speculation. No arts, no sciences. On the other hand, the most rude and barbarous of the whites, such as the ancient GERMANS, and the present TARTARS, have still something eminent about them, in their valour, form of government, or some other particular. Such a uniform and constant difference could not happen, in so many countries and ages, if nature had not made an original distinction betwixt these breeds of men. Not to mention our colonies, there are NEGROE slaves dispersed all over EUROPE, of which none ever discovered any symptoms of ingenuity; tho' low people, without education, will start up amongst us, and distinguish themselves in every profession. In JAMAICA indeed they talk of one negroe as a man of parts and learning; but 'tis likely he is admired for very slender accomplishments, like a parrot, who speaks a few words plainly. (Emphasis original)[24]

As Jordan reports, there certainly were some, particularly Quakers, who contended that Africans were naturally equal to whites, but oppressed under slavery. Yet, even comments from prominent abolitionists seem to reveal an underlying consensus on the superiority of white, Anglo-Saxon *civilization*. When men like Thomas Jefferson, Reverend Jonathan Boucher, Richard Nisbet, and others pointed to the native inferiority of the Negroes, or the lack of civilization in Africa, anti-slavery activists like Benjamin Rush and Arthur Lee made efforts to explain *why* the Negro seemed barbaric and inferior. Their attempt to rationalize "brutish," "ignorant," "idle," "crafty," "stupid," "thievish," and deceitful characteristics in terms of environmental factors like climate, culture, and population density amounted to a concession to the supremacy of Anglo-Saxon civilization and the barbarism of blacks.[25]

The protection of domestic slavery in the U.S. Constitution was not dismantled in the early years of the nation because, as Gary

Nash has suggested, a "belligerent white supremacism" prevented Northerners from supporting abolition proposals presented to Congress in 1790. Aside from the economic problem of how to pay slave owners for emancipating their "property," Northerners appeared to be convinced by arguments that blacks and Africans were an inferior and barbarous people. In a series of articles published in the *American Museum* in 1789 and 1790, Reverend Samuel Stanhope Smith, vice president of the College of New Jersey and moral philosopher, attributed all differences in color, complexion, and figure to environmental causes and the "state of society." Smith had divided the world into regions of skin color and civilization levels. "Encircle the globe," he wrote, and you will find that "[t]he black prevails, under the equator; under the tropics, the dark copper; and on this side of the tropic of cancer, to the seventh degree of north latitude, you successively discern the olive, the brown, the fair, and the sanguine complexion."

Smith did believe that all races were descended from a common ancestor; but he turned environmentalism on its head to *justify* slavery. While hot climates made skin dark, so too did societal factors. "Nakedness, exposure, negligence of appearance, want of cleanliness, bad lodging, and meagre diet" discolored and injured the form of "savages." By contrast, the "British," "Irish," and "Germans" were the "fairest people in Europe," and also the most civilized.

Many Americans were "pale," and "sallow," especially in the "laboring classes" of society, but with economic development and progress in manners, Americans were sure to become more refined, and consequently, more "fair." Though it would be "impossible that a savage should ever be fair," the implication was that slavery in America was progressive for the otherwise barbaric African. Even under the vile conditions of servitude, the Africans were daily becoming more "ingenious and susceptible of instruction" due to the change in their mode of living as well as to society and climate.[26]

The racial contract certainly worked against Native Americans as well as African Americans. Native Americans, officially members of their own tribal governments, have been viewed through the prism of the "noble savage," as well as its alter, the wild savage. As the noble savage, the Indian was revered for his egalitarian spirit and democratic traditions by Franklin, Adams, and other Americans. As the "wild savage," natives of both sexes were viewed as uncivilized in their lack of "improvement" or development of the lands, as well as in their reversed gender roles, whereby women labored in fields, voted for tribal representatives, participated as official record keepers at tribal council meetings, divorced at will, and enjoyed a property system of matrilineal descent. Thus, patriarchal relations among whites served to distinguish European American "civilization" from Native American "savagery."[27]

In theorizing racial patriarchy, we must consider how the racial and sexual contracts defined social hierarchy. If we consider the sexual and racial contracts together rather than as separate systems, we begin to get the crude outlines of a hierarchy based on differences in which white males appear to be the most privileged and nonwhite females appear the least privileged. In this work, I am interested primarily in the relative positioning of white women in racial patriarchy. If we position white women in the racial and sexual contracts, it is reasonable to suggest that they would be partially privileged, by race and class, and partially oppressed, by gender. With respect to class, the positioning of white women is ambiguous. The racial contract posits them as privileged, insofar as they are beneficiaries of white supremacy; but the sexual contract posits women as oppressed, in that laws of marriage, inheritance, and commerce gave economic control to men and barred women from equal opportunity in education and commerce. Nonwhite men would be partially oppressed by race, as "sub-human," but partially privileged by sex, as "men."

The intersectionality of race and gender hierarchies certainly poses questions with respect to actual experience in a lived pecking order. The main question that concerns this work is the relative positioning of the two intermediate groups in the hierarchy of racial patriarchy, white women and nonwhite men. Although racial ideology was based on the differentiation between white and the not-white other, I have focused more on African Americans than Native Americans within the category of the nonwhite. This focus is arbitrary, pertaining to my situatedness as a professor in a predominantly African American university. The institution of slavery undoubtedly played a decisive role in the development of white supremacy, but it seems no less likely that Anglo-American identity and "civilization" were also defined through the subjugation of natives. Although Native American nations were officially recognized in treaties and diplomatic relations, such recognition has been inconsistent at best throughout our history.

Institutions and Practices of Racial Patriarchy

To ask about the relative positionings of white women and black men in a general fashion is to inquire about which of the two difference contracts took primacy. Whether the "real" issue in any given political struggle is at bottom race, gender, or class, is a *result* of power and perspective, not something fundamental to it. Whether race or gender difference is primarily at play depends on *whose* perspective one takes in a particular time and place. A determination of primacy is thus always provisional, contingent, situated, and ultimately contestable. It requires historical investigation into the ways that specific persons actually used language to communicate the ideals, myths, stories, and customs that shaped their communities. We might begin by considering whether and to what degree black men were able to participate as signatories to or beneficiaries of the sexual contract. We would also need to inquire how white women "became white," in Mills's language, that is, to what degree white women participated as signatories and/or beneficiaries to the racial contract. I have partially considered the latter question in another work, and will develop it further in Chapters 4 through 6.[28] An important focus here is the sexual contract and the issue of patriarchal privileges available to black men.

Manhood, Hierarchy, and the Question of Black Patriarchy

One way to begin an inquiry on black manhood and patriarchy is to consider whether and how black men were included in the category "man." Did the hierarchy of men include nonwhite men in its ranks, or were only white men considered in the putatively universal "men"? In what ways were black men admitted to or excluded from patriarchal authority in the early American Republic?

Mark Kann's discussion of masculinity in *A Republic of Men* is a good place to begin. Kann studied discourses of manhood circulating in the Revolutionary and founding eras. He argued that four categories of manhood appeared in a hierarchy within a "grammar of manhood." In essence, the grammar of manhood identified the virtues and privileges of men, as well as their vices. It drew a line between patriarchs and those subordinate to them, which included all women as well as lower orders of men within male hierarchy.

At the bottom rung of the four classes of men is the category of the "disorderly man," which comprised the impoverished "wanderer," the sodomist, the "bachelor," the adulterer, and the drunk. Disorderly men failed to display the basic male virtues of industry, sobriety, and/or heterosexual marital commitment, and were thus generally considered to be unworthy of the franchise. At the next level, the "family man," considered worthy of citizenship, was characterized by the possession of a wife and children, and real property, or sometimes just a wife and children without real property. The "better sort" of man, who ought to fill the ranks of political office, was characterized as a trustworthy leader, often marked by social class, education, and strong community ties. Finally, the "founder" or "hero" was a patriarch among patriarchs. His extraordinary intellect and abilities in crisis situations justified heroic measures, and placed him in some ways above the law.

Kann acknowledges that the founders' grammar of manhood describes a hierarchy of *white* men. "Most founders saw blacks as 'outsiders' or 'outcasts from humanity.'" Although Kann relegates enslaved and free black men with or without property to the "disorderly" rank, he also notes a racial distinction in that the white "disorderly" man was always viewed as behaviorally, rather than naturally, defective. Disorderly white men were thought capable of joining the ranks of family men and the better sort if they reformed themselves through the manly virtues of industry, sobriety, military service, education, and/or marriage, or if they were reformed by the alleged superior virtue of wives.[29] Kann does not suggest, for example, that all men, regardless of color and culture, were distinguished from all women, and then separated according to masculine virtues. Rather, the grammar of manhood establishes a hierarchical ordering within European American culture, which suggests that racial and ethnic differences were fundamental, and once accomplished, followed by gender difference within white supremacy.

Marriage and Coverture: The Mainstay of European American Patriarchy

In the European American community, the hierarchy of most men over most women was instituted through marriage, but unmarried women were also subjected to patriarchal control. It is necessary to understand how legal marriage functioned to establish or codify gender hierarchy in Anglo-American law before we can address the question regarding whether black men enjoyed patriarchal privileges in their own communities.

The marriage contract was defined through the law of coverture, which positioned wives as men's subordinates. The English jurist William Blackstone defined coverture:

> By marriage, the husband and wife are one person in law; that is, the very being or legal existence of the woman is suspended during the marriage, or at least is incorporated and consolidated into that of the husband: under whose wing, protection, and *cover* she performs every thing; and is therefore called in our law-french a *feme-covert*; is said to be *covert-baron* or under the protection and influence of her husband, her *baron* or lord; and her condition during her marriage is called her *coverture*. Upon this principle, of an union of person in husband and wife, depend almost all the legal rights, duties, and disabilities that they acquire by marriage.[30]

Under the law of coverture, a married woman lacked many of the rights associated with being an individual. Historians agree that the American Revolution was much more revolutionary for white men than white women because the law of coverture, a mainstay of European monarchy, was preserved. Although many men were rewarded for their wartime sacrifices with the vote, and state-building created political opportunities for male heads of households, women were not granted any rights for their wartime sacrifices. One American author was explicit in comparing the masculine social compact with the feminine marriage contract. By entering the marriage state, women renounced some of their natural rights, as did men upon entering civil society.[31]

Coverture legally excluded married women from the category of the modern, rights-bearing individual. The wife shed her father's name and adopted the name of her husband's family. Wives who entered marriage with property ceded control of it to their husbands, unless they took special pains to create "separate estates" through the court system, which was rarely done, even among women from wealthy families. Wives could also be "corrected" by their husbands through the use of physical punishment. Normally a wife could not make business contracts without her husband's consent, and any wages that she earned could be legally appropriated by her husband. He was legally recognized as the single authority in family government, and was given sole power to represent the family's interests with the outside commercial and political world.

Unmarried women had more freedom, but were not on a par with male patriarchs. As "feme soles" they could operate as individuals with the rights of contract. Single women and widows were permitted to write wills directing the inheritance of property, which married women could not do.

But unmarried women were economically disadvantaged in other ways. A review of the scholarship on women and the laws of property suggests that single and widowed women did not have the economic power that men could enjoy. Marylynn Salmon has argued that shifts in inheritance laws during the late eighteenth and early nineteenth centuries may have privileged women and girls. The abolition of primogeniture and double shares for eldest sons where fathers left no wills would seem to have allowed females a larger share of inheritance property. However, others have offered several measures indicating an actual loss of inheritance power and outright property ownership among women as the eighteenth century progressed. For example, Joan Hoff noted that the percentage of women who were named sole executrixes decreased; and after 1750, there was an increase in the proportion of wills that gave wives no interest in land, or gave them only a life interest rather than outright ownership of property. A life interest prevented a widow from willing the property to whomever she wanted after her death, and therefore diminished her personal volition to do with the land as she wished. Double shares for sons and outright ownership of land obviously allowed them a disproportionate freedom. In Virginia and Massachusetts, there is evidence that sons rather than wives were more likely to be named as sole executors of estates upon the death of male heads-of-households. And regular dower rights diminished.[32]

According to Linda Kerber, the erosion of dower rights was the most important legal development directly affecting [white] women of the early Republic. Whereas widows traditionally inherited a life interest in the estate equal to one-third of the property upon the death of a husband, children began to receive an equal share with their mothers; thus, if a woman had more than two children, she was not guaranteed one-third the estate. Hoff has also noted that a widow's dower rights were not protected from creditors outside the family, whose claim to family resources increasingly took priority during the post-revolutionary credit crisis. Toby Ditz's study of inheritance patterns in Connecticut showed that most sons inherited enough property to underwrite their status as heads of households, while most daughters did not. "The short shrift given to daughters and widows was part of a general pattern designed to ensure that sons attained the status of independent men." Elizabeth Crane reported that tax assessments indicated that the proportion of women owning real property declined from the late seventeenth century to the late eighteenth century, and their holdings, in absolute numbers, also went down, especially in New England. It is difficult not to conclude with these authors that the general trend throughout the late eighteenth and early nineteenth centuries was for white women to become increasingly dependent on patriarchal heads of households.[33]

Although it is generally agreed that marriage was the mainstay of modern patriarchy in the Anglo-American community, there has been no real examination of whether and how marriage supported the development of patriarchy in the black community. An inquiry on the relationship of black men and patriarchal power would require an examination of scholarship on black family life in the late eighteenth and early nineteenth centuries. A minimal understanding of why black patriarchy was frustrated in the early Republic requires an examination of the transition from slavery to freedom in the "first emancipation," in the North.

The "First Emancipation" and Black Family Life

During and after the Revolution, northern states moved to abolish slavery. Except for New Jersey, every northern state passed an immediate or gradual emancipation act during the Federalist era. Vermont outlawed slavery in its original constitution in 1777. Massachusetts did so in 1783 by a court ruling in a case in which a slave petitioned that slavery violated his natural rights. Pennsylvania (1780), Rhode Island (1784), Connecticut (1784), and New York (1790) adopted gradual emancipation laws, guaranteeing freedom to future generations of blacks. New Jersey was the only state north of Delaware and Maryland to remain a slave state, which it did until 1804, when it passed an act. Those born before July 4, 1804 were enslaved for life. The children of those born after that date would be free. By 1800, 60 percent of blacks living in the North were free. The remaining 40 percent included those who would remain slaves for life, and those who would be freed through gradual emancipation when they reached a certain age of adulthood, or by other methods.[34] The black community of the post-revolutionary and early national periods thus included free and enslaved blacks.

Marriage and family life were profoundly affected by the status of family members as free or enslaved. Where it existed, the institution of slavery took priority over the institution of marriage. Free blacks could legally marry other blacks, but most states in the South, and two states in the North—Massachusetts and Pennsylvania—had laws against interracial sex and marriage. Whereas slaves and indentured servants were legally prohibited from marrying in the South and in many northern states, legally recognized and religiously sanctioned marriages among the enslaved were common in New England.[35]

But one's status in slavery nullified the protections of coverture; if either husband or wife was enslaved, the owner retained his or her right to treat his or her slave as property. Thus, patriarchal power of husbands over wives would have been disrupted at best. Neither labor, living conditions, nor visitations between husband and wife were under the legal control of the husband as was the case within most Anglo-American marriages. These conditions suggest the primacy of the racial contract over the sexual contract. Indeed, several black feminists have argued that black women enjoyed a kind of equality in their own households for that reason.[36]

A major problem in the black community was keeping the family unit physically and geographically intact. The legal authority of the white patriarch to discipline members of his household, including slaves, with physical punishment or estrangement was not abridged by the right of a slave husband or father to be patriarch of his own family.

Economic forces encouraged slave owners to break up families by selling members to others in different towns, counties, or states. As more states moved to enact gradual emancipation laws, the struggle to maintain an intact nuclear family did not disappear, and in some ways may have been intensified. Gradual emancipation laws, economic and agricultural changes, and the end of the foreign slave trade in 1808 created new incentives in the domestic slave trade. To circumvent manumission, many slave owners from the North and upper South sold those who would have been emancipated to prospective masters farther west and south, where slavery was protected, and the demand for labor remained high. Several states enacted laws forbidding this practice, but, as James and Lois Horton have reported, no one seems to have been convicted for this crime.

Personal tragedies thus persisted long after emancipation laws had been passed. The story of a slave mother named Isabella, better known today as the women's rights advocate Sojourner Truth, was not atypical. Sometime after New York passed its gradual emancipation law, Isabella's young son was illegally taken from her and given to her mistress's daughter as a wedding present. When Isabella protested to her mistress, she was scolded for making such a fine fuss over a "little nigger," and told that the remaining children were enough for her to look after.[37]

Property Ownership and the Frustration of Black Patriarchy

Another factor that frustrated the development of black patriarchy was the general lack of property in black families. Economic power was a major component of patriarchal authority. Therefore, the many factors that contributed to the lower economic class of African Americans would have also contributed to the frustration of black patriarchy. Property acquisition was more difficult for blacks for several reasons. Slave status of ancestors or oneself meant that African Americans were less likely than European Americans to receive inherited wealth or property.

Additionally, property rights were sometimes different for whites and blacks. For example, it was illegal for a black person to own real estate in New Jersey until 1798, but according to Elizabeth Bethel, servants and enslaved persons in Massachusetts were permitted to own land and transmit it to their heirs subject to the same laws as whites throughout the eighteenth century. Even where there was no racial or ethnic distinction on the right to own property, actual ownership patterns were markers of racial difference.[38]

The continued existence of slavery meant that many African Americans had to purchase their own and many times other family members' freedom. Such was the case for Absolom Jones, co-founder of the first African American church in the North. Jones purchased his wife's freedom as well as his own in 1784, when he was 38. The cost of freedom obviously had a disparate impact on blacks, in that white men and women could be free simply by birth, or in the case of indenture, after a limited period of service. Thus, it is also clear that the transition from slavery to freedom ate up resources that might otherwise have been devoted to the acquisition of property in the black communities.

As a consequence of the racial disparities in property and wealth, issues of prime importance to white women were irrelevant to black women. The erosion of dower rights and the decline of separate estates were issues of little relevance in black women's lives. Most African Americans had not reached the level of economic development to be concerned with inheritance patterns or the loss of control over one's property to one's husband in marriage. With regard to property ownership and rights, they had less to lose and more to gain in legal marriages than their white sisters. As several black feminists have noted, marriage and family life provided a vital source of strength for men and women during and after slavery.[39] Where families were intact, enduring family units provided a terrain in which Africans and African Americans could maintain some cultural autonomy and give meaning to daily life.

Property ownership patterns exacerbated racial differences. Figures on property ownership among blacks are difficult to find, but there is no question that free blacks were less likely than whites to own land or houses, whether they lived in urban or rural areas. Gordon Wood reports that the majority of white men were freehold owners,[40] and we know that such was not the case for black men. The census of 1790 lists almost 60,000 free blacks, two-thirds of whom lived in New England and the mid-Atlantic states. By the end of the century, New York and Philadelphia had the largest populations of free African Americans. In general, free persons of color received less money than whites for the same work, whether they were artisans, teachers, laborers, or farmers. Freed men and women who lacked property generally lived as tenants on farms, or in white households in the cities, often indenturing themselves as an intermediate step between dependence and autonomy.

Shane White reports that in the 1790s in New York, a few blacks owned their houses, but the vast majority of free blacks lived in rented accommodations. In Philadelphia, as Gary Nash reports, many blacks began to acquire property in the 1790s, such that by 1820, nearly 12 percent of black families were middle-class property owners. But those who were not property owners are reported to have occupied the worst slums in the city, where numerous families were forced to be crowded into dark, dirty, and damp cellars.[41] Blacks in the major cities were much more likely to live in a part of a house that was occupied by several families.

Labor Patterns

The proximity of family members under the same roof in the absence of a white patriarch and mistress was an improvement in the quality of life for most liberated blacks. But it did not necessarily empower black men as patriarchs. Discriminatory hiring and wage practices in the peacetime economy made survival and the acquisition of wealth and property difficult for most.

James and Lois Horton report that in most cases African Americans were excluded from all but the most undesirable, dangerous, and lowest paid jobs in society. They estimate that two-thirds to three-fourths of all blacks in antebellum northern cities worked at jobs requiring little skill and no formal education, and poverty led many to petty crime. It is also true that the occupations of minister and teacher came to fruition only after men like Absolom Jones, Prince Hall, and John Talisman were kicked out of white churches and white-run schools. The ghettoing of the black urban labor market combined with the segregated professional sector obviously marked a racial division of labor.[42]

Black survival often required that wife and children be bound to whites as indentured servants, or working for wages. The absence of persons in the household, as well as the decentralization of economic power, would have likely compromised the ability of a "head of household" to exercise patriarchal authority. Without property, a man cannot bestow inheritances, and thus the power to write a will becomes moot. In addition, those who could not meet the property requirements for suffrage could not vote. Property and income were required to support a wife as a domestic "bourgeoise." The absence of a dependent bourgeois wife and nonworking children was thus another factor that created racial difference and prevented the equal development of black patriarchy in the early Republic.

Labor patterns reinforced race and gender hierarchy. The more prestigious the profession or craft, the more likely the opportunity was foreclosed to nonwhites of both sexes and white women. The racial division of labor reinforced what Mills calls a "moral geography" separating dark and white spaces. The evidence for this is especially clear for Philadelphia, which had the largest black population.

In that city, some African Americans were successful as entrepreneurs and professionals. The black school and church movements provided an avenue for black teachers and ministers. Many more were skilled laborers and artisans. Black Philadelphians worked as carpenters, tailors, painters, paperhangers, brass founders, cabinet makers, cigar makers, coopers, gunsmiths, jewelers, silversmiths, plasterers, potters, shipwrights, wheelwrights, and hatters. As Nash reports, the number of skilled occupations increased steadily from 1795 to 1811, and the number of skilled black artisans listed in the city directory increased as well from 1795 to 1816. At the same time, those occupying the lowest class of unskilled laborers was predominantly black. Highly skilled artisans and the emerging industrial sector preferred immigrant and native white labor to black labor.[43]

The racial segregation of labor may have been less pronounced in New York with its gradual emancipation act, which slowed the early development of a separate black community. But class differences between white and black were still notable. According to Shane White, one in three blacks in New York City lived in a white household between 1790 and 1810, and most were probably domestic servants. In that city, a "free" black was much more likely to remain dependent on whites, because New York's gradual manumission act was essentially an extension of slavery into the first quarter of the nineteenth century. It stipulated that anyone born after July 4, 1799 was "free," but would serve the owners of their mother until the age of 25 for females and 28 for males. As we shall see, Abigail Adams took advantage of New York's extension of slavery, making use of a black boy of 15 bound out to her during John's term as vice president.

Free blacks living in independent households were more likely to be skilled than those in white households. White estimates that at least 40 percent of the free black heads of households were either dock laborers or mariners in the first decade of the nineteenth century, which may explain why there was a greater tendency for black women to head households than white women. New York blacks were more than twice as likely to possess a skill than were Philadelphia blacks. Much of the skilled black labor developed during the extended period of servitude after 1799. Skilled artisans were the largest group of slave owners in New York, and slaves were often trained as apprentices. Free mulatto immigrants also tended to possess artisan skills. After the turn of the century, as in Philadelphia, those entering professions and small proprietorships grew. One occupation, the oyster trade, was dominated by New York blacks; and two occupations had zero black representation: merchants and lawyers.

Black women were also active in the work force, and their labor distinguished them from black men and white women. Some were bakers, seamstresses, and market sellers, but by far the most common occupations for black women were washers and domestic workers. They were more likely than white women to work outside their own homes, and when they did, they suffered a narrower range of occupational choices than black men. Many turned desperately to prostitution. Some of the city's brothels were run by black women, whose services to white men appear to have impeded efforts by neighbors to have them closed. The public-private split that marked male and female space in the white community was thus much less pronounced for black women than it was for white women.

White women were encouraged in the popular literature to avoid public places, and be content in domesticity. Historians' reports of the labor patterns show another side of the same story. Before and during the Revolution, white women were employed in a variety of skilled trades and crafts. They were silversmiths, tin workers, bakers, lumberjacks, gunsmiths, fish picklers, brewers, milliners, harness makers, potash manufacturers, upholsterers, dry cleaners, dyers, seamstresses, woodworkers, stay makers, tavern- and inn-keepers, midwives, coach makers, embroiderers, rope makers, founders, tanners, and barbers.

By the 1790s and early 1800s, a middle class of white women developed. Increasingly, only poor women would be employed in the paid labor force, while their better-off sisters became the American bourgeoises, whose lives were wholly domesticated. Separate, gendered spheres began to crystallize in the post-revolutionary period. In the European American community, mothers who had worked for pay, or run family businesses with their husbands, aspired to provide for their daughters' refinement and education. These daughters were much less likely to be as economically productive or entrepreneurial as their mothers.[44]

By contrast, according to Gordon Wood, men in northern states in the 1790s would become increasingly identified with their labor; at the same time, the concept of property would transform from a static conception connoting leisure and independence from labor, to a dynamic one identified with the fruits of one's labor. For white men, work supplanted leisure as the sign of trustworthiness and virtue in political leadership. The nonworking landed gentry were increasingly criticized for their "idleness," and suspected as being promoters of the interests of the aristocratic class, rather than of the common good.

The failure of Anglo-Americans to recognize nonwhite men and women as virtuous and trustworthy on account of their labors presents yet another example of cognitive dissonance. Opportunities in productive labor and the respect it accorded thus became a marker of gender and race. Denying black men honor and reputation prevented the identification of white and black men as men; it also prevented a parallel development of gender hierarchy in the black community.

Military Service and Patriotism

The military was another institution that created and maintained race and gender hierarchy. Many enslaved men won their freedom through service in the war. But discriminatory recruiting and enlistment practices of the armed forces resulted in few African Americans receiving stipends and benefits to which white soldiers were entitled. Whereas most white male war veterans were rewarded with land, a stipend, or both for their services, most African Americans were not. Initially blacks were banned from the militia and the army; many tens of thousands fled to the British cause for the promise of unconditional freedom.

In 1779, the U.S. Congress officially recruited slaves as soldiers, reversing its prior ban. According to Benjamin Quarles, most slaves who fought for the patriots did receive certificates of manumission, and a few received land or stipends. But those who fought in place of their masters with only verbal promises of manumission after the war could be required to turn their wages and bounty of land over to their masters. Those who fled masters to enlist could be, and often were, returned to bondage after the war, even if the master was a loyalist.[45]

Free blacks who enlisted did not always receive land and pensions. The story of Cato Howe, Plato Turner, Quamony Quash, and Prince Goodwin—four black veterans who settled a piece of land outside of Plymouth they called the Parting Ways—is instructive. Entitled to benefits but lacking the education and wherewithal to pursue them, they lived most of their adult lives on the edge of poverty. Eventually they did receive stipends for revolutionary war service, but only in old age, after having desperately ceded their property rights to a local white man who fought for their benefits and thereby received his rents.[46]

Women were officially banned from serving in the armed forces, although a few of them did serve disguised as male soldiers, and many more were desperate camp followers who served as cooks, washers, and nurses to their husbands and other men. But women were not held accountable for political loyalty, as men were. In his 1978 book on the development of American citizenship, James Kettner noted that men made the transition from British subjects to American citizens by swearing allegiance to the revolutionary governments. The early years of the Revolution were likened to a "state of nature," without laws, in which a social compact would be formed through the voluntary allegiance of those who elected to become signatories. As dependents of their husbands or fathers, however, women's oaths of allegiance were generally neither required nor sought—another indication of the sexual nature of the social compacts.

The gender difference on political allegiance affected mostly the white community in cases of property seizures. For example, in cases involving seized property of loyalist families, family property could be seized on the basis of the husband's political allegiance alone. But wives could be entitled to seized property on the grounds that they couldn't legally have a political will separate from that of their husbands, thus they could not be held accountable for their husbands' decisions to join the British. A married woman was "bound to obey" her husband, except in activities involving "murder or treason." Joan Gundersen, Wayne Bodle, and Linda Kerber have all presented case studies that demonstrate the various states' refusal to view married women as capable of independent political allegiance, and thus citizenship. Courts had the opportunity to allow married women to declare their own political allegiance, and subsequently hold them accountable for their decisions. Despite the urging of some lawyers to consider women as independent persons capable of political commitments, they chose to preserve the law of coverture.[47]

Public celebrations such as national holiday parades generally prohibited white women and black men from participation, except as
spectators. The issue was more a matter of racial politics, because
most of the national holidays celebrated political and military victo-
ries, which were already determined to be the province of men. Shane
White reports that as freed blacks moved from rural to urban areas in
the early nineteenth century, they came face to face with whites who
resented their presence, and any sign of African American achievement. They excluded African Americans from most ceremonial events
of the new Republic, including Washington's birthday, Independence
Day, the ratification of the U.S. Constitution, and the opening of the
Erie Canal in 1825.[48]

Suffrage and Federal Rights

In social contract theory, the right to vote is probably the primary sym-
bol of the citizen's signature to the social compact. By consenting to the
original compact and forming a constitution, one "signs on" to the social compact and its structure of government. Once the constitution
has been written and ratified, the right to vote symbolizes continuing
consent to the established social and political order. The right to vote
was originally controlled by state governments. Constitution-making
was restricted to white males of property in the United States, but the
ratification of state constitutions included black male participation in
some places, and voting for representatives had been practiced by
women and nonwhites in Massachusetts, New Jersey, and possibly Virginia before the U.S. Constitution was ratified. From about 1790 to the
1850s, race and gender became qualifying factors for the franchise,
while property was gradually eliminated as a qualifying factor. Women
and blacks were disfranchised while white males were increasingly enfranchised.

The increasing trend to restrict the franchise to white men suggests
that the consent of nonwhite persons and white women was viewed as
irrelevant. With respect to the vote, black men appear to have been
more privileged than white women. In colonial times, unmarried
women who met legal property qualifications were allowed to vote,
along with men of similar wealth, married or unmarried. A few
wealthy baronesses were known to have exercised political rights and

wielded social and economic power. But after independence was declared, women became disfranchised in the new state constitutions. New York was the first state to specify "male" suffrage in its constitution, in 1777; the other states followed suit soon after. According to Joan Hoff, none of the new state constitutions granted women the right to vote except New Jersey, which then disfranchised women and blacks simultaneously, in 1807. The use of the petition also appears to have declined after independence, suggesting that, in general, the whole concept of women as rights-bearing citizens was rejected.[49]

The effort to disfranchise blacks on account of race would have been complete but for a few northern states in which black citizens retained the right to vote. During the ratification of the Articles of Confederation (1777), free Negroes could vote and were citizens of New Hampshire, Massachusetts, New York, New Jersey, and North Carolina. Several new states that were admitted to the Union, including Vermont (1790), Kentucky (1792), and Tennessee (1796), made no provisions for excluding free blacks from suffrage. Along with Maine (1819), they were the only states that entered the Union prior to the Civil War that did not restrict the suffrage to whites. In Maine, New Hampshire, Vermont, Massachusetts, and Rhode Island, free black men could vote without restriction.

As gradual emancipation acts were passed and the numbers of free blacks increased, other states moved to restrict their voting rights. Maryland disfranchised blacks in 1783; Delaware and Kentucky did so in 1792 and 1799. As new states formed, they followed suit, disfranchising blacks repeatedly up until the post–Civil War Reconstruction era. Connecticut was the only state in New England to disfranchise blacks, in 1819. In New York, black men were required to present an election certificate after 1811; and in 1821, that state included a discriminatory voting provision in its new constitution that burdened black men with a higher property qualification and longer residency period to exercise the right to vote.

In short, all states except Massachusetts, Vermont, Rhode Island, and New Hampshire either restricted or abolished the right of free black men to vote. By contrast, between 1790 and 1825, the franchise expanded to include white adult males regardless of property holdings in most states.[50]

Other rights defined by the federal government also employed differences in race and gender to restrict full citizenship to white males. The right to travel was racially encoded. Although some persons of color did obtain passports, others were barred from getting them. To travel within the United States, African Americans were required to carry official passes certifying their status as free persons. The acquisition of these passes was financially and practically burdensome. Only white men had the right to carry U.S. mail. As early as 1810, the federal government barred African Americans from working for the U.S. Postal Service. In 1790, Congress restricted naturalization to "free white" aliens, refusing to make nonwhite immigrants citizens of the United States. New state constitutions quickly moved to allow foreign-born white men property rights associated with naturalization, and all the rights that stemmed from them, including suffrage and the right to run for and hold elective offices. White women could be naturalized, as James Kettner and Linda Kerber have pointed out, but their membership in the United States did not make them independent citizens.[51]

Literacy and Education

The lines of racial patriarchy were also defined by literacy and access to formal education. Studies on literacy suggest that white men were the most privileged, but white women were more privileged than black men, who were more privileged than black women. Education in reading and writing was generally available to anyone who was free and had the money to hire a private tutor, or send their child to a private school. Several of the founders, including Thomas Jefferson, Noah Webster, and Benjamin Rush, argued that systems of public education were essential to the maintenance of republicanism; but, as Lorraine and Thomas Pangle have argued, school taxes were unpopular, especially among the more affluent families who sent their own children to private schools and did not want to subsidize the education of the masses. Most areas of the country, including towns, remained without a system of public schools until well into the nineteenth century.[52]

Within white colonial communities, the education of males and females was distinct. Formal, private education was available to white girls in New England in the colonial period, through dame schools. Few families sent their daughters to these private homes of dames who provided care and taught reading to very young children. A 1647 law in Massachusetts required every town of at least 50 families to provide instruction in reading and writing in English; towns of more than 100 families were required to provide for a Latin grammar school. To comply with the law, towns began to pay dames of dame schools for basic literacy instruction, which may or may not have actually included writing skills. As towns developed and populations increased, town leaders typically hired a Latinist to head the central school, but had women teach in "women's schools" at the outskirts of town. Women were increasingly hired as "town teachers" starting in 1713 and throughout the eighteenth century, in various Massachusetts towns as well as in Connecticut and New Hampshire. In general, these women taught reading and sometimes writing during the summers to the younger girls and boys, while men taught more advanced subjects during the winter to older boys; but as the demand for education grew, women gradually began to replace men and perform their roles in these lower-tier schools. Girls did not attend the upper-tier Latin grammar schools, and women did not teach in them. Well before 1750, "woman's schools" developed in which reading and sometimes writing was taught to boys and less often girls.

Because the education of boys was mandatory, whereas that of girls was not for most of the eighteenth century in New England, universal literacy among American-born males was achieved sooner. The extent of the literacy gap varies by study. Literacy has been measured by looking at signatures on wills and deeds, and comparing those who signed to those who made a mark. An early study by Kenneth Lockridge, based on a small sample of wills, estimated that illiteracy was nearly wiped out among men in New England by 1795, while half the women were still illiterate. More recent studies using deed data have pushed the estimate of female literacy upward. One study estimates that literacy among women in 1795 who were born after 1766 reached 80 to 83 percent, closing the literacy gap among whites in New England by around 1800.[53] These figures are all based on estate documents, and thus contain a built-in race and class bias.

One study of Rhode Island town records on the interrogations of transients, those without property, shows a much lower figure. In that population between 1750 and 1800, 77 percent of white men were literate, but the literacy rate for nonwhite men and for white females was at 21 percent, while nonwhite women suffered the lowest literacy rate, at only 6.3 percent.[54] The closing of the literacy gap between white men and white women of property-holding classes, and the same literacy rate for transient nonwhite men and white women, together suggest that literacy rates were mainly dependent on class, especially after 1795.

In many, especially southern, slave states, there was a legal prohibition against literacy instruction for slaves, and this undoubtedly put most African Americans at a disadvantage when compared to most whites, by the 1770s. In the North, slaves were not prohibited from reading, but few masters taught their slaves to read, and even fewer sent them to school. It was common for northern abolitionists to exemplify educated African Americans as evidence that blacks had the *ability* to become literate, and thus civilized. If they could become literate like any white person, then they could be civilized, meaning that they would still be under the control of white society and its norms when emancipated.

This argument was launched against others who claimed that blacks were naturally mentally deficient or of a subhuman species. Thus, for example, when the Boston slave Phillis Wheatley published a book of poems, northern abolitionists like John Hancock and the Reverend Samuel Mather proclaimed that a "young Negro girl, . . . an uncultivated Barbarian from Africa," could read and write, and assimilate to the Anglo-European tradition. Others, particularly Thomas Jefferson, refused to validate Wheatley's intellect, and dismissed her mastery of Western, neoclassical style as "colorless" and thus not authentically "Zulu" or African. In this view, black literary accomplishment could only be unnaturally "imitative" of white culture, of which a black person could never really be part.[55] In any case, free African Americans were more likely to be hindered by economic necessity, and thus more likely to be uneducated and illiterate than European Americans.

The near universal literacy of middle-class white women allowed for the establishment of over 400 female academies and seminaries between 1790 and 1830, followed by hundreds more before the outbreak of the Civil War. According to Kerber, "no social change in the early Republic affected women more emphatically than the improvement of schooling, which opened the way to a modern world."

The degree to which the "modern world" was opened to white women through the new academies is relative. Access to college education was restricted to males, and generally to white males of the wealthiest families. The expense and pressures of an agrarian economy prevented most white men from seeking a college education. Women of the wealthiest families were barred from colleges, but black men were sometimes admitted to them. John Russwirm's attainment of a degree from Bowdoin College was exceptional, as even elite men of free black communities were far less likely than whites to have a college degree.

Female academies and seminaries typically offered a curriculum that was more advanced than that of primary school, but less rigorous than what was offered in the colleges and universities for men. The curriculum for the first female academy established—The Young Ladies Academy in Philadelphia—included reading, writing, arithmetic, English grammar, composition, rhetoric, and geography. It did not include natural philosophy, advanced mathematics, or the classics, which were typical courses in men's colleges. Indeed, Priscilla Mason's much quoted valedictory essentially justified women engaging in oratory, and articulated a critique of patriarchal society, "our high and mighty lords," for closing off the church, the bar, and the Senate to women while degrading their minds and dooming them to "frivolous employments."[56]

The practical curriculum of most ladies' academies represented a compromise between those who argued that women could reason equally with men and therefore should have identical curricula, and those who argued that intellectual accomplishment would masculinize the fair sex and encourage white women to abandon ascribed duties in motherhood and domesticity. In that compromise, white women were educated to balance accounts, read maps, speak and write in correct English grammar—all of the practical skills that were necessary for managing a household without threatening the sanctity of the marriage contract or the patriarchal separation of spheres.

And yet, as Mary Kelley has demonstrated, near universal literacy among white women did validate the female intellect, and the propriety of reading for women. It undoubtedly stimulated them to consider alternatives to the conventions by which they lived. Beyond that, it also appears to have led to the organization and establishment of female literary societies and to teaching as a woman's profession. Women were typically paid less than half of what a man might be paid for the same work, but teaching was one profession that did not compromise the virtues that a white woman was supposed to display. The universal literacy of white women in the North by the turn of the century facilitated the development of epistolary and community networks for white women. This intellectual development undoubtedly exacerbated the gap between white women and nonwhites of both sexes, and may have even been effective in facilitating the development of communicative rationality, or more open-ended egalitarian discussions in families. But it appears not to have altered white women's economic, legal, or political status.[57]

When middle-class white men had access to universities and colleges, and middle-class white women had access to seminaries and academies, the better-off free African Americans of both sexes were learning the basics of reading, writing, and arithmetic. The universal literacy of middle-class white women gave them an advantage over most African Americans in the last decade of the eighteenth century and beyond. Differences in educational opportunities were linked to articulated differences in human nature, as well as economic advantages.

By the 1760s, the number of white females who were taught to read and write in families and private schools made the question of literacy moot. The debates on female education that began in the 1760s and came into full bloom in the 1790s centered on the *propriety* of educating females, given that they ought not be encouraged to move beyond their proper sphere of domesticity. But during the same period, the debate on blacks and education centered on whether those of African origin or descent had the *ability* to become fully literate in English.

Religion

Religious practices and institutions were also reinforced by race and gender hierarchy. Women and blacks were categorically viewed as naturally more sinful than white males, which justified their subordination. Historians have documented that blacks were originally viewed by European Christians as heathens.[58] In the sixteenth and seventeenth centuries, the absence of Christianity provided a justification for the enslavement of Africans and Native Americans, as well as the racial distinction between the white indentured servant and the black slave. As slaves adopted Christianity, whites relied on physical differences to articulate racial difference and white supremacy. This difference was carried over in the post-revolutionary North, where racially segregated seating and worship services existed. The rude and discriminatory treatment of blacks by whites in Philadelphia forced blacks to develop self-help societies and churches.

The black charitable organizations and churches created solidarity among free and enslaved blacks. When Richard Allen and Absolom Jones, along with other parishioners, were dragged from worship services for sitting in a new balcony of St. Georges Episcopal Church, they raised money to form Philadelphia's Free African Society, and subsequently founded the Saint Thomas Protestant Episcopal Church. Other black churches and charitable societies developed in New York and Boston, creating a kind of parallel "bourgeois public sphere," to use Habermas's term, in which free and enslaved blacks could discuss their experiences and strategies openly, as equals.[59]

White women also developed community ties through religion in the late eighteenth and early nineteenth centuries. Through these ties they may also have enjoyed discursive equality amongst themselves, as the predominant group in congregations. Yet ideologies of gender difference and the restriction of the ministry to white males may well have kept white women from using churches to develop progressive strategies as blacks of both sexes did in their churches.

In eighteenth-century English and American literature, white women were often viewed as the descendants of a sinful Eve,[60] whose vanity and curiosity led her to eat the forbidden fruit and cause the subsequent fall of mankind. Because of their "natural" propensity toward sin, they were encouraged in conduct literature to be more pious, temperate, and modest than men. For the same reason, women's virtue was considered more important than men's. The notion of women's greater propensity toward sin was also used to explain their suffering in childbirth and to justify their subordination to men in families.

Even in the mid-seventeenth century, women outnumbered men in congregations, which were almost always led by male ministers. As commercialization and industrialization developed in the Northeast, men were even less of a presence among congregations. Nancy Cott has argued that this development and the domination of congregations by white women led to an ideological change in which women would be viewed as naturally suited for religion by nature, as well as by an emotional temperament of tenderness and sensibility, developed in domesticity. Some suggested that the white woman's religiosity made her the spiritual equal of man, but neither the domination of women in white churches nor the new ideology would disrupt patriarchally controlled churches. Cott suggested that the Great Awakening from 1798 to 1826 in New England enabled women to have a bourgeois public existence, as charitable associations and maternal societies emerged and multiplied.

But the development of "woman's sphere" did not allow most white women discursive equality with white men, either with respect to reason or revelation. Catherine Brekus's recent study on female preaching from the mid-eighteenth century to the mid-nineteenth century confirms this view. There were examples of female exhorters in the North and South who claimed to be directly influenced by God, and were even sought by preachers for their advice. In the southern colonies, in particular, white women were allowed to speak publicly and serve as deaconesses and eldresses in Separate Baptist Churches in the 1770s. But even in the South, white women never argued that women should rule, or be ordained, and they never questioned female subordination to men. In the North and the South, ministers encouraged women to subordinate themselves—to "learn in silence with all subjection" and to "know their place" in plantation hierarchies. According to Brekus, female preachers of the late eighteenth and early nineteenth centuries resigned themselves to serving as men's helpmeets or assistants. The ministry remained the province of white men, whose sermons tended to reinforce sexual difference and the domesticity of white women.[61]

Concluding Remarks

A theory of racial patriarchy in the early American Republic requires an integrated examination of white supremacy and male supremacy. To start, it requires an examination of the sexual and racial contracts underlying social contract theory, which have been separately identified by Carole Pateman and Charles Mills. The study of male supremacy and white supremacy as two separate systems has led to awkward universals, which suggest that patriarchy privileged "men," and racism privileged "whites," when we know that patriarchal practices did not privilege black men in the same way as white men, and white privileges did not grant white women privileges equal to those of white men.

The rudimentary theory of racial patriarchy presented here posits a unified system of hierarchy in which the category "white" was theoretically positioned above the category "black," while the category "male" was positioned above the category "female." I raised the issue of primacy, that is, the question whether racial hierarchy was a priority over gender oppression (or vice versa) because the determination of which hierarchy is operative in a particular historical context is important to find possible remedies or solutions, however partial or transitory.

The evidence collected and presented on institutions and practices suggests that with respect to property ownership, white women enjoyed particular advantages over black women. Comparing white women with black men with respect to class and property ownership becomes difficult for two reasons. First, there appear to be no studies providing comparative data between the two groups. Second, it has always been difficult to determine women's class position relative to that of men because of the restrictions of coverture. It is difficult to evaluate women's property ownership when marriage allowed husbands, not wives, sole authority in general to direct family income and assets. The "embourgoisement" of white women, or their particular experience of "woman's sphere" of domesticity, thus appears to have been a function of race *and* class.

With respect to labor and suffrage rights, black men may have fared better than all women, yet were not as privileged as white men. In terms of military service, black men appear to have gained at least some recognition, in the form of property. This was not the case for white or black women, who were excluded from remunerative military service more completely than black men. Black veterans were shunned from displays of patriotism in public celebrations that heralded white veterans. And black women received none of the recognition that white women received for their patriotic sacrifices. Regarding literacy and education, despite the few African American men who were admitted to colleges, many more white women had access to ladies' seminaries and academies. Further, on average, white women seem to have fared better than nonwhites in terms of literacy, which reflected both racial prohibitions and exclusions as well as class differences between most whites and most blacks.

The theory of racial patriarchy cannot predict the exact positions of white women with respect to black men or black women; it cannot determine whether race, class, or gender is primary. Actual positioning can only be approximated through historical investigation of particular persons in specific contexts. In developing a theory of racial patriarchy, it is not my intention to make blanket universal assumptions about lived experience, but rather to pose questions about lived experience in light of known ideas circulating in political discourses of the period under study. Through the theory, I suggest that "natural" differences articulated in the political theory and ideology of the Revolutionary and founding eras were in important ways reflected in institutions and practices. All of the major societal institutions and practices, such as marriage, property relations, employment, the military, schools, and churches, seem to have supported the separation of spheres and the dominance of white men as citizens above other noncitizens.

But this cursory historical investigation highlights the theory's *indeterminacy* with respect to lived experience. The theory of racial patriarchy is intended to prompt micro-level investigation across categories of race, gender, and class to test the theory's premises. It provides a theoretical context against which to interpret how particular individuals were defined by differences, or alternatively, how they deployed, utilized, escaped, or negotiated these categories.

From what we have examined in late eighteenth-century America, race appears to have been primary to class and gender for two reasons. First, Gordon Wood's assessment that property ownership was near universal for white men stands in stark contrast to the near universal propertyless status of black men in the early Republic. Second, marriage relations were largely determinative of gender relations, establishing patriarchy, but the marriage contract was largely racially bound. As a general rule, black men did not enjoy patriarchal privileges in families the way white men did. And, although white women generally did not enjoy equal property rights with white men, they were much more likely to be property owners than black men were. White women were also more likely to reap the benefits of having shared property formally owned by their husbands than were black women.

The general positioning of white women in racial patriarchy, and the issue of primacy become clearer when we examine specific historical issues. Sometimes it is not possible to disentangle a racial issue from a sexual one. As we shall see in the next chapter, race and gender norms were bound together in an "ideology of the fair sex" that circulated in popular discussions, letters, and magazine articles in the post-revolutionary period. This ideology effectively encoded distinctions that separated white women from white men on the one hand, and white women from nonwhite women on the other.

3

The Ideology of the "Fair Sex"

The theory of racial patriarchy suggests that white women were ambiguously positioned in the hierarchy of gender and race relative to white men and nonwhite persons of both sexes. This ambiguity was neither happenstance nor inexplicable, but culturally produced through discourses on the "fair sex" which circulated through letters, essays, satire, and ordinary conversations.

In contrast to the ideal of the empowered republican mother, held by many American historians today, actual discourses on the "fair sex" in the late eighteenth and early nineteenth centuries situated white women instrumentally rather than as discursive equals capable of participating in an ideal speech situation. In fair sex ideology, white women of propertied classes were already doubly positioned, as subordinate others with respect to white men and as superior subjects with respect to nonwhites. This double positioning precluded the ideal of communicative rationality across gender lines within the Anglo-American community, and between the races in society in general.

Two implications follow regarding fair sex ideology and its function in racial patriarchy. First, strategic deployment and ordinary usage of the term "fair sex" produced white women as a special category: a racialized sex group that lost consciousness of itself as bounded by race and class, retaining the memory of its identity as one based on gender alone. Once the discourse was deployed, one understood universals like "females," "ladies," and "the sex" to mean white and middle class without having to make these specific references.

Second, repetition and redeployment of fair sex ideology served as an act of "signing on" to racial patriarchy. Fair sex parlance was a means by which individuals consented, explicitly and then tacitly, to the social order. If the first proponents of the virtues and vices of the fair sex deployed the term strategically, others further removed would deploy it unselfconsciously. Fair sex ideology would thus lose consciousness of itself as strategic, and become something ordinary, understood, reified, and dogmatic. In parallel fashion, the hierarchies of racial patriarchy, though somewhat disrupted by egalitarian rhetoric of the revolutionary American Enlightenment, would be justified and strengthened during the founding era, such that *their* disruption would then require justification.

Fair Sex Ideology and English Literature

Combing through the popular literature of late eighteenth century America, and in particular, of post-revolutionary America, one discovers that women were often referred to as "the fair sex." A crude genealogy of the term fair sex in the American post-revolutionary period reveals that the association of white women with a political duty to civilize men was neither original to America nor politically progressive.[1] The utterance meant both "white female" and "more virtuous gender." Usage of the terms "fair sex" or "the sex" dates back to the European Renaissance. It involved the articulation of racial difference, in which the word "fair" referred to light skin tone, civilized beauty, and moral purity. The "fair" European was contrasted with the "sooty" or "jetty" Negro, the "pale" Asiatic, and sometimes even the off-color "sallow" of the Native Americans and southern Europeans. Simultaneously, it involved an articulation of gender difference: "the sex" referred to females as the repository of sexuality that had to be reserved, contained, and excluded lest its passion corrupt rationality.

According to the *Oxford English Dictionary* (*OED*), the oldest meaning of the word "fair" or "fayre" (c. 888) is beautiful, or good looking, chiefly in reference to the face, almost exclusively of women. The terms "fair sex," "fair one," or the French "le beau sexe" to describe women can be traced to 1440. As early as 1340, "fair" referred to conduct, actions, and arguments, as in kindly, benignant, peaceable, or favorable. At this time "fair" also referred to freedom from disfigurement, as in clean, unsoiled, or unstained, as well as freedom from moral blemish, as in impartial or morally pure. By 1551, just when the English are reported to have had first contact with Africans, fair became a reference to skin tone and hair color, meaning light as opposed to dark, and white as opposed to black.

As Jordan has reported, the most striking feature of the African to the Englishman was his color. The English encounter with the Africans in the 1550s and beyond brought together the lightest people on Earth with the blackest people on Earth. Quoting the *OED*, Jordan notes that the word "black" conveyed many meanings associated with evil:

> deeply stained with dirt; soiled, dirty, foul . . . Having dark or deadly purposes, malignant; pertaining to or involving death, deadly; baneful, disastrous, sinister. . . . Foul, iniquitous, atrocious, horrible, wicked. Indicating disgrace, censure, liability to punishment, etc.[2]

Shakespeare deployed all of these meanings of the words fair and black in *Othello* (1604).

The dual meanings of the term fair sex were expressed a century before the American Revolution, in England.[3] A text search in the *English Poetry Database* for the words fair sex results in several seventeenth-century poems.[4] Consider "The Pleasures of Love and Marriage," by Richard Ames, published in 1691, in the wake of the Glorious Revolution. As a response to misogynist degradations of women as the descendants of a sinful Eve, Ames' 26-page poem set out to describe the virtues of the fair sex:

> *Divinist Sex*, compos'd of purer *Mold*!
> (We only the *Ore*, but you the *Gold*.)
> How shall I justly Treat so vast a *Theme*,
> Where *meanly* to *Commend* were to *Blaspheme*?
> How shall I give your *Virtues* half their due,
> In *Living Verse*, and *Numbers* worthy you?

Ames characterizes the fair sex with the virtues of beauty, a smiling kindly face and softness and charm that inspire male creativity and industrious domesticity ("The bolder Male abroad for Food does roam,/ And leaves th'industrious Female Close at home"). The beauty and domesticity of wives are romanticized by suggesting that theirs is an equally or perhaps more commanding power than that of men in "the world."

> In *Politics* and *Architecture* Skill'd,
> *Men* boast they *Empires* raise and *Cities* Build:
> Monsters and Thieves are the Destruction hurl'd
> By them; 'tis they pretend to Rule the *World*;
> When *Women* kept it in its constant state,
> While they their first *fair Copy* [Eve] imitate
> Encourage *man* in all his *sweat* and *toils*,

> And richly pay his pains with *Love* and *Smiles*.
> 'Tis *Woman* makes the ravish'd *Poet* Write,
> 'Tis Lovely *Woman* makes the *Soldier* Fight;
> The Merchant sails to China or Peru,
> Farther than *Janson* or *Mercator* Knew;
> And *Caravans* through Sandy Desarts rome,
> but to the same *account* their *Labours* coam,
> To bring a *Mistress* silks or Spices home.
> If them with welcom *Smiles* she's pleas'd to meet
> Down go their *Gold* and *Jewels* at her Feet.
> Should that *soft Sex* refuse the World to Bless,
> Twou'd soon be *Chaos* all, or *Wilderness*;
> A *Herd*, without *Civility* or Rules,
> A *Drove* of Drinking, Cheating, Fighting *Fools*; . . .
> Twas *Beauty* first made *Laws*, did Monsters bind,
> Reform'd the *World* and civiliz'd *Mankind*.
> (Emphasis in original)[5]

A virtuous wife figures as the muse for men's poetry, the beauty behind men's laws, and the source of inspiration for men's actions in the world. The soft, smiling faces of women inspire men to work hard and fight to bring them delights such as spices, silk, and jewels. The fair sex is credited with the inspiration for and maintenance of civilization. Without them, men would be but a herd of rough, dishonest, belligerent fools. The mind of woman is fanciful, characterized by a natural, untutored "Wit," which makes her conversation delightful, a source of pleasure and harmony in men's lives.

> *Man*'s like a *Lute* unstrung, until he be
> By *Conversation* turn'd to *Harmony*
> And *that*'s it self, if *Woman* from it stays,
> As *dull* as when an *ill Musician* Plays.
> Woman's the *Salt of Life*, without a *Grain*
> Of which, attempts for *Mirth* were all in vain;
> Where e're she treads like *Sunshine* guilds the ground
> And throw an air of *Life* and *Pleasure* round.[6]

Woman's virtue also lay in her modesty or "complaisance," the opposite of pride. Their "sweet arts of complaisance" lend them to be the best tutors of men, particularly those who have been corrupted into fashionable fops by visiting France. As for the women that have succumbed to fashion and vanity themselves, they are excused as merely trying to please men.

> Where did they learn their *Pride* unless from you?
> If they're infected, 'Tis with your Disease;
> Unless *fantastick*, they can never please.[7]

Interestingly, virtues of chastity and purity are measured by the whiteness of a woman's skin.

> If you a *Virtuous Woman* tempt in vain,
> Who still repells you with deserv'd disdain,
> Who all your weak *designs* secure can mock,
> Firm seated on an *Alabaster Rock*.
> Her Snowy *Bosom* not more pure and fair,
> Than the *white Guest* still inhabits there, . . .

The association of beauty and virtue with fair skin and hair is also represented in Gould's poem "To My Lady Abingdon" (1709):

> Of some bright Dames w'ave been by *Poets* told
> Whose Breasts were heaving Snow, and Hair of flowing Gold:
>   Whose eyes were Lights able to rule the Day,
> In which ten Thousand *Cupid's* basking lay, . . .

Again, fair sex ideology was present on the other side of the Atlantic well before the American Revolution.

The Fair Sex and American Independence

During the War of Independence, women were called upon to contribute to the war effort and to do much of the work left behind by men who served as soldiers or legislators. As Mary Beth Norton and Linda Kerber have documented, white and black women asserted themselves as patriots (and loyalists) during the Revolution. Sometimes as a response to male patriots' calls for help, other times upon their own initiatives, women made political contributions by circulating petitions, leading the boycotts on British tea and clothing, spinning and weaving homespun linens, and raising money for the revolutionary army. Many wives also served as "deputy husbands," conducting business as heads-of-households while their husbands were away fighting or legislating.

They provided food and shelter for soldiers in their homes, and some women became camp followers of Washington's Army, serving as cooks, laundresses, and nurses. A few, like the African American Deborah Sampson Gannett, dressed in men's clothing and fought as soldiers. Others fended off the British in their own homes, or attacked them in food riots.[8] Though never completely accepted in the public sphere during the war, white women were praised for their patriotic efforts.

In the post-revolutionary era, however, one detects a shift in public opinion. Virtues of female patriotism that were useful to win the war—like fortitude, bravery, intelligence, assertiveness, independence, and even aggression—were increasingly viewed as a threat to propriety and civilized manners. In the late 1780s to the turn of the century, popular discourses on the fair sex seem to have reasserted many of these feminine virtues and adapted them for the needs of the new nation. Uttered in the parlance of the New World, the words involved an articulation of race, sex, and class differences. Discourses on the fair sex converged into a kind of ideology that produced white, middle-class femininity.

By ideology, I do not mean any sort of tight theoretical strategy but rather a loose collection of discourses that came together in the early national period. Discourses in conduct literature, short stories, poems, and political essays produced a fairly stable system of ethics, which took as its object white women, and prescribed for them norms of virtuous behavior. The creation of norms for white middle-class women was done through specific language usage, and magnified through the literacy gap, discussed in the previous chapter, that ensured a predominantly white, middle-class readership.

In the 1790s, the utterance fair sex encoded race, gender, and class norms embedded within the racial, sexual, and social contracts. It served as signature to these contracts, and thereby produced racial patriarchy in ordinary, day-to-day social relations. Many popular writings deployed the terms "fair sex" explicitly, while others directed to "women" would carry the same messages, already understood to be directed toward white, middle-class women. By the turn of the century, more often than not, all the "fair" would be women, and all the "women" would be white.

Taken together, articles that mentioned the fair sex in passing or as a central focus attributed certain virtues to white women, or encouraged them to acquire them. They also warned against vices to avoid, those actions that would be taken as inappropriate for white womanhood.

The virtues included softness, meekness, delicacy, domesticity, sympathy, agreeableness, self-restraint, modesty, politeness, purity, piety, subordination, and deference to husbands. They also included industry, frugality, and literacy. Each of the virtues was defined by a contrast with its opposite, or corresponding, vice. These included: obstinacy, contention, pedantry, ambition, publicity, vanity, luxury, licentiousness, dissipation, intellectualism, and masculine pride.

Racial and ethnic overtones were also deployed to delineate the boundaries of moral behavior. Some of these virtues would demarcate race, class, and gender difference simultaneously, such as domesticity and delicacy. Alternatively, race, class, and gender boundaries might be drawn by an author's suggestion that the particular virtue or behavior was a marker of "civilization." Travel essays, for example, frequently described the differences between civilized and uncivilized behaviors by using the words "barbaric" or "savage" to describe practices of Africans or even southern Europeans. Other virtues, like industry and sympathy would be directed universally, but what counted as industry or sympathy might depend on one's gender, class, and ethnicity. None of these virtues or vices defined white womanhood by itself, but taken together, the virtue/vice binaries in discourses on the fair sex would create white womanhood as a category and define its boundaries.

All of the virtues ascribed to the fair sex were articulated within two linked contexts: marriage and American nationalism. These two contexts contained within them a consciousness of gender and ethnic identity. Marriage was described and understood as a woman's primary vocation in life, the institution on which her happiness and economic survival depended. But marriage was limited by and constitutive of European American cultural norms. Through the European American marriage contract, with its doctrine of coverture, a specific type of patriarchy was established. Pateman has called it "dual" or "modern" patriarchy, to describe the gendered separation of spheres typical of republicanism, combined with the modern invention of *representative* government. The American marriage contract did not resemble Native American marriage contracts, Asian marriages, or African marriages. That they did not was a point of racial and ethnic pride for Anglo-Americans. The institution of marriage in the United States shared a racial and ethnic heritage with England and northern Europe, but was infused with and shaped by the struggles peculiar to U.S. national development. Anglo-American nationalism was conceived through Anglo-Americans' image of themselves as heirs of British culture, including its republican tradition, North American empire, and racial or ethnic consciousness. During the Revolution, Anglo-Americans thought themselves to be of virtue superior to those of the corrupt mother country. But they also suffered a kind of inferiority complex as colonists—enough for Otis and others to assert their shared race and color with British subjects of the mother country, and for Jefferson to underline the Anglo-Saxon origins of American liberty.[9]

Early Nationalism and the Crisis in Virtue

After the war, the most immediately pressing national problem in the Anglo-American view was the postwar credit crisis. A great many European Americans owned land, but during and after the war, hard currency was scarce for almost all. As a form of postwar retribution, Britain denied Americans credit, demanded hard currency for past debts, and closed off West Indies trade to Americans, which had previously provided a means of securing money to pay for English goods. The credit crisis infiltrated American society from top to bottom. As coastal merchants were squeezed for cash, they pressed inland shopkeepers for cash as well, who were then forced to demand cash from farmers, who had been accustomed to bartering farm products for goods.[10] The crisis in credit was fueled by an increasing imbalance of trade between the United States and Britain, as Americans craved the finer products the mother country produced through her more developed manufacturing base. In addition to the "embarrassments of trade" when Americans reneged on their obligations, state and national governments found themselves unable to pay even the interest on debts owed to Holland and France for their assistance during the War of Independence.

The people responded to these economic pressures in two ways: by taking advantage of law, and by disregarding law. As Wood reports, large groups of people formed committees and associations to press their legislators for debt relief measures. They took advantage of their new rights in political participation to subvert private contracts and the rights of proprietors. State legislatures often granted their constituents' wishes, and passed laws allowing for the printing of paper money, the extension of credit, and even the confiscation of property. When legislators refused to do this, angry mobs who stood to lose their property denounced the government and its laws as tyrannical, and many simply defied them, as in Massachusetts in 1786, when the Shays rebels forcefully closed the Springfield court to stop its foreclosures, and again in Virginia in 1787, where rebels actually burned courthouses.

Because the credit crisis affected "good," industrious people and not just the riff-raff, some were sympathetic to debtors. James Warren, for example, complained to his friend John Adams shortly before Shays's Rebellion that Massachusetts government did nothing for its constituents to alleviate the credit crisis. "Paper money, Tenders of Lands, etc., suspension of Law Processes, and a variety of Expedients are proposed and nothing adopted." It seemed to him that there had been a "total change in principles and manners" since the days of the Revolution. The rich were now exerting their power over everyone else, supplanting republicanism with the pursuit of self-interest. If the government didn't do something soon, there would likely be eruptions of civil war. Adams saw things differently. He rejected that the government was at fault and emphasized that industry and import taxes, not debt relief, were the key to American viability. When the "state of anarchy" finally broke out in Shays's Rebellion, Adams was inclined to blame the people—"our countrymen have never merited the Character of very exalted Virtue."[11]

Some sympathized with the rebels, blaming the disorder on an "unequal and highly unjust distribution of property."[12] But most blamed the credit crisis on the vices of the people. Ordinary citizens imported foreign luxuries on credit, while sporting vices such as drinking, gaming, and speaking in profanities. Worse, these uneducated men were now dressing like their betters and emerging as leaders in business and politics. The concept of equality had been taken to "democratic despotism." Violent rebels merely gave the most anarchic expression of a growing body of people who would subvert the fundamental principles of government to promote their own interests.[13] Many members of the mercantile and legal communities were shocked by the quickness of the citizenry to abrogate the rights of property. In their view, the sanctity of private property rights provided the primary justification for government, their abrogation providing the primary justification for the Revolution against the mother country. They complained that ordinary folks were failing to respect social distinctions of class and education necessary for any civilized nation.

In the next few years, the concept of virtue would be thoroughly domesticated and feminized. The crisis in virtue was viewed not as a crisis in manly self-assertion, but a crisis in *civilized* virtues. The binary civilization/savagery contrasted both the educated property owners with the rebellious mobs as well as the white folks of Anglo-Saxon ancestry with the brown and black peoples of the "barbarous" regions of the globe.

Reverend Thomas Reese spoke for many of his race and class in his observation that republican government required a "moral and virtuous people," but so many were "illiterate and uncivilized."[14] Given that illiteracy was nearly wiped out in the white community when his article was published, the reference had to include newly emancipated African Americans as well as the lower-class rebels, whom he described as "idle" and "profligate" "traitors," "incendiaries," and "vile creatures."[15] Satirical articles in the *American Museum* played on race, gender, and class in their various representations of Shaysites as dumb oxen, savage anarchists, and effeminate consumers of luxury.

The Virtues and Vices of the Fair Sex: A Reassertion of Gender, Class, Ethnic, and Race Hierarchies

As Carroll Smith-Rosenberg has argued, discourses on virtue arose in the 1790s in response to the postwar economic crisis and the apparent disorder as a new class of impoverished persons came onto the scene through the emancipation and manumission of slaves.[16] American fair sex ideology developed out of these discourses on virtue. The virtues and vices in fair sex ideology would be tied to marriage, as woman's lot, and the norms of marriage would be tied to Anglo-American nationalism. As such, this loose system of ethics would define gender as well as race, class, and ethnicity. It would articulate femininity through Anglo-American traditions, and thus also norms of masculinity, whiteness, and nationalism.

Fair sex discourses were often based on explicit or implicit claims about "natural" differences between whites and nonwhites, and men and women within the white community. In the 1790s, authors defined masculine nature as strong, robust, rugged, and superior to feminine nature in bodily constitution. The gender of the author was frequently ambiguous, as essays were published anonymously or with pseudonyms; but we can be sure that the authors and distributors of fair sex ideology were male and female and generally white. In these discourses, the intellects of men were described as having a "more extensive reach" and greater stability than that of women. Women were defined as beautiful, delicate, irresistibly soft and charming, romantic, and more self-sacrificing in love than men, their minds described as "intuitive and instinctive," "transparent," "susceptible," or clogged by "cobwebs." Sexual difference seemed to legitimate coverture in marriage contracts by suggesting that women's weaknesses necessitated men's protections. As "Philo" put it, "[b]y a superiority of constitutional firmness," nature "evidently designed *us* to be the guardians and protectors of our defenceless sisters, to shelter their feeble barks from the storms and tempests which continually agitate and foment the billowy ocean of life."[17]

Such differences in body and mind necessitated marriage. Man, it was said, could not be what he ought to be except in conjunction with woman. Over and over again, authors reasserted what poets had written in the seventeenth century in England, that without the civilizing effects of the domesticated fair sex, man would be only a miserable, sorry brute. The Anglo-American marriage contract was explicitly unequal, involving an exchange of a woman's obedience for a man's protection and affection (cherishing). Most writers accepted this inequality, and reminded female readers of their contractual obligations to be obedient to husbands.

Obedience was defined in terms of its negatives—"obstinacy," "opposition," and "contention." Authors suggested that since a girl could only fulfill her nature in marriage, she must be early cultivated to the habit of obedience. Its opposite, "obstinacy," was the worst fault a girl could possess. Women were "the counterpart of man, taken out of man, to be subject to man; to comfort him like angels, and to lighten his cares." Without wifely obedience, a married couple's whole life would be spent in opposition and contention, hindering the happiness of themselves and others. A wife ought be "ready of submission to the enterprise and power of man," but not in such a crude manner that could be identified with the "despotism" or "slavery" of the harems of Turkey or Egypt. She should internalize her subordinate role. As one writer advised, "[w]omen should not let their condescension appear strongly, as if they are submitting to a tyrant. They should cheerfully fulfil the obligation they had entered into at the altar—love, honour, and *obey*."[18]

Within domesticity, the husband/father ought to be the central focus. "Every man ought be the principal object of attention in his family." His home was his castle. He had a right to feel happier there than at any other place, and it was woman's responsibility to see to it that he did. The author of "General Remarks on Women" cited 1 Corinthians (3:12), which states that Jesus is the foundation on which man must build his house. This author extended the metaphor:

> Woman is not a foundation on which to build. She is the gold, silver, precious stones, wood hay, stubble; the materials for building on the male foundation. She is the leaven, or more expressly, the oil and vinegar of man. . . . Woman, who feels properly what she is, . . . rests upon man.

Christ was the foundation for man; man the foundation for woman, in that order.[19]

A few would resist the patriarchal marriage contract that required female obedience. As we shall see, all three women featured in this book—Warren, Adams, and Murray—challenged or disregarded the notion of wifely obedience in their own lives. The same year that Wollstonecraft's *Vindication of the Rights of Woman* would be published, one American author writing for the Philadelphia *Ladies' Magazine* stated her objection to wifely obedience on the grounds that it made a wife a slave.

> Where I have sworn or even promised to obey any man, I must on honour consider myself as having sworn or promised to obey him in all things, and at all times. In a word I have bound myself to be a *slave*, until he is pleased to release me, which in the matrimonial world is an occurrence that I believe seldom happens.

If any obedience was required in marriage, it ought be mutual. Marriage "ought never be considered a contract between a superior and an inferior." It should rather be a "reciprocal union of interest, an implied partnership of interests, where all differences are accommodated by conference."[20]

Such a bold expression of objection was rare. By "conference," this author was demanding communicative rational action and the ideal speech situation, wherein truth and rightness are determined and decisions made on basis of the equal right of all speakers to make and contest claims. Most of the writings on female manners and virtues would leave the vow of obedience uncontested, and build upon that foundation. Domesticity was linked to a woman's duty to obey. By fulfilling her function to maintain the household and render it pleasing for her husband, a woman upheld her marital vows, and could better expect her husband to uphold his.

A few authors even suggested that if a man strayed from his wife, it was her fault.

> It is doubtless the great business of a woman's life to render his home pleasing to her husband; he will then delight in her society, and not seek abroad for alien amusements. A husband may, possibly, in his daily excursions, see many women whom he thinks handsomer than his wife; but it is generally her fault if he meet with one he thinks more amiable.

If he should stray, one author's recommendation to wives was to visit the mistress and seek to understand her secrets. "The School for Husbands and Wives" told a story about how one clever wife did just that, and was well prepared for her husband when he came home from work. She threw her arms around him immediately, without talking, set him down in an easy chair, brought him a lighter garment to wear, and cooled him with a fan. Another author left open the possibility that a husband could stray without any fault on the wife's part. What was a woman to do? She should first take an impartial look at her conduct, and if she truly had exhibited no manners that could possibly have "given offence" or "created disgust," then she ought keep her behavior the same as before, ignoring his infidelity. "For to resent or to retaliate, neither her duty, nor her religion will permit." Though it would be one of her most difficult tasks, she must "carry smiles upon the face when discontent sits brooding upon the heart."[21]

Domesticity as a virtue for white women imposed a kind of moral geography that kept them out of politics and the bourgeois public sphere, both of which were viewed as scenes of self-interest, competition, and corruption. Of course many women enjoyed going out in public to dances, card parties, and theatrical amusements; and poor women of all colors existed in public spaces to work. Jefferson's disdain for women in public was not an unusual sentiment. The presence of the fair sex in public entailed the "promiscuous" mixing of the sexes, threatened the wifely obedience and self-restraint that was the cornerstone of Anglo-American propriety. As Shane White reports, theatrical performance, rituals, dancing, music, games, feasting, and drunkenness were tolerated (and vicariously enjoyed) through African

American culture, when white Americans in the North allowed their slaves to celebrate Pinkster and Election Day. The cultural antithesis of the lewd black folks drinking, dancing, and drumming was the purity and innocence of the domestic white woman. "One of the greatest beauties of the female character," it was commonly suggested, "is that retiring delicacy, that modest reserve, which avoids the public eye."[22]

Authors followed the ideas of Reverend James Fordyce, linking the virtue of *modesty* with domesticity. In *Sermons to Young Women* (1766), which was widely read in the United States, Fordyce warned that it was "impolitic" for a woman to make herself "cheap" by being seen too much in public, "[T]he majesty of the sex is sure to suffer by being seen too frequently, and too familiarly. Discreet reserve in a woman, like the distance kept by royal personages, contributes to maintain the proper reverence." Like most pleasures, women were "prized in proportion to the difficulty with which they are obtained." Women who led "too public a life" signaled their loose morals, and could expect to be attacked.

> [I]f a young person will be always breaking loose through each domestic inclosure, and ranging at large the wide common of the world, those destroyers will see her in a very different point of light. They will consider her as lawful game, to be hunted down without hesitation.

Women were told not to think of a husband as a "downright brute" for denying his wife the pleasure of appearing every day in public. A fashionable wife who engaged in the everlasting dissipation of balls, plays, and other public amusements signaled her lack of merit and could not possibly retain the esteem of her husband. Anglo-American authors followed suit, contrasting the vicious life of the city and public spaces with the virtues of domesticity. Surely the daughters of fashion were in a state most painful of any, obliged as they were to cover hatred with the smile of friendship and anguish with the appearance of gaiety. A woman could be more genuine and happier at home. There she would find her family "virtuous and happy, where affection takes place of duty, and obedience is enjoyed, not exacted."[23]

Modesty was linked to *piety* and *bashfulness*, other virtuous characteristics that helped one cultivate self-restraint. "Lavater" warned that women were "raging and monstrous" without religion. "A woman with a beard is not so disgusting as a woman who acts the free-thinker; her sex is formed to piety and religion." Bashfulness also served to restrain a woman from free thinking and acting. "Bashfulness is certainly an inestimable quality in the composition of a woman's manners, and ought to have a particular ascendency over the conduct of everyone who would not wish to do violence to the delicacy of her sex." While certainly not an important virtue for maintaining a family in the absence of a husband during the war, it was now, in peacetime, a necessary feminine virtue to attract and keep a husband.

Any and all personality traits related to female assertiveness or individualism were now taken to be vices. "Nothing can appear more ridiculous, than to see a handsome female descending beneath her native dignity, by the abruptness of her behaviour." A good woman guarded her thoughts, words, and actions as if her well-being depended upon it. She did not play with the "wanton glances of her eyes" or replenish her cup when the toast came around. Even talking with a man was suspect. "Is there a man with whom thou delightest to talk? Let not thine ear be too familiar with thy discourse." The ideal woman was a good conversationalist, but she remembered to "blush" in mixed company. She acted with modesty, humility, and deference, not pride, ambition, or confident self-assertion.[24]

Articles with titles such as "On the Happy Influence of Female Society," "On Politeness," and "Scheme for Increasing the Power of the Fair Sex" began to reassert, in peacetime, the necessity of women's softness, domesticity, and complacency to support men's individual toils in the external "world." Female conversation was to be soft. The author of "The Pleasures of Female Conversation" declared that female conversation was "light and airy"; it relieved the [male] mind from more intense studies which frequently cast a gloom over the countenance. Without it, men would be "dull and stupid beings, utterly unacquainted with good manners" and fit only to be "placed in a beargarden to terrify the beasts into tame submission and easy compliance."[25] Male conversation was rough, rugged, competitive, and libertine. Robust and enterprising men needed "female softness" and the "lenient balm of endearment" to "smooth their rugged nature" and "wear off the asperities they daily contract[ed] in their business and connections with one another."[26]

The *polite conversation* of ladies was also deemed the perfect antidote to "masculine pride." While men's competitiveness was accepted as an obnoxious hindrance to civilized conversation, women were advised that their role was to buffer that spirit of competition by "yielding."

"The best way for a married woman to carry her points is to yield sometimes. Yielding in a married woman is as useful as fleeing is to an unmarried one."[27]

Polite conversation was also defined in opposition to political discussion. As Norton and Kerber have separately documented, male authors of Europe and America warned women explicitly that they were out of their proper sphere when they broached the subject of politics.[28] Thomas Jefferson objected to women's interests even in the U.S. Constitution. In 1788, he shrugged off Angelica Schuyler Church's comments and questions about the Constitution by telling her that "the tender breasts of ladies were not formed for the convulsions of politics." To use Habermas's concept, white women were not to enjoy any sort of "ideal speech" that was becoming the hallmark of democracy and modernity for white men. The virtue of delicacy demanded self-restraint, obedience, and subordination to men in ordinary conversations.[29]

Female delicacy was linked with domesticity and the necessity of keeping women out of the public realm. In proposing that women and children be used for cheap labor during the post-revolutionary labor shortage, Alexander Hamilton disregarded the idea that the moral purity of ladies depended on their exclusion from the corrupt, public world. But he was surely in the minority among leading thinkers. Several of the founders explicitly advanced or implicitly agreed that the public/private split for white women was necessary to preserve white femininity and moral order in the community at large. As Noah Webster put it, "such is the delicacy of the sex, and such the restraints which custom imposes on them, that they are generally the last to be corrupted." Many men had been restrained from a vicious life, and some of the worst men had been reformed by their attachments to ladies of virtue. Keeping company with such women was the best security against the temptations of a dissipated life.[30]

To be obedient without appearing slavish, a woman should be *agreeable* and avoid showing a "sour disposition." A cross wife spread the contagion of discontent throughout her household. Everyone disliked her, including her servants. "A virtuous woman communicates only happiness." She was grateful to providence, and never showed negative emotions like rage or jealousy. She avoided calling attention to her own suffering, because that would be un-Christian, an insult to Jesus Christ who knew true suffering, and to God, who ordained that woman suffer.[31]

Women were encouraged to be agreeable by invoking the virtue of *sympathy*. As Joan Tronto and Rosemarie Zaggari have argued, sympathy was considered an important political and social virtue, especially in the Scottish Enlightenment. Americans following writers like Hume and Hutcheson echoed the importance of sympathy to restore human "felicity." Sympathy was defined as "a principle in the breast of man which disposes him to take an interest in the joys and sorrows of others, and to heighten the former, and alleviate the latter by all means in his power." Sympathy was considered important for the maintenance of a republican polity. In this, white women could play a leading role. "[T]he fair sex is peculiarly susceptible of the tender emotions of sympathy."[32]

Sympathy was also linked with notions of racial difference and Anglo-American civilization. At times the virtue of sympathy was tied to an abolitionist sentiment. In "Address to the Heart on American Slavery," for example, readers were urged to practice the virtues of sympathy and benevolence with respect to the slave woman's plight, separated from her children and "spoiled" by "the hideous groans of men with the clanking of chains" at midnight.[33] But the use of sympathy to criticize the Europeans and the barbarous Africans with whom they consorted in the slave trade also surreptitiously promoted the civilization of white people.

Tales of Africans were told in women's magazines to encourage sympathy for the unfortunate Negro who had been unjustly captured. "Selico: An African Tale" set out to describe the virtues of one extraordinary family in the most barbarous region of the world. It likened the history of Africans to that of "lions and panthers." Their religion did not feature the God of reason, but made deities out of serpents. Their law was enforced by women with guns, or women inflicting tortures. The readers were reminded that even such a "degraded part of the human species" were still "men" and should therefore inspire their sympathy. "The African: A Sketch" described the European capture of "Sambo," who was described as a "harmless African," yet "manly and vigorous as the lion that ranges sole master of the forests." The author, "Julia," called upon the "more enlightened part of creation" to cease staining their characters and put an end to the slave trade.[34]

The sympathy that increasingly became identified as a feminine virtue bears resemblance to what Carol Gilligan and her followers have called the "ethic of care."[35] Fair sex ideology linked sympathy, or caring, and the duty to alleviate the suffering of an Other with white womanhood. They considered it natural, that is divinely ordained, but a virtue that had to be developed. The ideal partnership was a companionate marriage. Companionate marriages required "politeness." Some would suggest that it was a mutual duty of husband and wife to maintain a "delicacy of manner" or "flattering deference."[36] But more often than not, writers advised *wives* to be deferential toward their husbands. They considered the "friendship" of husband and wife to incorporate female subordination.

Marriage was a woman's main vocation in life, and in marriage, women were to be completely other-directed. The "concord of souls" necessary to make a marriage happy required a "parity of understanding and temper." Women were counseled to shape their accomplishments, understandings, and desires around those of their husbands to create that parity of understanding that made for the companionate marriage. They were told that marriage was the most important aspect of their lives; thus preserving the esteem of their husbands would necessarily have to be their key goal in life. "[F]orm your taste exactly to his, . . . endeavor to attain to some degree of those accomplishments which your husband most values in other people, and for which he is most valued." The mind was to be cultivated to make the wife more "agreeable" to her husband.

The end of a wife's existence was to conform to her husband, and to take care of his emotions. "Be it your province, then to keep your husband's heart from sinking into the incurable disease of tasteless apathy." It was also the wife's duty to regulate her temper toward her husband, and to pay such an attention to his, to prevent it from ever appearing in a disagreeable light. Wives were urged to study their husbands' tempers so that they would know the proper "seasons" to address him with particular subjects. A wife should never press her claims with her husband, but rather "imperceptibly" obtain the power of guiding his concurrence or denial. In short, the virtue of "sympathy" was about being other-directed in one's care, and may have included these ideas about a wife's duty to make her husband the center of her identity.[37]

Fair sex ideology limited the debates on female education. As several have documented, the rise of female academies prompted discussions about what sort of education was appropriate for the ladies. Feminine virtues of meekness, mildness, and delicacy were conceived in opposition to intellectualism, employment, and political debate. Women were repeatedly warned *not* to become intellectual. "Men in general look upon one of our sex that possesses an uncommon degree of understanding, with a jealous, and not infrequently, with a malignant eye."

A wife's education must not threaten her husband's superiority over her: "A wife must endeavour to heighten the charms of a mistress, by the good sense and solidity of a friend. If she reads a new work, a poem, or a play, it must be to form her taste, that she may be able to entertain the man she loves."[38] Women should accept the "empire" which belonged to them: "the heart, . . . secured by meekness and modesty." They must not engage in discussions of "war, commerce, politics, exercises of strength and dexterity, abstract philosophy, and all the abstruser sciences," which were "the province of men." Those who did were "masculine women" who mistook their "true interests" by pleading for equality. Invoking the traditional virtues of the fair sex, American authors declared "mildness of disposition," "amiableness of heart," "agreeableness of countenance," and gentleness of manners the proper characteristics for the finely and delicately woven fair sex, who was not designed for "arduous employment."[39]

Intellectualism in women was unattractive. "Philo" ridiculed the ugliness of "female disputants." To prevent the spread of such corruption, he recommended that "our young ladies" *not* become the "complete mistresses of the sciences." "[T]hey would not only find them burdensome, but useless in the particular spheres in which nature has designed them to move." One author told the story of "Amelia," a young woman who had been tragically educated in Latin and Greek classics:

> Hasten to thy tasks at home,
> There guide the spindle and direct the loom;
> Me glory summons to the martial scene;
> The field of combat is the sphere of men.

Poor Amelia had lost her mother, and had been inappropriately educated by her father, who cultivated her unusual abilities. Amelia learned quickly, devouring her books, but "[i]nstead of that deference and respect which she had vainly expected, desertion and contempt were the natural consequences of learning." To console herself, she:

> retired to her closet to discover why the same causes in subjects scarcely different should produce such discordant effects: for she well knew that learning in men was the road to preferment, an introduction to the best company; that it was patronized by the rich, and admired by the poor; and that both sexes united in the applause of learned men, whilst sad experience convinced her that consequences very opposite were the result of the same quality in women; that with them learning was obnoxious to envy, and exposed to neglect and desertion.[40]

Amelia should have been told that the classics were "repugnant to female delicacy." A woman who learned them became intimidating and ineligible for marriage. Proper reading for a female included poetry, novels, and plays; Greek philosophy led to political debate which was likened to the masculine activity of war.[41]

Fordyce's *Sermons* had advised women to avoid knowledge that would lead them astray from "those family duties for which the sex are chiefly intended," or impair those softer graces that give them their highest lustre. In such cases they would relinquish their just sphere. Many American writers agreed. "Man may for wealth or glory roam,/ But woman must be left at home;/ To this should all her studies tend,/ To this her great object and her end." A young woman should thus learn "needlework to perfection," and all that was necessary to understand the proper management of a house; she should be acquainted with "the various seasons and provisions, the price of markets, and in short the whole economy of a family."

The American writer "Ignotus" agreed. "Believe me, Sir, when they are sensible of their own abilities and power, we shall soon be subject to their tyranny, and despotism of petticoat-government." Ladies should receive sufficient information only to "become good housewives" and superintend the "inferior concerns of the family." For "[i]f once a man raises his wife to an equality with himself it is all over, and he is doomed to become a subject for life to the most despotic of government."[42]

These feminine virtues showed their instrumentality in writings that encouraged men to get married. Men were encouraged to marry in part because women's domesticity would support their industriousness away from home. *American Museum* published an article "On the Happiness of Domestic Life," which encouraged men of ambition to get married because a supportive wife and loving children would provide the necessary "rest and repose" to balance their hard work in the world. Here the fair sex serves once again as muse. Having a family domesticated a man, made him more focused on earning a living and less prone to the dissipations of the bachelor: "He who beholds a woman whom he loves and an helpless infant looking up to him for support will not easily be induced to indulge an unbecoming extravagance, or devote himself to indolence."[43] Marriage promoted conservatism, order, and prosperity.

One might wonder why a woman would marry, that is, why she would agree to or become signatory to the sexual contract. Aside from purely economic reasons, women were given a strong incentive in fair sex discourses that emphasized wives' power to civilize men and children through marriage and family life. As Linda Kerber, Jan Lewis, and Ruth Bloch have documented, women were told that virtuous behavior was essential to the survival and development of the American nation.[44] Men's natural attraction to women led them to follow women's lead. If women would be virtuous, then men would necessarily follow.

For example, the author of "A Dissertation on Industry" urged that if the ladies would stop indulging their passions for fancy dresses and instead made industry fashionable, men would do the same and economic distresses of the nation would be alleviated.[45] The commencement address for the 1795 graduation ceremony at Columbia College, entitled "Female Influence," claimed that the "fair" were "possessed of a power literally unlimited" that they could use to reshape the nation. Women were advised to discourage intimacy with men whom they would regard unsuitable husbands, and use their conversation to civilize potential suitors. Their pure, delightful wit without a "stain" or "sting" would encourage men to eliminate all "ferocious" and "foreboding" principles. The "gentleman, the man of worth, the Christian," would all "melt insensibly and sweetly into one another."

In marriage, a woman's virtuous influence was expanded. Her angelic presence discouraged "profanity, libertinism, gaming, prodigality, and a long train of crimes and follies" which otherwise vilify the manly character. Through her economy and frugality in household management her husband could build a fortune, and through her charity and benevolence to the less fortunate, he could take pride that virtue reigned triumphant. Her influence with children was equally important for national economic development. By assuming the duty of educating her children (mainly a father's prerogative in the early eighteenth century), she could encourage, manage, and check the growing faculties of their souls, inculcating reason and religion, and thereby secure the triumph of the "Genius of Liberty." In short, by channeling her ambition toward her husband and children, she could civilize the nation and achieve her "Fame."[46] Practicing the virtues of the fair sex thus extolled many benefits. It would make women attractive and marriageable; lead men to practice virtues in and outside of marriage; and allow women to develop their highest potential as civilizing beings.

Institutionalizing Fair Sex Ideology through Female Education

Proposals for female education generally incorporated the ethics of fair sex ideology. Benjamin Rush is frequently presented as a liberal reformer, but his plan for female education was not intended to disrupt female subordination, or the separation of spheres. To those who feared educating women would make them more difficult to control, he wrote: "[T]his is the prejudice of little minds. . . . If men believe that ignorance is favorable to the government of the female sex, they are certainly deceived, for a weak and ignorant woman will always be governed with the greatest difficulty." Noah Webster defined a standard for female education that would not disrupt patriarchal authority: "In all nations a *good* education is that which renders the ladies correct in their manners, respectable in their families and agreeable in society. That education is always *wrong* which raises a woman above the duties of her station."[47]

As Linda Kerber has reported, there were several persons who criticized the narrow or contracted education of females, and came close to advocating equality in education. They included Judith Sargent Murray, Abigail Adams, Mercy Warren, Gertrude Meredith, Thomas Cooper, and Philadelphia Ladies' Academy graduate Priscilla Mason. At least one author had in mind educating women in "civil polity and philosophy" for the eventual "emancipation of the fair sex." But such sentiments were not shared widely enough to influence the sex-based curricula of female seminaries and academies, or to admit women into university education until late in the nineteenth century.

Indeed, as we shall see in later chapters, Warren, Adams, and Murray had difficulty resisting the norms of fair sex ideology, despite their attempts to criticize various aspects of it. Female education was designed to empower the fair sex for their instrumental roles as wives and mothers of citizens. Rush's essay, "Thoughts upon Female Education, Accommodated to the Present State of Society, Manners, and Government in the United States of America," figured the virtuous woman as the industrious helpmeet who facilitated her husband's accumulation of wealth:

> The state of property in America renders it necessary for the greatest part of our citizens to employ themselves in different occupations for the advancement of their fortunes. This cannot be done without the assistance of the female members of the community. They must be the stewards and guardians of their husbands' property. That education, therefore, will be most proper for our women which teaches them to discharge the duties of those offices with the most success and reputation.[48]

The wife appears to be defined in opposition to the citizen, the proprietor, and the competitive individual of contract who are all identified in the husband. Since men's "numerous avocations" in "professional life" would take them out into the world, they would have to rely on women to assume "a principal share of the instruction of children." Young ladies would have to be educated to secure their concurrence in instructing their sons in the principles of liberty and government.

Ladies' curriculum would include English, religion, geography, history, arithmetic, and vocal music, keeping in mind the ideal woman set forth in the book of Proverbs. Anglo-American women were warned that if they did not cultivate the virtue of industry, their "idleness, ignorance, and profligacy" would be the harbingers of national ruin; theatrical performances "of a buffoon" would be more worthy of commentary than "the patriot or the minister of the gospel."[49]

Noah Webster seemed to stress the same instrumental rationality. The future wives of citizens should learn to speak and write in perfect (Americanized) English. They were not to learn French or read romance novels, since such would seem to infect American virtue and promote a class of idle, refined women of fashion. A woman should be educated to improve her "domestic worth." Since most were likely to marry men who had to work as mechanics, shopkeepers, or farmers, they would not be "above the care of educating their own children." Thus, their education "should enable them to implant in the tender mind such sentiments of virtue, propriety, and dignity as are suited to the freedom of our governments."[50]

By promoting industry and the education of children as virtuous female activities, the ideology of the fair sex was instrumental in shaping men and children to become industrious and law-abiding persons who respected the right to private property as fundamental. The ideology of the fair sex thus seems to have facilitated the transformation of political concepts like reason, liberty, and virtue from radical to conservative meanings. Where liberty and freedom had been defined through revolutionary rhetoric as the right to have a say in representative government, as well as the right to private property, those words were now being defined in popular literature and in political theory as the respect for private property rights, law, and order. As many have argued, virtue became feminized and civilized to promote passivity, domesticity, industry, and rule-following, all instrumental to the development of a capitalist racial patriarchy.[51]

Defining American Femininity through "Uncivilized" Foreign Women

The definition and promotion of Anglo-American female virtues was also accomplished through negative examples of nonwhite femininity around the globe. As early as 1775, Thomas Paine articulated both gender and ethnic differences in his "Occasional Letter on the Female Sex."[52] The letter begins with an articulation of natural sexual difference:

> O Woman! Lovely Woman!
> Nature made thee to temper Man.
> We had been Brutes without you.

In this early example of American fair sex ideology, Paine sets out to validate all women, and to give particular consideration to the women of "civilized nations." He begins with a statement that all women are oppressed around the globe, in part by nature and in part by social customs. Nature is cruel to women, who must risk their lives in childbirth, suffer the "cruel distempers" of menstruation, and then become de-sexed by menopause. But society adds to these miseries, especially in uncivilized countries. "More than half the globe is covered with savages; and among all those people women are completely wretched."

Similar to Thomas Jefferson's view of African American men in *Notes on the State of Virginia,* Paine's view was that men in "barbarity" were "cruel," "indolent," and acquainted with little more than the physical aspects of love. When not engaged in warlike activity, they indulged in idleness, and made slaves out of their wives. Wives were kept in separate beds and not allowed any conversation or correspondence with their husbands. The Indians all exercised a despotic authority over their wives, who were considered property. They made their wives procure all the food, and then they prevented them from eating until they had their fill.[53]

In the East and in Africa, women suffered in the Seraglio; and in Turkey, Persia, India, China, and Japan, the excess of oppression stemmed from the "excess of love." Asia was "covered with prisons" through which men exercised mastery over women. There the "lovely sex" were forced to serve their husbands with the "most tender affections," or worse, "the counterfeit of affection." They were "confined to their own apartments," and debarred from business and amusements. In one country they were affronted by polygamy; in another they were enslaved by indissoluble ties which "joined the gentle to the rude, and sensibility to brutality." As one went north, despotic passion was changed into "a spirit of gallantry," which employed wit and fancy more than the heart. As one went further away from the sun, passion became either "composed into a habit of domestic connection," or alternatively, "frozen into a state of insensibility," under which the sexes scarcely chose to unite their society.

Even in the "civilized" nations, where women were deemed most happy, they were constrained in their desires in the disposal of their goods, robbed of freedom by the laws, made the slaves of opinion and appearances, and "surrounded on all sides with judges who are at once their tyrants and seducers." In all climates, man had been either an "insensible husband or an oppressor." However, all men had not been "equally unjust to the fair"; in some countries public honors were paid to women, which is what he urged ought to be the case for American women.

Despite Paine's criticism of laws which "robbed" women in civilized countries, all he pleaded for was minimal public recognition of women's virtues. Women's names should be "some time pronounced beyond the narrow circle" in which they lived, and have their tombs inscribed with emblems of love or friendship, so as not to deny them of public esteem.[54] Thus even Paine, who was considered a political radical and somewhat of a feminist for his time, did not in any way suggest that the "rights of man" be extended to women. Although American women were oppressed by men and laws, they had it better than women of the barbaric nations. Woman's lot was misery, but in civilized countries, women were allowed to temper man's brutality.

In the early national period, travelogue essays repeated fair sex ideology. Foreign nations were described through the gender relations of the people. Foreign women were praised when they demonstrated the ethics of the fair sex, and criticized when they did not. The women of Mount Etna in Sicily were praised as "naturally mild and amiable." Unlike other Sicilian women, they showed "candour and cheerfulness" in their countenance, and their gestures displayed "serenity of mind" and a "desire to oblige and be useful."[55] But the French Creole women in St. Domingo (Haiti) epitomized the social evils of undomesticated women. "Accustomed to command, they grow obstinate if controlled; when their wishes are gratified, they sink down to their usual apathy." The power that Creole women enjoyed only corrupted them and the rest of society. They ate at nonregular intervals according to their desires, and fed on nonnutritious foods like chocolates, sweets, fruits, and coffee, rejecting out of hand "simple and wholesome aliment." They were uneducated, capricious, ugly, and full of rage; they were excessively tender toward their children, and "indifferent" toward their husbands. These slaves of passion, power, and luxury were contrasted with the American fair sex, who were praised and encouraged to be "lovely and complying" wives. "Be persuaded, then, o amiable sex! To confine your dominion to the power of your charms and to procure the happiness of your subjects, by the allurements of virtue!"[56]

In similar fashion, the Greek women of the Island of Lesvos served as a negative model of Amazonian tyranny. They were criticized for having "arrogated to themselves the department and privileges of the men." Unlike the customs of other countries, the eldest daughter inherited while the sons, "like daughters everywhere else," were "portioned off with small dowers, or, which is still worse, turned out pennyless, to seek their fortune."[57] The eldest daughter acted like a tyrant with her inheritance, enjoying "every sort of liberty" with the family's fortune, spending as she pleased, treating her husband as an "obsequious servant," and her parents as inferior dependents. She was distinguished by vice and a "haughty, disdainful, and supercilious air."

The perversion of power between the sexes pervaded all aspects of life. In all their customs, gender was reversed. "Manly ladies" straddled the horse, while the men sat sideways; the husband took the wife's name; and the wife was head of household rather than her husband, who dared not interfere with her management. This article was immediately followed by another which urged the fair sex to "guard against the infatuation of vanity and ambition, for ambition is the ruin of the sex, and humility is the only antidote against it, lovely humility!" The point was obvious: a patriarchal family was the center of civilized republicanism, while a matriarchal family produced a tyrannical "amazonian commonwealth."[58]

The Production of "White Women" as Intermediaries in Racial Patriarchy and U.S. Nationalism

Fair sex discourses created a system of ethics that contributed to dominant thinking on race, ethnicity, and gender in the last two decades of the eighteenth century. The ethics marked a retrogression to marriage within monarchy, adapted for life in republicanism. By promoting discipline among white women to suppress claims to knowledge, authority, and equality, the ethics of fair sex ideology revived traditional patriarchal relations in the home. They promoted wifely subordination and distorted speech within families, not free rational discussion among equals. Second, these ethics imposed a moral geography that separated public, male spaces from private, feminine ones. In short, fair sex ideology helped to establish republicanism through dual patriarchy. Third, the ethics served nationalist ends, as they defined femininity through specifically *Anglo-American* patriarchal relations. Fourth, fair sex ethics promoted economic stability by normalizing middle-class values through virtues of industry and obedience, which were supposed to encourage men and sons to be more or less productive but passive law-abiding citizens. The ethics of the fair sex thus seems to have supported commercial development and racial patriarchy.

Because discourses of the fair sex were set in the context of gender and ethnicity or race, they produced femininity as well as American whiteness. They positioned the white woman as partially oppressed and partially privileged. "Woman," or "the sex," figures as the other of "man," but she is posited as subject through another articulation of alterity, the barbaric or savage other. As the "fair" she is positioned in the "civilized" world, where she is permitted and encouraged to be the "civilizing" sex. "Civilization" encodes whiteness, Anglophilia, and Western industrial progress. Through this ambivalent positioning, as man's Other taking another Other, the white woman becomes an intermediary. White supremacy and male supremacy become inextricably bound in fair sex ideology. Acceptance of the terminology and its system of ethics, through various repetitions in ordinary language, constitutes a signature to both the sexual and racial contracts in one fell swoop. White female identity would have incorporated both patriarchy and white supremacy; an individual could not separate them if he or she adopted the common parlance of fair sex ideology, which infiltrated everyday communications.

The circulation of fair sex ideology renders the issue of the ordering of the contracts much less important than their interrelatedness and intersectionality. Because fair sex ideology represented the adoption of both the racial and sexual contracts, it is likely that anyone who spoke its terms accepted both race and gender hierarchy. If we reject the notion of woman as the weaker sex and assume instead that white women were as capable of rationality as were white men, and further, that as men were becoming modern subjects, pursuing their own interests, women were on some level doing the same, then a few hypotheses relating to female subjectivity and agency emerge.

The first hypothesis invokes a claim of inseparability. It would be difficult for any Anglo-American woman to refuse one contract while signing on to the other. Fair sex ideology mutually reinforced gender and race hierarchy simultaneously. We would expect that in most cases, as a woman became a "lady" under its virtues, she also became more white. The adoption of fair sex discourses would likely represent a double signature.

The 1807 act to disfranchise all women and all blacks in New Jersey illustrates this inseparability. Judith Klinghoffer and Lois Elkis noted the curious absence of white female protest in their study of the "petticoat electors." They suggested that the politically sophisticated Federalist widows of New Jersey probably understood that their voting rights were firmly tied to those of blacks and aliens. "Consequently, they may have preferred to lose their right of suffrage rather than reenfranchise those they considered inferior to themselves." Fair sex ideology was used by one contemporary to explain this curiosity. He remarked that the "bill introduced into the State Assembly" for "depriving the fair sex of their right of voting at elections" resulted from their previous votes for men who were too aristocratic, "for ladies have the reputation of hating democracy as well as demagogues." It seems reasonable to suppose, as Klinghoffer and Elkis have done, that the ladies opposed the part of democracy that placed them on an equal footing with blacks.[59]

The second hypothesis I call the reward claim: Any white woman who adopted fair sex language would stand to incur external benefits from the dominant culture. These benefits might include a limited political voice, access to information, power, and property. The privileges would be based largely on literacy, specialized education, and domesticity, privileges afforded through race and class hierarchy. The benefits relating to white supremacy would include an appearance of virtue, and a limited but nonetheless authorized moral voice in family morals and manners; and a subjectivity that came from whiteness. Class benefits would have included education, literacy, and "embourgoisement," or exemption from wage labor.

Through fair sex ideology, Anglo-American women "became white" in Charles Mills's words, and it was in their interest to do so, because whiteness underwrote women's middle-class standing and their limited autonomy and authority as "civilizing" beings. The only costs that such a compliant white woman might incur would be intrinsic or internal. For example, if a white woman believed in sexual equality, but complied with fair sex ideology to maintain race and class benefits, she might feel and express an inner sense of frustration. Uneducated white women, women of color, and those who worked outside of the home, or cared for the children of wealthier women, would not be so privileged.

The inverse would also hold: Any white woman who challenged fair sex ideology, or its behavioral norms, might stand to gain internal benefits, such as peace of mind, integrity, or creative expression. But because challenging fair sex ideology also entailed a challenge to racial patriarchy, she would be vulnerable to extrinsic costs: negative labeling by the dominant culture for having exceeded the boundaries of femininity. She would have violated the norms of patriarchy, middle-class values, and Anglo-American ethnicity. She might be labeled an obstinate woman who destroyed marital harmony; an impious monster, an immodest or "loose" woman, a female pedant, a "disputant," and an "amazon." These labels carried with them further risks, of spinster-hood, ostracism, and financial distress.

Finally, the third hypothesis for this work is the "feminist" claim: that a white woman concerned mainly with gender issues would attempt to view issues of sexual inequality in isolation from race and class issues, such that women of color, uneducated, or poor women would be largely invisible or irrelevant to her critical or reformist vision. In other words, a "feminist" would attempt to challenge the sexual contract while leaving intact the racial contract. She would attempt to challenge ascriptive virtues and vices that pertained to woman as the weaker, subordinate sex; but she would not challenge the ascriptive virtues that posited white women as the more sympathetic or civilizing force in society. This strategy is basically an attempt to maximize one's own power as a white woman by equalizing the opportunities between white men and white women without giving up racial privileges. Women who adopted this strategy for expressing their subjectivity would be heralded by the feminist movement as "early feminists."

The three hypotheses above may be useful to examine the political thought and experiences of three white women: Mercy Otis Warren, Abigail Smith Adams, and Judith Sargent Murray. All three women were born and raised in Massachusetts. Adams and Warren knew each other well, and corresponded for many years. Murray, the youngest, knew of the other two women, and met Abigail Adams when Mr. Adams was vice president, but did not have much of a relationship with either woman. All were intellectual, privileged white women whose husbands were educated and renowned. All came from wealthy, established families whose names were well known in the state. In the following chapters, we examine how each of these women contended with fair sex ideology and the politics of racial patriarchy in her own way.

4

The Philosopher Queen and the U.S. Constitution

Mercy Otis Warren as a Reluctant Signatory

When we think about American founders, we think about famous men, like Thomas Jefferson, George Washington, James Madison, John Adams, and Alexander Hamilton, who were active in the movement for independence, the framing of the Constitution, and as executives in early administrations. Although most American government textbooks include a section on the Antifederalists, most Americans do not recognize the names Robert Yates, John Lansing, Elbridge Gerry, George Mason, Luther Martin, Richard Henry Lee, and Mercy Warren. And yet, the opponents of the proposed Constitution raised objections that led to the drafting of the Bill of Rights, without which ratification in several states would not have occurred. That is why they too must be considered founders.

Mercy Warren was the most sophisticated of the Antifederalist American founders. Her objections to the proposed Constitution were backed up by an original theory of republican politics that drew its inspiration from the entire Western tradition of politics and political philosophy. As a woman, Mercy Warren did not have access to a Harvard education, like her brother James Otis, her husband, James Warren, or her friend, John Adams. During the battles of the War of Independence, however, the rules of gender were loosened, and women could more easily discuss politics without being chastised for leaving their proper sphere. Mercy Warren was extremely well read. She was also a prolific writer.

Warren's political thought shows its roots in her correspondence as early as 1774, but her mature political theorizing came to fruition late in her life, after all her five sons were grown. Born in 1728, she was 50 years old when her Antifederalist essay came out, and she was 77 when her masterpiece, *History of the Rise, Progress, and Termination of the American Revolution* (1805), was published. Taken as a whole, her corpus of writings display a system of politics which makes reference to the ancient Greek and Roman republics; the Roman Empire and its demise; the virtues and principle beliefs of Christianity, Machiavellian thought, and the idea of the state of nature and the social compact so characteristic of modern political thought.

Textbooks rarely mention Mercy Warren, and very few teachers of American history or government are aware of her contributions to American political thought. Reasons behind Warren's marginality today no doubt relate to the exclusions she experienced in her own day. Few women were educated in political philosophy or history, so it would have been easy to dismiss her views as the inexperienced opinions of a woman with too much time on her hands. John Adams suggested the same when, after he read her history, was disappointed with the way she characterized him. Warren was a dissenter who wrote on the "losing" side of history. She stepped out of favor much earlier, when she and her husband began to sympathize with the Shays' rebels in 1786; things did not improve after Mercy Warren published her anonymous essay criticizing the Federalists.

The principal reason for Warren's continuing obscurity is that her writings demand much of the reader. They make references to figures and events from earlier historical periods including Socrates and Athenian politics, the Roman republic and its decline, Machiavelli, and the Exclusion crisis leading to the Glorious Revolution in England. Warren's analyses of the political events in her own day were framed in terms of this history of Western civilization. An understanding of that history is required to understand Warren's own republican theory, which itself is required to understand why she couldn't "sign on" to federalism and the proposed constitution. In this chapter, we will examine Mercy Warren as an unwilling signatory to the U.S. Constitution. In particular, we will consider whether her rejection of the Constitution was in any way related to a rejection of the sexual and racial contracts of racial patriarchy that were embedded in it.

Warren's self-conception far exceeded the boundaries of fair sex ideology, but she heeded fair sex norms or at least carefully negotiated them in her communications with others. She was aware of her exceptional breeding and education, and considered herself intellectually superior to most women and most men. She became embroiled in revolutionary political debates and was perfectly comfortable asserting herself as an interlocutor, at least with her acquaintances, and sometimes with those whom she wanted to make acquaintances, including George and Martha Washington, John and Abigail Adams, and Henry Knox. Warren's ideal of republicanism was expressed throughout her entire corpus of published and private writings. These included her plays, poems, letters, her Antifederalist essay, and her three-volume masterpiece, *The History of the Rise, Progress, and Termination of the American Revolution* (1805). In various works, she describes herself as a "theorist," "philosopher," "patriot," "genius," and "politician."[1]

Warren's Theory of Republicanism

Warren's theory of republicanism drew its inspiration from the Enlightenment thinkers, especially Locke, Jefferson, and Hume. She subscribed to many elements of modern social contract theory, such as a concept of natural rights, the right to private property, the positing of a universal human being capable of rationality and sympathy (or benevolence), and she believed in the idea of popular sovereignty. But her central concern of how to maintain virtue in a republic distinguished her from modern social contract thinkers, and perhaps more important, from the Federalists, whose theories did not rely so much on the virtuous characters of individuals. In Warren's ideal republic, much that is classical in origin is blended with the idea of the voluntary social compact. Elements of classical political theory were represented by her concept of natural hierarchy, her understanding of the "manly" virtues, the privileged place of the philosopher in republicanism, and the priority of the soul and its virtue over external goods or commercial development.

Warren's writings show a constant preoccupation with the classical battle of virtue and corruption of republics, which determined their *physis*, or natural cycle of birth, growth, and death. Nearly every letter, play, poem, essay, and treatise that she wrote reflected her fear of the degradation of virtue and the fall of republicanism. This fear drove the writing of her *History* and underlay most of her correspondence:

Let it never be said of such a favored nation as America has been, as was observed by an ancient historian, on the rise, the glory, and the fall of the republic of Athens, that "the inconstancy of the people was the most striking characteristic of its history."[2]

Warren subscribed to the classical privileging of reason over passion, identifying virtue with rationality, and vice with uncontrolled appetites or passions. Her hierarchy of humanity seems similar to one we find in Plato's *Republic*. What distinguished the "worthy few" in Warren's mind from the "avaricious adventurers for place" and the "licentious mob" was their level of education and appropriate use of reason, to promote the public, rather than private, interest.

For Warren, the polis was the center of life, and private activities ought all be congruent with the public good, on which happiness in earthly existence largely depended. Like Socrates, she privileged the pursuit of philosophy and the philosopher above the particular maneuvers of politics or politicians. Yet her concept of citizenship was more participatory, invoking the active life envisioned by Aristotle. For Warren, the citizen was defined as one who was "destined to command as well as to obey."

Warren's political thought was also heavily influenced by Christianity. A belief in God understood through the teachings and example of Jesus Christ is frequently repeated in her personal correspondence. Her religious understandings were integrated with her political thought through covenantal theology. As Harry Stout conveys, within this theology, God entered into covenants with nations and individuals promising to uphold them provided they acknowledged no other sovereign, and remained devout.[3] For Warren, the covenant was embodied in the Declaration of Independence, which she described as having been drawn under the auspices of God:

This celebrated paper, . . . begins with an assertion that all men are created equal, and endowed by their Creator with certain unalienable [sic] rights, which nature and nature's God entitle them to claim; and, after appealing to the Supreme Judge of the world for the rectitude of their intentions, it concludes in the name of the *good people* of the *colonies* by their representatives assembled in congress, they publish and declare, that they are, and of right ought to be, Free and Independent States; in the *name* of the fountain of all just authority, relying on the protection of

Divine Providence, they mutually pledge to maintain these rights, with their lives, fortunes, and honor.[4]

Resistance to the mother country England was only secondarily about constitutional rights and political liberties, as these appeared to be the ideal institutional and social guarantees that both reflected and protected the integrity of the covenant. During the hostilities between Britain and the colonies, Warren frequently expressed her faith by urging others that prayer and virtuous behavior were more important to win the War of Independence than bloodshed, and that Divine Providence would decide the war.

Warren's religious beliefs also informed her understanding of virtue. Life on Earth was temporary, and one could bear the worst calamities knowing that, with the grace of God, painless existence would come in the afterlife for the worthy few. Earthly existence was but a test of character, and the virtuous would be rewarded by heaven. These religious beliefs helped her cope with the anxiety of war, and the threat of living under a despotic government. One letter to Abigail Adams demonstrated this view. Because of their Christian beliefs, she told her, they need not kill themselves, like ancient heroines, who felt that virtue required suicide when they or their people were overtaken by tyrants. One could instead practice spiritual surrender, and even maintain a kind of contentment, knowing that Providence would reward the truly virtuous in the end.[5] Warren's republican theory held the Christian virtues of charity, benevolence, compassion, and submission as equally important as the classical "manly" virtues of intelligence, military bravery, honor, and self-sacrifice.

Warren began to articulate her theory of republicanism during the founding period, in the context of the ratification debates for the proposed federal Constitution. As Russell Hanson has noted, the founding period was a struggle among persons for custody of the republican ideal. The word "republic" comes from the Latin, *res publica*, which means "of the public," the commonweal, hence "commonwealth," or rule for the common good. American colonists distinguished between particular institutional arrangements and republicanism, maintaining the latter as an ideal by which to judge the former, in much the same way as we would argue over what is and is not a "democratic" solution today.[6] Confronted with a view of republicanism so new and different from her own facilitated the development of her political theory. Warren responded to the proposed Constitution in a point-by-point fashion to raise her criticisms. The particularity of the criticisms forced her to come to terms with her own ideal, which she later articulated in the publication of her three-volume *History*.

Warren's political theory was founded on a complex conception of human nature. Like modern social contract theorists, she held that humans were endowed with certain natural rights, which included the right to self-government, freedom of conscience, and the rights of the people collectively to form a government of their own choosing. At the same time, she maintained a classical view that in order to choose well, individuals had to practice the virtues. Hence, individual character had a profound impact on whether the social compact would be virtuous or corrupt. She begins her *History* with a statement on human nature:

> The study of human character opens at once a beautiful and deformed picture of the soul. There we find a noble principle implanted in the nature of man, that pants for distinction. This principle operates in every bosom, and when kept under the control of reason, and the influence of humanity, it produces the most benevolent effects.[7]

By nature, human beings were neither good nor evil, but imperfect beings with conflicting propensities. Here rationality is classical, the self-control which aims for the public good, and not the modern conception of efficiency in achieving one's private interests. One who is rational is not egoistic and interested, but "benevolent."

Human nature was shaped through practices in the world. Human practices took place within specific cultural contexts, and some contexts were better environments than others for the cultivation of virtue. The noble principle could easily be corrupted by social and economic conditions.

> [W]hen the checks of conscience are thrown aside, or the moral sense is weakened by the sudden acquisition of wealth or power, humanity is obscured, and if a favorable coincidence of circumstances permits, this love of distinction often exhibits the most mortifying instances of profligacy, tyranny, and the wanton exercise of arbitrary sway.[8]

Virtue and vice here are Socratic, conceived as the product of a "civil war of the soul" between reason and appetite. The disturbance of social and economic classes through a "sudden acquisition of wealth or power" created the conditions in which Reason, or "the moral sense," was susceptible to being overtaken by "ambition and avarice." These were the primary sources of corruption from ancient Rome to the British monarchy of George III.[9]

Like other Enlightenment thinkers, Warren postulated a universal view of human nature. She attributed differences between ethnic populations to environmental factors. For example, in her *History*, she takes as axiomatic the existence of a single species of humankind, and when comparing the savage nature of Native Americans to the civilized Europeans, she notes that Europeans were once brutish tribes themselves. Differences between white Europeans and "Indians" or "Africans" are related to environmental factors such as the level of development, literacy and religion, the distribution of wealth, and the state of the economy.

Warren's concept of a universal human nature also crossed gender lines. In a letter to her son Winslow, she criticized Lord Chesterfield's writings for attributing vice only to females. In these comments she wrote that human nature was "the same in both sexes." By this she did not mean that men and women had identical makeups in all things, that they acted or thought the same, or that they should perform the same roles or have the same rights. She meant that both men and women experienced the same conflicting tendencies in the soul. Both sexes could "reach the same degree of perfection or sink to the same stages of pravity which so often stamp the disgrace on the human form."

It was bad custom, not nature, that "branded licentious manners in female life with peculiar marks of infamy."[10] The same applied to the origin of female stupidity, or "the eager pursuit of trifles"; it resulted from "the different education bestowed on the sexes, for when the cultivation of the mind in the early part of life is neglected, . . . we see ignorance, stupidity, and the ferocity of manners."[11] This view was consistent with Warren's claim that humans were neither good nor bad by nature, but had the potential to be either, depending on social circumstances and the use of reason. The practice of virtues was equally important for both sexes, their vices equally devastating to republican politics.

Human beings were endowed with natural rights that ought be translated into civil rights. Following Locke, whom she admired, she held that men entered into a social compact to preserve the "absolute rights" vested in them by "the laws of nature." Political society was necessary because natural rights could not be preserved "without the mutual intercourse" of "friendly and social communities."[12] Natural rights included the right to self-preservation, freedom of conscience, and private property. Wherever the first rudiments of society have been established, "the right of private property has been held sacred" (1988, 13). Thus, the Stamp Act, which levied a duty on "all bonds, bills of lading, public papers, and writings of every kind for the purpose of raising revenue for the crown" amounted to taxation without representation, and justified resistance, as her brother James Otis had argued earlier.[13]

The fundamental principle of "free government" was the "equal representation of a free people." By equal representation Warren did not mean to suggest that all inhabitants should have the suffrage. She meant that no party or faction would dominate the government. The key distinction between republicanism and despotism was the republican commitment to a government that served the common good. A republican government was not to be instituted for "the profit, honour, or private interest of any man, family, or class of men" but would strive to represent the common interest, and thereby promote a substantive equality among men.[14]

Like her Antifederalist compatriot the "federal farmer," Warren subscribed to the radical *delegate* theory of representation. As delegates, representatives were supposed to take instructions from their constituency. If the government failed to "guard the life, liberty, and property of the community," the voters retained the right to reject the decisions of their representatives, call for a revision of their conduct, put others in their place, or demand further time for deliberation. And if the government did not obey the will of the people, the people retained the right to dissolve it:

> It is true the ferocity of the human mind is such, that the great law of self-preservation has made it necessary to select some by mutual consent, to rule over others; but when that power is abused by a cruel and arbitrary sway, the same law authorizes a resistance.[15]

Warren allowed for the concept of civil disobedience only when the government was truly violating first principles. For the most part, people obeyed the laws, as they should. But when government failed to represent the people's interest, the people retained their ultimate sovereignty and could, she believed, justly disobey the law. This sort of radical sentiment got the Warrens into trouble with the Adamses and other

Federalists, who considered lawlessness to be a definitive sign of corruption.

Warren located the ideal conditions for republicanism in "the simple life."[16] For Warren, republicanism had the best chance of flourishing within a level of social development between two equally undesirable extremes, corrupt civilization and "savagery." Her utopia was an agrarian one, unacquainted with the arts of civilization, uncontaminated by luxury, hence fertile ground for those virtues "which spring up in the soil and are most congenial to the nature of man." Warren was emphatically not an advocate for "the savage life." Similar to Rousseau, she held that human virtues and rationality could not be developed in a state of nature where anyone could take the law into his own hands. "In a state of nature," Warren explained, "the savage may throw his poisoned arrow at the man whose soul exhibits a transcript of benevolence that upbraids his own ferocity, and may boast his bloodthirsty deed among the hordes of the forest without disgrace." Warren appreciated literature and wanted to see America boast in its acquisition of science and of empire; but this empire should be based on republican principles. It should avoid the imperialism of those nations "prompted by avarice or ambition to infringe the natural rights of their fellow man," as well as the debasement of the species that occurs in primitive societies, "where there is little distinction but what arises from the imperfection of human nature which makes it necessary to submit to some subordination."[17]

The vision here is once again classical, anamnestic of the Socratic disdain for luxuries, and Aristotle's theory of "polity," his ideal form of government, itself based on the "best life" represented by an agrarian or pastoral people.[18] Warren's "simple life" centers on the yeoman farmer.[19] The yeomanry included all property freeholders who cultivated their own land,[20] such as her husband-legislator James Warren. Her neoclassical conception of public virtue centered on a "heroic love for the public good, a profound reverence for the laws, a contempt for riches, and a noble haughtiness of the soul." As a tiller of the soil, such a man existed in a kind of nascent society, that just and happy medium between wild savagery and those high stages of civilization and refinement that corrupted purity, piety, sobriety, and public-spiritedness.[21]

The yeoman was marked by his independence, industry, frugality, and patriotism. As a freeholder, he was dependent on no one for his subsistence or his ideas. His reason was less likely to be corrupted by the vices associated with wealth, such as luxury, idleness, or domination, or with poverty, such as slavishness, bad work, and rebellion. Enjoying the fruits of his labors in the provision for his family, he was poised to defend his freehold if it were threatened. The yeoman was neither desperate nor distracted by artificial cravings for luxuries. His time was fully occupied with agriculture, the cares of his family, religion, and reading, which would not permit him to distinguish himself by sudden wealth or frivolous acquisitions. The ideal of the yeoman farmer preserved that rough, satisfying equality in which none desired to dominate another. The yeoman farmer was also patriotic. Since his life and livelihood depended on his tie to the land, his "manly arm" would rush to defend it were it threatened by a foreign or tyrannical power. He readily understood that his private life depended on the stability of his community. Like the Spartan soldier, the yeoman farmer was poised for a virtuous life, and served as Warren's ideal of male citizenship.[22]

A Vision of Woman Citizenship

Warren's political theory also contained a vision of woman citizenship. The marriage contract incorporated women into the polity by stipulating different roles for men and women. The husband took part in ruling through his vote and voluntary services as a soldier and/or legislator. In turn, he was ruled by the state created under his compact.[23] Wives were represented and ruled by men through the republican state, but they also influenced men and children through their practice of republican and Christian virtues, without which the republican state and society could not exist. "The virtuous education of a young family is a work of the highest importance," she told a female friend.[24] Warren's neoclassical definition of the citizen, as one "destined to command as well as to obey," thus allowed for sexual difference. Warren's definition of woman citizenship is one of the best examples of what several historians have called the "republican motherhood" or "republican womanhood" ideal.[25] The sexual, racial, and ethnic aspects of her thought and identity become clearer through the more exacting lens of fair sex ideology. Fair sex ideology also helps us understand why Mercy Warren was so angry about federalism and the federalist Constitution.

Warren's conception of the virtuous mother and wife was inspired by ideals of womanhood in ancient Sparta and Puritan Christianity. The Spartan woman displayed republican virtue by courageously sending men to the battlefield to defend the republic. She sacrificed her emotional attachment to her husbands and sons for the greater good of preserving the republic, as the female heroine Maria does in Warren's play *The Ladies of Castille*.[26]

A wife's duty was to practice the private virtues that strengthened marriage and supported her husband's efforts to serve the republic. A husband was affected by his wife's virtues and vices. It was imperative that she maintain the strictest virtue, lest she become selfish or frivolous and instruct her husband to satisfy her personal desires rather than the public good. During the War of Independence, for example, Warren told Abigail Adams that their duties as wives of prominent patriots was never to wish their husbands to do anything repugnant for "our own sakes"; they must suffer pain and poverty with their husbands rather than have them depart from their noble principles. During peace, a woman must also control her desires as a consumer. Warren urged her niece Sally Sever, a young wife, to avoid the vices of "ostentatious profusion," and its opposite, "disguised parsimony." If she instead exercised "taste marked with economy and liberality with discretion," she could look forward to a feeling of self-esteem. "[T]he soul will swell with the conscious pleasure of distributing happiness as the power increases."[27]

These standards of female virtue led Warren to rebuke Lady Sarah Hesilrige of Philadelphia for enjoying the balls, concerts, assemblies, and card parties of city life. The virtuous woman spent her precious time caring for her family, consoling the survivors of "the worthy dead," and improving her mind through literature; she did not waste her life "in the parade and pleasure of the gay world."[28]

More importantly, a wife had a duty to raise her children to be virtuous citizens. She should teach them not to be selfish, but to think of themselves as members of their community, and ultimately under the watchful eye of God. A good mother taught her adult sons to control their passions. Warren's letter to her son James upon entering Harvard typified her attempt to control her sons' sexuality: "Remember that once the barriers are broken down, and the bounds prescribed to virtue can be overleaped without horror, there is danger that a mind thus perverted will never recover the tranquility that arises from innocence."

Another vice that a man ought to avoid is too much fashion sense. A proper valuing of time did not permit wasting it with "idle amusements or the senseless folly of dress." Warren expressed "mortification" at the idea that college men were "more solicitous for the adjustment of the toupee than the composing of a syllogism or solving a problem in Euclid." And she warned her son Winslow to rise above the "tinsel of fashion" that makes one servile to the world of appearances. Mother Warren repeatedly warned her sons to avoid "criminal passions," "guilty gratifications," "the lowest gratifications of animal nature," the "monster vice," and "the most shameful debaucheries." In all of her admonitions against effeminacy, frivolity, gambling, dancing, masturbation, homosexuality, or premarital sex, she preached the priority of rational over appetitive pursuits in her capacity as a mother, and linked the fate of the Republic to the development of virtuous character.[29]

If she did her job well, her sons would be prepared to enter a virtuous marriage based on a shared, rational desire to serve the community. As husbands and fathers they would then be poised to recognize and fulfill obligations to the community associated with "manly virtues." The virtuous man "resist[ed] the first approaches of tyranny," and sacrificed his blood if necessary.[30] In peacetime, he used his vote carefully to choose virtuous leaders, or to serve the public himself. For example, Warren's husband James served on the Navy Board and as a Massachusetts legislator and Speaker of the House. Desiring prestigious employment for her sons as well, Mrs. Warren worked hard, albeit unsuccessfully, to secure public positions for Winslow and Henry after the war.[31]

The education that a mother gave her daughters was meant to prepare them for female citizenship as wives and mothers. Mothers and older women should dissuade their daughters and all young women from indulging in romantic fantasies and premarital sexual involvement. A young woman obsessed with romance could too easily become "the sport of [her] own passions." Even those with the most guarded virtue "may inadvertently stray into some flowery path," where reason was subverted by a "pleasing delirium." Romance excited the passions, and clouded women's judgment to "discriminate mankind."[32] Unwanted pregnancy and the attachment to a licentious man too often resulted from romantic indulgences.

Warren despised women who acted as temptresses, referring to them as "unworthy companions" who encouraged their "devoted victims" to engage in the "monster vice" of premarital sex through their "empire" over men's weakened minds. Careless sexual involvements outside of marriage typically hurt both sexes by permitting appetite to reign over reason. The forced unions that would occur would not be based on the rational friendship necessary for republicanism, but on vice and necessity. And if appetite prevailed in private life, how could men be expected to subjugate their appetites and make the necessary sacrifices in public life or war?

For Warren, the great business of life was "the regulation of the passions and the subjugating those appetites which tend to inflame them."[33] Self-government of a republic clearly depended upon individual self-government. Any lapse in the private rule of reason over the passions was viewed as a threat to liberty, independence, and republicanism. As guardians of virtue in their families, then, women were absolutely vital to the republican state; therein lies Warren's basic conception of woman citizenship.

It may be instructive to consider Warren's relation to the sexual contract of modern patriarchy by comparing her thoughts on marriage and gender with that of other contract theorists. She certainly subscribed to gendered spheres, by which women were identified with the private and men with the public. But as I have argued elsewhere, Warren was not necessarily an advocate of male domination.[34] If we hold Warren's marriage contract up against those of other contract theorists, hers appears less patriarchal.

For Warren, the foundation of marriage was rational friendship, which approached an ideal of communicative rationality, not conjugal right, as appears to have been the ideal for Locke, Rousseau, and Kant.[35] Marriage ought to be a "friendly union of hearts," wherein each person was "actuated by the love of what is truly excellent, with a mutual desire to please." But this desire was based neither on physical passion nor the delirium of romantic love. It ought to be an "endearing association" that brought "delight and satisfaction to a rational and well-informed mind." Warren stressed that mutuality, rationality, friendship, and intellectual stimulation were the stuff of a good marriage.[36]

For Locke, disagreement between husband and wife over things held in common was resolved through the husband's "rule," which was placed in the man's share as the "abler and stronger."[37] In Rousseau's political thought, subservience to men defined women's reason for being: the subjugated wife maintained stability in society. He urged that women be educated for subservience, and not develop their intellects, because "a brilliant wife is a plague to her husband, her children, her valets, everyone."[38]

Warren suggested in a letter to Sally Sever that female subordination in marriage "may have been so willed" by God "for the sake of order in families," but she also suggested that male dominance should be subverted. Women might find it necessary to seem inferior but they need not be so. "Let them have their little game, since it may have been so willed. It won't hurt you; it will amuse them." While appearing to be under a husband's rule, a woman "need not acknowledge such an inferiority." Rather, a wife should strive to "equal in all mental accomplishments the most masculine heights."[39]

Playing the game of condescension in marriage did not require a woman to submit to the final authority of her husband. Husband and wife could disagree on small matters: "A minute similarity of sentiment" was not necessary in marriage, but neither could Warren see how a couple could be happy if their "opinions and taste in life are generally variant."[40] Thus, Warren allowed for minor marital disagreements, and proffered no authoritative solutions for deep disagreements. If a marriage was based on a rational friendship between moral equals, as she thought it ought to be, the problem presumably would not arise; the couple would have enough in common to work out their differences. The "game" of female subordination, coupled with its subversion through intellectual pursuits, would seem to represent Warren's attempt to reconcile the limits of Christianity with Enlightenment rationality, especially the idea that women be included in the category of rational human nature.

Warren's Utopia: Intellect, Merit, and the Privileged Position of the Philosopher Queen

The exceptional woman, like the exceptional man, might make a greater contribution to the republic by writing political theory. Warren clearly considered herself a political theorist. Early in her writing career, Mercy Warren forged a bond between herself and British Whig historian Catherine Macaulay, on the grounds that they were both politicians and political theorists. Within her very long first letter to

Macaulay, Warren detailed her views of the loss of liberty in America, and then justified her political interests as a woman:

> You see, Madam, I disregard the opinion that women make but indifferent politicians. It may be true in general, but the present age has given one example [Macaulay] at least to the contrary, and pray, how many perfect theorists has the world exhibited among the masculine part of the human species either in ancient or modern times? When the observations are just and honorary to the heart and character, I think it very immaterial whether they flow from a female life in the soft whispers of private friendship or the Hundred in the senate in the bolder language of the other sex. Nor will one be more influential than the other on the general conduct of life or the intrigues of statesmen in the cabinet, so long as private interest is the spring of action which is induced to be the pole star that governs mankind from the King to the Cottage.[41]

Warren seems to be suggesting that since men have never devised a perfect political theory, talented women should not be dissuaded from making their attempts. Ideas ought be judged on their own merit, not on the sex of the thinker. She also suggests that under a corrupt government, where private interest pervades life "from the King to the cottage," women's political observations will never be allowed to be more influential than men's; patriarchal self-interest will be dominant. Perhaps Warren needed this disclaimer to give herself permission to broach the subject of politics with an authoritative voice.

Others validated Warren's sense of herself as a woman of exceptional intellect. As Joan Hoff has noted, Warren was validated primarily by men such as her husband James and, less consistently, John Adams.[42] James Warren encouraged Mercy to write to settle her nerves during the hostilities while he was away. On one occasion, he ordered her to "digest (i.e., devise) a system of politics" while he was at Watertown serving in the Massachusetts legislature, because he considered such work to be congruent with her intellect and personality.[43] He also sent John Adams a copy of her satiric play, *The Group*, which Adams published in England, and for which he praised her talent in superlative terms. "Of all the geniuses which [sic] have yet arisen in America, there has been none, superiour to one, which now shines, in this happy . . . exquisite faculty." Adams also encouraged her to write her *History*, suggesting that she was one of the few possessed with enough historical facts of the Revolution, and the ability to record them well.[44]

Mercy Warren internalized this validation, and considered herself a woman of genius and a guardian of virtue. This internalized identity allowed her to overstep the bounds of proper femininity as they would later be crystallized through the ideology of the fair sex. For example, although she repeatedly apologized for taking up John Adams's time and attention when writing to him while he was in England after the war, she couldn't help offering advice on moral issues, or questioning his character as an intrusive mother would interrogate her own son. Repeated interrogations as to whether he was now corrupted by the courtly life of the English monarchy no doubt offended Adams, but he did feel compelled to respond to her occasionally that he did in fact prefer his life back at the farm in Braintree, and that he was not corrupted by English luxuries or ideas.

As Jeffrey Richards has noted, Warren made reference to herself as an isolated, grieving genius in her poem "The Genius of America Weeping the Absurd Follies of the Day.—October 10, 1778, 'O Tempora, O Mores!'" Warren herself figures as "Columbia's weeping genius."[45] As the nation's guardian of virtue, Warren mourns the prevalence of vice: "a most remarkable depravity of manners pervaded the cities of the United States, in consequence of a state of war; a relaxation of government; the sudden acquisition of fortune; a depreciating currency; and a new intercourse with foreign nations."[46] Warren's ideal of woman citizenship thus placed ordinary women at the center of republicanism, as guardians of virtue. Their positioning in the private realm was not a liability, but a virtue, as the purity of their rationality was linked to their distance from the corruptions of politics. At the ordinary level, every woman could be the moral guardian in her own family. Extraordinary women could be founders and philosophers, guardians of virtue in the public realm through their writings, or as wives of politicians. Thus, while Warren was aware of fair sex ethics, she often exceeded or challenged them. In any case, Warren viewed the regulations of the passions as the most important business of life. This vision of woman citizenship, coupled with her delegate theory of representation, suggests what Warren was not willing to state openly: that upright middle-class white women were the heart of republican politics.

Despite Warren's vision of a woman-centered polity, she never challenged the actual development of separate spheres. She believed that she could work within them and circumvent the legal inequalities of the sexual contract through political ideals of virtue, her own conception of marriage as "rational friendship," and her view of motherhood as a role that allowed women to exercise moral authority. At times she took refuge in the virtues of the fair sex and the boundaries of separate spheres. She preached to younger women that "sweetness of temper," "gentleness," and "delicacy of manners" were the appropriate female virtues to compensate for want of brilliance. She even encouraged Sally Sever to teach her daughter the "habits of sweet condescension." She stated that condescension that "must always be made to appear the result of choice and not compulsion" was "the basis of female felicity."[47]

Warren probably did consider herself intellectually equal or even superior to most men, but the mere contemplation of acting as an individual in the public realm created anxiety for her. Although she sometimes resented that men had "consigned" women to the "narrow circle of domestic cares," she noted to Abigail Adams the *advantage* that women had there. They could conceal their neglect of mental improvements in the "obscure retreats" of their own firesides. By contrast, men were generally called out to a full display of their abilities in the "great school of the world," and were less able to hide their barren and uncultivated minds, or their deficiencies, despite their greater educational opportunities.[48]

Thus, when fair sex ideology became dominant in the 1790s and beyond, she took issue with only those aspects that oppressed her as a female intellectual. In 1805, when she was ready to publish her three-volume *History*, she appropriated fair sex ideology to justify her "right to write."

In her introductory "Address to the Inhabitants of the United States," Warren proclaimed that not all political attentions lay outside the road of female life. She acknowledged that there were "certain appropriate duties assigned to each sex," and that writing the history of war and revolutions was undoubtedly "the more peculiar province of masculine strength," and then proceeded to justify her own writing. Warren dares to characterize herself in the masculine, as a "philosopher" and a "historian," but never challenges the patriarchal separation of spheres directly. Instead she softens the blow with fair sex discourse, promising that she "never laid aside the tenderness of the sex or the friend." Her observations flowed from her "sympathizing heart" and her "concern for the welfare of society." She tells the reader she recoiled at the magnitude of her task with "hand often shrunk back" and a "trembling heart," but she persisted, in order to transmit the details to the "rising youth" of the country. Just as the reader is ready to type-cast her as the *passionate and irrational* fair sex, she immediately adds that she always endeavored that the "strictest veracity should govern her heart," and the most "exact impartiality" be the guide of her pen.[49]

Warren appropriated fair sex discourse to make use of its racial and ethnic privileging, as well as its limits on female agency, to introduce herself as a nonthreatening female interlocutor in American national debates. Fair sex discourse provided a foil that gave her authority without claiming that she was as qualified to write history and political theory as David Ramsey, John Marshall, William Gordon, or any other American man. She used fair sex ideology also to ask for leniency from critics. Her goal was not to produce a great work, but one that was merely "useful or entertaining, as to obtain the sanction of the generous and virtuous part of the community."

Warren and the Racial Contract: Denial, Displacement, and the Usurpation of "Slavery" in American Politics

To accurately evaluate Warren's positioning with respect to the racial contract, we have to go well beyond her appropriation of fair sex ideology. Warren's ideal of citizenship was bounded by class, in that male citizens came from the "intelligent yeomanry," who were by definition property owners with at least some education. Because the division of persons according to property ownership or lack thereof in the American states fell principally along racial lines, Warren's citizens were also likely to be understood as white. A more certain determination would require comparative analysis of her use of universal concepts in different contexts.

Specifically, it is instructive to examine her deployment of terms like human nature, freedom, slavery, virtue, vice, and rationality in the context of conflicts within the white community and those that took place between white and nonwhite communities. The major political conflicts that Warren wrote about concerned those within the white community in her own day—the conflicts between Britain and the colonies that led up to the War for Independence, North-South relations in the struggle for independence, and Federalist-Antifederalist conflicts in the constitutional period, after independence was won. In these, nonwhites appear in the background, never as having subjective perspectives of their own.

In her *History*, Warren provides a justification for the War of Independence by locating her own subjectivity and that of the patriots through several hypostatized others: corrupt British "tyrants," the "African slaves," and the "pusillanimous Asiatics." Warren uses the concept of slavery to highlight British abrogations of American freedoms. In a letter to Hannah Lincoln dated September 3, 1774, Warren justifies the War of Independence in natural law terms. The British acted as tyrants attempting to "sink the inhabitants of this land to a level with the African slave, or the more pusillanimous and effeminate Asiatic," and thus justified manly opposition.[50] The same ideas are repeated in her *History*, wherein she describes the contest as a struggle for the "native freedom and equal rights of man," which "ever revolts at servitude":

> A contest now pushed with so much vigour that the *intelligent yeomanry* of the country as well as those educated in the higher walks, became convinced that nothing less than *a systematical plan of slavery* was designed against them. They viewed the chains as already forged to manacle the unborn millions. . . . To the most moderate and judicious it soon became apparent that unless a timely and bold resistance prevented, the colonists must in a few years sink into the same wretched thraldom that marks the miserable Asiatic.[51]

Warren's use of the word "slavery," and markers like "African" and "miserable," "effeminate," or "pusillanimous" "Asiatic" employ white supremacy to recruit her countrymen for war against other whites. Her strategy involves sensationalism and *reductio ad absurdum*. She forges an identification of white colonists with enslaved Africans and colonized "orientals" only momentarily, to transport the concept of slavery onto British/American relations, invoking the binary pair colonizer/colonized.

The technique harkens back to and surpasses her brother's argument in "Rights of the British Colonists." There, Otis maximized racial difference between white colonists and the others to forge a racial identification between the mother country and white Americans. The colonists were not a "compound mongrel mixture of *English, Indian, and Negro*, but . . . freeborn *British white subjects*" who deserved the same rights as those of the mother country.[52] In asserting the rights of man, Otis at least extended the universal to blacks, arguing for abolition at the same time that he argued for white representation rights in the British parliament.

His sister does the reverse. She forges the identification merely to disavow it, as something outrageous. Warren's complicity with the actual practice of legalized unfreedom in the United States is glaring, as she does not criticize black slavery as a denial of natural rights.[53] For example, Warren admonished Lord Dunmore, the royal governor of Virginia, for having had "the inhumanity" to "declare freedom to the blacks" and to "arm them against their masters" in order to suppress opposition to the crown. "He excited disturbances in the black settlements, and encouraged the natives bordering on the southern colonies, to rush from the wilderness, and make inroads on the frontiers." Slaves are viewed as "domestic enemies" in southern and Chesapeake colonies, which had the "long habit of filling their country with foreign slaves."[54]

Warren does criticize slavery, but mainly as a means by which to assert northern superiority within the United States, not to denounce slavery per se as wrong. Northern slavery is all but ignored. She denounces slavery as a southern problem, an "embarrassment" as well as a source of corruption. It is a marker of southern aristocracy, and all of its vices: luxury, arbitrary rule, ignorance, and weakness.

> In the southern colonies, it is true, there was not that general attention to early instruction; the children of the opulent planters only were educated in England, while the less affluent were neglected, and the common class of whites had little education above their slaves.

The education of the slaves, or their right to equality, is not at issue; the point is that republicanism flourished in the North. Both knowledge and property were more equally divided in the colder regions of the North; consequently, a greater spirit of liberty was diffused. "Perhaps . . . wherever slavery is encouraged, there are among the free inhabitants very high ideas of liberty; though not so much from a sense of the common rights of man, as from their own feelings of superiority."[55]

Warren explains later that this assumed superiority became a problem for northern soldiers, "the bold and hardy New Englanders; the *full-blooded* Yankees," who, having few slaves at their command, had always been used to a greater equality of condition in rank, fortune, and education. The joke on racial purity is not lost. Yankees figure as pure and virtuous subjects at the forefront of the independence movement, having to deal with the backwards, corrupt, and possibly mixed-race Southerners.[56]

Warren also conveniently took no notice of the many blacks who fought and died for American independence. The blackness of Crispus Attucks, the first to be shot during the Boston massacre, was completely occluded in Warren's account of the Boston Massacre. She prefaces her description of the event in her *History* by telling us that continual bickering took place between the soldiers and the citizens, and that the insolence of the soldiers excited the African slaves to murder their masters with the promise of impunity. No doubt, more slaves joined the British than the Americans, but Warren's repetition of the problem of slave rebellion here is curious for its denial and inversion. In her description of the massacre, which follows her statement on slave rebellion, she fails to note that the first victim of the first battle of the Revolution was a black man named Crispus Attucks. Paul Revere, in the *Massachusetts Gazette*, reported that Attucks, an ex-slave in his late forties, was the first martyr of the American Revolution, and even John Adams put a quip in his diary that this "saucy" Negro was the "hero of the night." But Attucks appears only in the diminutive in Warren's book, as a nameless "boy" of the "lower class" who cast "opprobrious reflections" on a high-ranking officer, and thereby excited other lads to take the "childish revenge" of pelting the soldier with snowballs. The deaths of five men are considered "trivial," hardly worth recording, except that they provoked an overreaction by the soldiers, and alarmed "cool and temperate" persons "of higher condition" to inquire into the cause.[57]

"Slavery," the Rights of Man, and the Proposed Constitution: Warren's Antifederalist Argument

After independence was won, another conflict emerged, and once again Warren complained of impending slavery. Warren situates herself as an outraged and unwilling signatory to the proposed Constitution. She rejects the Constitution because it is a plan for "slavery," but she in no way rejects racial slavery or the racial contract. The "practical and wretched effects of slavery" will be realized:

when the inhabitants of the Eastern states are dragging out a miserable existence, only on the gleanings of their fields; and the Southern, blessed with a softer and more fertile climate, are languishing in hopeless poverty; and when asked, what is become of the flower of their crop, and the rich produce of their farms—they may answer in the hapless stile of the man of La Mancha—"the steward of my Lord has seized and sent it to Madrid."—Or, in the more literal language of truth, the exigencies of government require that the collectors of the revenue should transmit it to the *federal city*.[58]

Nowhere in the essay is there any concern for the actual practice of slavery, the "Great Compromise," including how to count slaves for representation, or the duration or abolition of the slave trade, which were certainly issues of tension at the Constitutional Convention. Warren's main concern is how the white people—especially, white men—will be enslaved by the creation of a new taxing entity in the federal government. The irony here is doubled: Warren is *not* talking about actual enslavement, and she is *not* a rights-bearing individual who will sustain a direct loss of political rights herself.

Warren's rejection was based on two kinds of criticisms: those that accused the delegates of corruption on a procedural level, and those that focused on the content of the proposed Constitution. Like all other Antifederalists, Warren considered the extralegal moves of the delegates an outrage. The liberties of the people were denied by the conspiratorial mode in which the Constitution was adopted, and the illegal method by which it was quickly being ratified. The people had a right to be included in the deliberations, but the Federalists had not allowed fair discussion or rational argumentation among the public. Moreover, the delegates far exceeded their authorized duties. None of the state legislatures had any idea, when they first appointed delegates for the convention, that they would return with a consolidated system that severely diminished state sovereignty, or that they would create their own terms for ratification. Whereas amendments to the Articles required unanimous consent by the state legislatures, now only nine states' approval would be needed for ratification of the Constitution.

Warren called the proposed plan a "many-headed monster, of such motley mixture, that its enemies cannot trace a feature of Democratick or Republican extract." It deprived white men of the rights of citizenship. Negative liberties, those freedoms from government so essential to preventing tyranny, were missing. First on Warren's list was the freedom of conscience. Freedom of conscience included religious freedom as well as the right to disagree with government, as the two were intertwined in her covenant theology. Liberty of the press was also left unmentioned in the Constitution. Citizens would also lose their natural right of self-preservation because every state lost the right to raise its own army. Defense would become nationalized with the institution of a standing army; yet just such an institution created the tensions between the British government and the American people that eventually led to the Revolution. The absence of a bill of rights eroded the rights to a free press, freedom of conscience, and jury trials in civil cases. But, more important, the proposed Constitution deprived people of positive liberty, the right to democratic self-government. In Warren's view, it terminated state sovereignty, and centralized power, emasculating local politics. Political participation would be contracted, and representation could not be adequate since the national government had to preside over all of the states.

Warren did not accept the Madisonian argument that the extended size of the territory under one government would preserve republicanism better than small sovereign states. Madison's claim that the extended reach of the national government would prevent the dominance of a single interest through the opposition of many interests and factions seemed to her to be an admission of the politics of self-interest, and thus of corruption. Further, she believed that the extended size of the Republic would necessitate enormous wealth and ambition to win elections. Wealth and ambition would thus supplant virtue and merit as the marks of distinction among classes.[59]

She urged American male citizens to resist "the fraudulent usurpation at Philadelphia," as they had resisted British tyranny in the late war. The Federalists "hoodwinked" the people to voluntarily forgo their natural rights. They deceived the supple multitude of the American "peasantry" who were not educated in the "systems of democratic theorists" and denied them the right to deliberate the system that would soon compel them to "blush at their own servitude."[60]

The Federalists had debased the whole concept of public virtue. By creating a system of politics based on man as a self-interested, corrupted being, the Federalists essentially dismissed the problematic of virtue and corruption on the individual level. The Federalists sought to avoid republican decline by recognizing a distinction between normative and positive political theory. In their view it was unreasonable to insist that the people acquire and practice Spartan virtues of self-sacrifice, frugality, and strict control of the passions; most were incapable of such discipline. And even if the individual characters of men were deemed central, there was no guarantee that a "good man" produced goods for the common benefit. The true basis of good political conduct might be the most base and selfish desires. What was important was the product—commercial empire and military strength, not the purity of individuals' intentions.

This sort of reasoning alarmed Warren, who viewed it as a loss of excellence or a degradation of standards. Hamilton, Madison, Adams, and other Federalists accepted men as selfish, egoistic, and competitive. The constitutional checks and balances acknowledged and sought to transcend the *passionate* nature of man. They themselves were motivated by desires for fame and immortality; they believed that the Federalist constitutional system would channel the egotism of like-minded men toward public service.[61] In Madison's constitutional design, the lack of perfect public devotion in the citizenry would be offset by a system that encouraged the brightest and most ambitious characters to ascend to political power. At the same time, power would be fragmented and shared by the legislative, executive, and judicial branches of government, so that no one person or institution could dominate public policy.[62] To Warren, it seemed that the Federalists authorized themselves to set up a system that rewarded similarly ambitious men who thirsted for nobility and aristocratic authority.

Indeed, there is some validity to this view. Since Madison regarded the people as neither "angels" nor "a nation of philosophers," he in particular sought to limit their political participation. As Richard Matthews has shown, Madison distrusted the demos deeply, even considering them one of the greatest "evils" of politics. The author of the Constitution feared majority opinion because the multitude would not have an extended, national view of the public interest. This fear grounded his argument for the extended size of the Republic and his *trustee* view of representation. The extended sphere of politics would serve to filter out parochial interests of local politicians. Representatives would serve as trustees who, once chosen, were left alone by the masses to set the agenda and govern the nation. And of course, the weakening of state governments would enhance the power of these same politicians.[63]

The Federalists successfully persuaded the public to accept their plan for government with its contracted view of citizenship by appealing to the self-interests of the people, with the negative liberties of individuals that they would hold as free Americans. They de-emphasized the cultivation of classical virtues, and in their place emphasized the cultivation and protection of private, nonpolitical rights. The most important of these rights was to be secure in one's possessions and property *against* public pressure for debt forgiveness or the redistribution of wealth, as Madison made clear in the tenth *Federalist*.[64]

In contrast with classical political theory, in which a virtuous citizenry was one of the central ends of a republic, the Federalists subordinated the development of virtue or goodness to other goals. No longer depending on the individual characters of men, the Federalist system would seem to avoid the decline that, for example, ancient Athens suffered after the death of Pericles. The concept of virtue was transformed. To be a good citizen now meant to obey the laws, show deference to leaders, and pursue one's economic interests with industry and a robust sense of individual rights.[65]

Virtue had lost its previous currency as a criterion for political leadership and success. By no means were the concerns for morality and virtue totally arrested; but these had become objects of the private sphere. Insofar as virtue and morality were heralded as important values in the public realm, the character of virtue was also privatized. For example, the Northwest Ordinance contained a stipulation that schools be established to teach morality and religion; but the kind of morality typically advocated had less to do with political participation than with minding one's own business. The founders' visions for national education stressed individualist ideology, inculcating pride for hard work and the creation of personal wealth. As men were encouraged in the early national period to display the new masculine virtues of individualism, the fair sex was encouraged to cultivate civilizing behaviors and manners, especially those that were instrumental for the production of a stable, commercially successful republic. These included, for example, serving as guardians of their husbands' property, so that husbands could concentrate on commercial enterprises.[66]

As Russell Hanson has argued, the Federalists consigned the people to a state of civic lethargy, and hastened the decline of civic virtue. I would add that this decline reflected and widened the gap separating public and private spheres and thus also exacerbated women's exclusion from public life. The privatization of virtue and failure to encourage citizens to develop a sense of moral and political responsibility necessarily transformed citizenship. The good modern citizen of Federalist ideology differed from the classical citizen in that the citizen of the United States would take part in being ruled, but generally not in ruling.

In Warren's view, virtue had been abandoned and ridiculed, and citizenship emasculated. She called upon fellow revolutionaries to resist the Framers. They were "avaricious adventurers for place," intoxicated with the ideas of distinction and preferment, who had subjugated every worthy principle to the shrine of ambition. The law of self-preservation thus called for a resistance:

> Self-defense is a primary law of nature, which no subsequent law of society can abolish; this primeval principle, the immediate gift of the Creator, obliges one to remonstrate against the strides of ambition, and a wanton lust of domination, and to resist the first approaches of tyranny, which at this day threaten to sweep away the rights for which the brave sons of America have fought with an heroism scarcely paralleled even in ancient republicks.[67]

Federalism was the new tyranny, representing the over-civilized arts of Machiavellian politicians. Warren is once again unequivocal that the deprivation of the rights of white men is an unacceptable form of domination.

Native Americans, Natural Rights, and Virtue

Warren equivocates on natural rights when she later considers the political conflicts between her own countrymen and the Native Americans. She recognizes them as innocent victims of European and European American conquest. She points out that the warriors of the distant tribes "molested young settlements" in self-defense. They possessed valor, and were tenacious in guarding their hunting grounds. Their hostility toward whites originated in "the same impulse that in human nature prompts all mankind, whether civilized or savage, to resist the invaders of his territory." In other words, the natives were protecting their natural rights.

But Warren's view of natural rights was culturally based, resting on a prior notion of "civilization." The natives were barbarians, an "unhappy race of men." They lived in huts, without arts, sciences, manufacturing, or any evidence of developed rationality: "See the naked hunter groaning out his fierce soul on his native turf, slain by the tomahawk of his own savage tribe, or wounded by some neighboring hordes that prowl through an existence little elevated above the brute." The virtuous life was not possible in savagery. A virtuous existence required a republican structure, and Warren was either unaware of or unwilling to recognize the republican characteristics of the Iroquois Confederacy that inspired founders like Franklin and Adams.[68]

Assimilation was certainly a better solution than extermination, which Warren feared would be the fate of natives by Europeans, in the United States and all over the globe. Against those who claimed that the Indians were savage by nature, Warren pointed to the Moravian sect of the Muskingum tribe. They had professed themselves Christians, and refused to participate in war against the white Americans. Indians such as these demonstrated traits of reason and humanity, the dignity of human nature.

The problem was thus one of environment and culture, not nature. The ancestors of the most refined and polite nations were once but "rude, ignorant savages, inured to all the barbarious [*sic*] customs and habits" of present native peoples. There was no inherent difference in the intellectual capacity of nations, but adventitious circumstances allowed some to become civilized more rapidly than others. The American natives lacked the advantages of education to display genius and ability equal to the Europeans who had hunted them.[69]

Interestingly, Warren finds the relationship of colonizer to colonized acceptable for white/Indian relations. She does not consider the dominance of Europeans over Native Americans a form of enslavement, and there is no obligation here to "remonstrate against the strides of ambition" or the "wanton lust of domination." To reconcile the inconsistency of her views of natural rights as they pertained to white persons and native persons, Warren suggested that white and native conflict was perhaps all part of God's plan. Like the American Revolution, the war with the savages was all about the extension of the Enlightenment. It was Providence's way of diffusing "universal knowledge" over a large part of the population that remained enveloped in "darkness, ignorance, and barbarism." It was thus the impending duty of the American government and those with fairer complexions to "soften and civilize" the "rude nations of the interior," supplanting their "ignorance and ferocity" with arts, agriculture, science, and true religion.[70] Although the property rights of the natives have been violated by white imperialism, it was acceptable because the Indians might be better off under white domination.

"Civilization": The Foundation for Hierarchy in Warren's Republicanism

"Civilization" grounds white supremacy in Warren's political theory. Natural rights, gender, and citizenship are not universal at all, but completely dependent on an extremely ethnocentric vision of civilized society. Colonization was deemed acceptable when more civilized white people dominated a less civilized or barbarous dark people. But it was not acceptable when the dominating society was "too civilized" and therefore lacking virtue. That is why she believed the Americans should resist the domination of the British, but persist in their domination of natives. The British were overcivilized and ruined by luxury and domination; the savages were undercivilized, in need of "humanity." Thus, Warren's concept of civilization explains why, in her mind, the deprivation of rights was totally unacceptable for white Americans, but totally acceptable for blacks, and somewhat acceptable for natives.

"Civilization" grounds a hidden hierarchy within Warren's republican ideal. Just as Plato privileged philosophy above the practice of politics, which was itself privileged above commercial engagement, Warren privileged the philosophers above the yeoman-citizens, who were valued above the money makers and speculators, as well as the propertyless or enslaved rabble. Federalism left intact most of the hidden hierarchy as Warren envisioned it; nonwhite, uneducated, and propertyless persons still occupied the bottom rung. It was the displacement of the philosophical and intellectual virtues that Warren could not withstand. Their displacement was akin to the corruption to which Socrates alludes in Plato's *Republic*, when the most rational fall under the sway of the appetitive, those of a lesser "metal."

Concepts of virtue and civilization also ground the white woman's political existence. As Lester Cohen has noted, the denigration of civic virtue ushered in a paradigmatic change that undercut Warren as a republican theorist.[71] Warren seems to make Gordon Wood's point—the

Constitution represented the "end of classical politics" and the beginning of liberal individualism. Only for Warren, the stakes were higher than they were for most men. Virtue and its protection provided the foundation for her own political theory, and more importantly, empowered her as a philosopher and a woman to write about politics. Her political theory, voice, and "right to write" were now usurped by the denigration of civic virtue and the active citizen.

Despite the devastation of Warren's conception of woman citizenship that would have seemed to accompany federalism, Warren is silent about the degradation of woman citizenship in her Antifederalist essay. Warren wrote the Antifederlist pamphlet anonymously, and her pseudonym, the "Columbian Patriot," presents her as a man furious about the degradation of male citizenship, completely unconcerned about the sexual contract within federalism. I have argued elsewhere that this silence has much to do with Warren's anxiety of authorship as a woman, as well as her need to appear disinterested and pure, rather than as the advocate of the "party" of women. But the silence about women is not seamless. One passage in her Antifederalist essay betrays a sense of how she viewed the effects of Federalist politics on women:

> When patriotism is discountenanced and public virtue becomes the ridicule of the sycophant—when every man of liberality, firmness, and penetration, who cannot lick the hand stretched out to oppress, is deemed an enemy to the State—then is the gulph of despotism set open, and the grades to slavery, though rapid, are scarce perceptible—then genius drags heavily its iron chain—science is neglected, and real merit flies to the shades for security from reproach—the mind becomes enervated and the national character sinks to a kind of apathy with only energy sufficient to curse the breast that gave it milk.[72]

The metaphor of a Federalist government as a mother suckling a dependant infant is curious for what it may portend regarding Warren's views on federalism as well as motherhood. Under a Federalist regime, the "national character" of the citizenry would be weakened to infantilism. As dependent infants, the citizenry are too weak to resist the mother/government that "enslaves" them. The despotic mother rules by her overarching, dominant presence, not by her exemplary virtue. She keeps her male citizens "enervated" and "apathetic" so that they have "only energy sufficient to curse the breast" that sustains them. The mother that is federalism sustains despotism through her "milk," and thus stands as a corrupt contrast to Warren's woman citizen ideal, who sustains the republic with her virtue. Warren represents the transformation of virtue as its utter debasement, in which impotent sycophants displace men of "liberality, firmness, and penetration." The male citizen is effectively destroyed. And so too is the female citizen, for without him, she cannot exert her subjectivity or her rule, and therefore cannot exist as a citizen, but only as one who is ruled by others, a slave.

It may be that Warren's compulsion to forge and disavow an identification with slavery is as much or more about the condition of white women than of the yeoman farmer. After all, white men were still to retain the suffrage. It is white women who became the most severely emasculated. Granted, Warren's husband did fly to the shades, leaving his political career behind in the wake of federalism; but hers was the only recognized genius here that would "drag heavily its iron chain."

Warren's rejection of the proposed Constitution and federalism was not based on a rejection of either the racial contract or the sexual contract, as both of these were congruent with her concept of civilization. Her unwillingness to sign on represented a tribute to her rage with the disruption of a fundamental hierarchy that lay beneath her republican ideal. Warren's assumed hierarchy was the mechanism by which she authorized her own political participation and political theorizing. Federalism confronted and disrupted this assumption by displacing and marginalizing classical philosophy. No longer could she sustain the fantasy of her exceptionalism with respect to the sexual contract and fair sex limits as a philosopher, theorist, or political genius. These vocations lost their privileged position, along with civic virtue, as the foundations of republicanism. The death of that fantasy made her angry.

The incompatibility of Federalist politics and Warren's conception of woman citizenship explains why Warren did not celebrate the American founding, even after the Bill of Rights were added to the original Constitution. Warren did not give up easily, nor did she disintegrate in complete submission to the boundaries of the effeminate and enervated fair sex. At the age of 77, when many of her contemporaries were already dead, she began to publish the volumes of her *History,* her life's masterpiece. She would not be silenced, would not obey, and would not succumb to claims of mental inferiority that were being popularized through fair sex ideology. Her advice to a young female friend in 1790 was to *resist* the marginalization of women in politics and the public realm:

We lessen the dignity of our own sex when we accede to the opinion that our conduct individually is of little consequence to the world. The first rudiments of education are implanted by the feminine hand, and early traits are seldom wholly eradicated from the bosom of those who must tread the public stage and regulate both the religious and political affairs of human life.[73]

Warren seemed to be saying that though the Federalist order marginalized women from politics, women must not marginalize themselves.

To return to our central question regarding Warren's refusal to sign on to the social compact as represented by the Constitution, we must note that despite Warren's claim that the Constitution was a plan for "slavery," she had no objection to the racial contract, including racial slavery. Warren's comments about slavery concerned the deprivation of morality among *slaveholders* rather than the natural rights of the enslaved. Her refusal to approve of the Constitution probably did concern the sexual contract, however. Warren's own theory of republicanism included separate spheres as well as a vision of sexual equity, but the sexual contract within federalism was far more restrictive. The diminution of virtue and the displacement of classical political philosophy in federalism severely privatized domesticity and most individual behaviors. Without an emphasis on virtuous behavior and political participation, the foundations for Warren's vision of woman citizenship could not exist. Federalist theory, practices, and institutions also diminished Warren's power as a woman and an intellectual. At the same time, fair sex discourses were becoming dominant in shaping gender ideology. However insightful Warren may have been as a republican intellectual, she would now be reduced to the ranks of the privatized fair sex. No wonder she was angry.

5

From Revolution to Racial Patriarchy

The Political Pragmatism of Abigail Adams

If perticular care and attention is not paid to the Laidies we are determined to foment a Rebelion, and will not hold ourselves bound by any laws in which we have no voice, or Representation.
—Abigail Adams, 1776

Government of States and Kingdoms, tho God knows badly enough managed, I am willing should be solely administered by the Lords of the Creation. I should contend only for domestick government, and think that best administered by the female.
—Abigail Adams, 1796

The most remarkable thing about Abigail Adams as a political thinker is that she completely reversed her political principles within two decades. During the mid-1770s, as hostilities intensified between England and the colonies, Abigail supported American independence. At that time she spoke the language of the Enlightenment. Noting the ramifications of a universalized human being with natural rights, she opposed the institution of slavery as an abhorrence to republican principles. She also criticized patriarchal privileges. She denounced the "tyranny" of men that excluded women from "ingenious" education, deprived them of proprietary and political rights, and subordinated them in marriages. But by the early 1780s, she had dropped her criticism of gender inequity, and the rest of her public life bears testimony of a journey away from a utopia of equal rights toward hierarchy and conservatism. The language of fair sex ideology would replace her talk of natural rights, and her acceptance of racial patriarchy would replace her egalitarian ideals. As the wife of a rising politician who would fill the offices of a foreign minister, the first vice president, and second president of the United States, Mrs. Adams gradually merged her political goals with those of her husband and signed on to racial patriarchy.

What I will undertake here is a narrative of Abigail's intellectual journey from radical revolutionary to advocate of racial patriarchy. This theoretical journey will necessarily entail brief coverage of historical details, because Abigail was actively engaged in the political events of her day. She was a doer more than a thinker, a politician more than a philosopher, an achiever more than a perfectionist. As a doer, politician, and achiever, her views stemmed from praxis in a world in which men and women vied for power, competed over resources, and articulated different visions of the nation and its foundational principles.

Abigail Adams tested but was careful never to exceed the boundaries of proper femininity. The views that she held were seldom outside of the mainstream Anglo majority, and when they were, she kept them close to home. She would not publish anything in her own name during her lifetime. Her prudence with respect to sexual boundaries, as well as her willingness to support her husband's career, is probably why she was able to attain greater fame than the more intellectual Mercy Warren. Abigail had neither the depth of insight nor the philosophical or historical understandings of politics that Mercy had, but Mrs. Adams was hardly dull. She was sharp, politically savvy, organized, and resourceful.

Abigail Adams was a political pragmatist *par excellence*.[1] She had an unusual ability to feel out a political situation, grasp its perimeters, and work within them. She experimented with her political positions in her correspondence. When her views were met with resistance, she typically changed them so as not to be in conflict with those in power around her. Lacking the formal education that her husband had enjoyed, she read on her own and never allowed her limitations, such as a difficulty with spelling, to prevent her from writing letters and articulating important household or political information. Occasionally, she did contemplate the nature of man, religious duty, and political principles, but compared to Mercy Warren, she was more interested in *what* was happening in the world than why.

Reviewing Abigail's political journey thus offers a small window into the era in which she lived. It was an era during which radical thinking came into being, created a nation, and was subsequently deemed a threat to civilized order.

Abigail's Acceptance of Patriotic Duty

The story of Abigail's pragmatism really begins when she takes on the commitment to be the wife of a frequently absent husband-politician. The couple had already been married ten years when John asked Abigail to join him in the revolutionary struggle. She would make sacrifices by permitting his absences and by managing the family and estate without him.[2] Abigail accepted the challenges as her patriotic duty.

Once she made the agreement, she proved competent to maintain it. Volumes of correspondence exist between John and Abigail Adams in the decade from 1774 to 1784, during which John was absent in a variety of capacities. In 1774, he traveled as a lawyer on the Maine circuit, until he was elected to the first Continental Congress. In the years between 1774 and 1784, John served the Congress on many committees, and as a foreign minister in France, Holland, and England, until he was elected vice president in 1789. In that decade, John and Abigail lived separately, except for a few brief returns home, as John became a minister plenipotentiary to France, and later to England in anticipation of a peace treaty between the two countries.

While John was gone, he instructed Abigail on managing the farm and educating the children. Although she was initially overwhelmed by her duties as a "deputy husband," Mrs. Adams adapted to her husband's absence and coped on her own. For the first two years, life was difficult. She complained to her friend Mercy Warren of her struggles:

> I find myself . . . not only doubled in Wedlock but multiplied in cares to which I know myself unequal, in the Education of my little flock I stand in assistance of my Better half.

Her hired hand had also left to serve in the army, and she reported feeling "obliged to direct what I fear I do not properly understand." Similarly, she wrote her husband that she scarcely knew which way to turn and felt "uneaquil to the cares" which fell upon her, especially as the "Directress of . . . Husbandry and farming."[3] Wartime farming was made especially difficult by the labor shortage and rapid inflation. Abigail wrote John that she could scarcely get a day's work from the money paid, and that the rate was so high it was almost impossible for her to live.

Within a year, however, Abigail seemed to be doing quite well on her own. In the summer of 1776, she had herself and the children inoculated against small pox without her husband's knowledge or consent. Soon the farm was more productive than it had been under John's direction. General James Warren, Mercy's husband, was certainly impressed. The following spring he wrote to John:

> I don't doubt but Mrs. Adams Native Genius will Excel us all in Husbandry. She was much engaged when I came along, and the Farm at Braintree appeared to be under Excellent Management. I tried to persuade her to make a Visit to her Friend Mrs. Warren, but she cant leave Home this Busy Season.[4]

To meet the challenge of inflation and a labor shortage, Abigail curbed her consumption and worked to improve the productivity and profits from the family farm. She was willing to adopt a lower standard of living to save money, and to take part in patriotic boycotts. She no longer bought sugar, molasses, coffee, tea, or imported clothes. "I can live without any of them," she wrote, "and if what I enjoy I can share with my partner with Liberty, I can sing O be joyfull and sit down content." At the same time, she set goals for farm production:

> I hope to have 200 Bushels of corn and a hundred & 50 weight of flax. English Hay we have more than we had last year, notwithstanding your ground wants manure. We are like to have a plenty of sauce [garden sauce, i.e., from vegetables] I shall have fat Beaf and pork enough, make butter and cheesse enough.[5]

Her efforts appeared to be successful. She had contracted no new debts, and managed to pay off previous debts; "one of our Labourers Prince I have paid seven months wages to since you left me. Besides that I have paid Bracket near all we owed him which was to the amount of 15 pounds lawfull money." Additionally, she set up a cider press, had existing equipment repaired, and bought new equipment that John wanted but had been unable to procure. As Mary Beth Norton has argued, Abigail Adams was one of those women who became stronger and more confident as a deputy husband during the American

Revolution, despite the wartime inflation. "I should do exceeding well," she wrote John, "if we could but keep the money good, but at the rate we go on I know not what will become of us."[6]

Abigail's competence in running the farm and providing for her family is especially impressive given that she became pregnant during John's brief recess from Congress in October of 1776, and delivered a stillborn baby the following July. Moreover, there were rumors that Howe's army would invade Boston, which certainly caused her anxiety. Not once did John return to comfort or assist her during the pregnancy, despite many desperate requests from his wife.[7]

When John received his congressional commission as Minister to the Court of France in November 1777, Abigail was disappointed. However competent she was as a deputy husband, she wanted her husband home. Again she consented to his absence as her duty to the public good. In the summer of 1778, she could not keep up with inflation and pay her workers, but neither would she borrow money.

> Debts are my abhorrence. I never will borrow if any other method can be devised. I have thought of this which I wish you to assent to, to order some saleable articles . . . a trunk at a time, containing [goods worth] ten or 15 pounds Sterling.

As a retailer of European ribbons, fabrics, handkerchiefs, tea, and dinnerware, from which she could supply her family and sell to others, Abigail demonstrated her competence and independence. Importing foreign goods soon became her regular practice. She credited her retail business as the means by which she was able to pay the high taxes, which many others had not been able to pay. John began to refer her orders to mercantile houses in Bilboa and Amsterdam between January 1780 and July 1782. Both of these merchant houses exported goods and sent invoices directly to Abigail Adams.[8]

In addition to taking care of her own business, Abigail also provided support for John's career, keeping him informed of military and political details and attending to his interests with the Congress. As early as 1776, John came to depend on his wife's information.

> You take it for granted that I have particular Intelligence of every Thing from others. But I have not. If any one wants a vote for a commission, he vouchsafes me a Letter, but tells me very little News. I have more particulars from you than any one else. Pray keep me constantly informed.[9]

Apparently Abigail was more impartial and less self-interested than John's colleagues.

When John returned to Europe for the second time, as Minister Plenipotentiary to France in the fall of 1779, communications between them were strained. Abigail seemed to be more disturbed by this than John. John did not have firsthand information from Congress to share with her, and was often too busy to write as frequently as she needed him to regarding business in Europe. In addition, of course, letters were lost in transmission, especially when ships were overtaken by the British.

In the winter of 1779, Abigail wrote James Lovell for information. Lovell was another member of Congress from Massachusetts. Abigail asked if she was entitled to the annals of Congress, and asked Lovell to send her copies, as well as any newspapers he had. Lovell graciously complied. After almost a year of receiving privileged information, she had established enough of a rapport with Lovell to inquire about exchange rates that were affecting her husband's salary.

> I am not seeking Sir for communications improper to be made to a Lady—only wish to know from time to time any important and interesting matters which may take place. I find that Congress are drawing Bill[s] at 25 for one upon Mr. Laurens and Jay to the amount of 100,000 Sterling. . . . Why I ask do they demand only 25 when 30 has been currently given here and 40 at Philadelphia[?] You may always give me the go by, when I ask an improper Question and I shall take no umbrage but it will not be one I suppose to inquire after Mr. Adams's accounts and vouchers and to ask what has ever been done with them?[10]

Lovell did not give her the "go by." Abigail was successful in this request, and it is significant that she asked gingerly, always including a mention of the proper boundaries of the fair sex as she proceeded to nudge beyond them. Lovell appeared to respond to her every query and irritation, in addition to sending her copies of official reports. Abigail then forwarded the papers to John, with a summary of the latest news from Congress. In addition, Abigail provided Lovell with detailed information from John about what was happening in Europe.

Abigail also maintained a regular correspondence with John Thaxter, her cousin, who served Mr. Adams as a secretary on his second mission to France. Thaxter provided her descriptive travelogues that included details about the terrain, architecture, and people in Europe. He also made mention of her two boys, John Quincy and Charles, who made the voyage as well. The comfort that Abigail felt having warm letters from this relative enabled her to voice political opinions to which her husband seemed impervious. As we shall see, she received more empathy from Thaxter on issues of gender inequality than from her husband, which enabled her to clearly articulate the patriarchal aspects of tyranny that still prevailed in what they all considered to be the most liberal country in the world.[11]

Adams's connections to these male political figures made her the envy of Mercy Warren, who felt quite out of the loop, as her husband was less involved in politics than Abigail's and had been voted out of the Massachusetts General Court in 1778. Mercy Warren was clearly disappointed with James's failure to be reelected, and quickly blamed the public for their inability to recognize and appreciate all her husband had done for them. She expressed to her husband, and to the Adamses, that he was too good for his constituents, and his principles too pure for the dirty business of politics. In June 1778, she told James that she wanted him home to take care of her anyway, and hoped that his duty would not separate them in the future. James Warren also made himself unavailable to the public. He had refused a judgeship in 1776, was voted out of office to the General Court in 1778, and resigned from his congressional appointment to the Navy Board later the same year. He refused his seat as an elected member of Congress in 1782.[12] Mercy made frequent requests for "particulars" that Abigail would fulfill at her discretion, sometimes leaving Warren feeling slighted.

Abigail unquestionably fortified her own intelligence by gathering information and communicating it to John. The communications this role afforded her were also important because they allowed her to have something of an emotional affair with John Lovell. She rarely received a tender letter from her husband, as his were almost exclusively about political facts. By contrast, Lovell's politically informative letters to Abigail gushed with sweetness and flattery. She poured out to him "the Natural sentiments of the Heart," to which her own husband did not respond. Lovell responded by referring to her as the "amiable Portia," "lovely Woman," and his "lovely anxious friend" in his flirtatious yet informative correspondence. The letters between Abigail and Lovell heated up for a year, until Lovell became too suggestive and Abigail had to chastise him for crossing the line. A more businesslike rapport continued until Abigail joined John in Europe in June 1784.[13]

Separation and Revolutionary Radicalism

In this decade, from 1774 to 1784, Abigail developed the most radical political positions of her life, and gained a reputation as an extraordinary woman in her own right. The first radical view that she articulated in writing was about race. On July 9, 1774, John relayed a story about a casual meeting he had with William Tying, the loyalist sheriff who had just been made a British colonel by General Gage, his wife, and a few other members of the Bar and the Court. They got into a discussion about the "Affrican trade," in which a judge named Trowbridge remarked that the trade of "making Slaves" was very humane and Christian. Mr. Adams agreed. "It makes no great Odds, it is a Trade that almost all Mankind have been concerned in, all over the Globe, since Adam, more or less in one Way and another," which occasioned a laugh, he told his wife.[14]

A few months later, Abigail touched on the subject of slavery. She reported hearing of a "conspiracy of Negroes." Apparently, there were some enslaved blacks who attempted to gain their freedom in Boston by offering their loyalty and services to the governor. Her commentary on the subject displayed empathy for the enslaved. Slavery, she insisted, conflicted with Enlightenment principles, and its practice in the American colonies was hypocritical. "It always appeared a most iniquitous Scheme to me—fight ourselves for what we are daily robbing and plundering from those who have as good a right to freedom as we have. You know my mind upon this Subject."[15]

As John began to rely on Abigail for information, she began to ponder her own sense of political capacities, and suggested to her husband, in a now famous letter, that revolutionary ideals be applied to liberate women. On March 31, 1776, Abigail wrote to John:

> I long to hear that you have declared an independancy—and by the way in the New Code of Laws which I suppose it will be necessary for you to make I desire you would Remember the Laidies, and be more generous and favourable to them than your ancestors. Do not put such unlimited power into the Hands of the Husbands. Remember all Men would be tyrants if they could. If perticular care and attention is not paid to the Laidies, we are determined to foment a Rebelion, and will not hold ourselves bound by any laws in which we have no voice, or Representation.

That your Sex are Naturally Tyrannical is a Truth so thoroughly established as to admit of no dispute, but such of you as wish to be happy willingly give up the harsh title of master for the more tender and endearing one of Friend. Why then, not put it out of the power of the vicious and the Lawless to use us with cruelty and indignity with impunity. Men of Sense in all Ages abhor those customs which treat us only as vassals of your Sex. Regard us then as Beings placed by providence under your protection and in immitation of the Supreem Being make use of that power only for our happiness.[16]

As Edith Gelles has noted, there has been a virtual "Abigail industry" of 150 years of scholarship on Abigail Adams;[17] there is no consensus, however, on the meaning of Abigail's 1776 plea to John and his congressional colleagues to "remember the ladies."

Recent scholarship on Abigail Adams has been highly critical of claims that she was any sort of feminist. Some, such as Linda Grant DePauw and Joan Hoff, have echoed Janet Whitney's 1947 claim that Abigail was never serious in her threat that the ladies would rebel if they were not given rights of representation. These scholars deny that Adams ever meant to argue for woman suffrage; she was only half-serious in making a limited plea for restrictions against the right of men to physically chastise their wives.[18] Others, such as Lynn Withey and L. H. Butterfield, emphasize the possibility that Abigail did mean to argue for women's rights, including suffrage, despite her general contentment as a wife and mother. They highlight a conundrum, namely, that Abigail Adams sometimes acted and thought as a radical republican and advocate of woman's rights, and at other times as a conservative reactionary and traditional eighteenth-century wife.

Several points of Abigail's letter support the argument that she was a suffragist. First, she decried the power that husbands were granted over wives as unlimited and tyrannical. This was a direct application of revolutionary reasoning to "domestic government." Abigail rejected the legal tradition of coverture, which established the relation of husband to wife as one of lord to vassal. Enlightenment thought rejected the notion that some were naturally the political inferiors of others, and Abigail applied this to gender. Second, her letter demonstrated an understanding that the link between coverture and representation was virtual representation, which was contradictory to American republican principles. Coverture dissolved the separate legal identity of the wife, who was in theory represented by her husband in matters of contract and political obligation.

Scholars have widely accepted that the Revolution was fought in part to reject *virtual* representation, in favor of a theory of *actual* representation, by which the American colonists would be seen on a naturally equal footing with British subjects in the mother country. The slogan "no taxation without representation" signaled American men's rejection of the idea that they were represented by the British parliament while being denied the right to vote for any of its members. Abigail suggested that women also had a right to "sign on" to the social compact explicitly and not tacitly. They would not "hold themselves bound to any laws in which we have no voice or representation." In other words, she rejected the idea of virtual representation as it was practiced through coverture and the exclusively male franchise.

On the other hand, Abigail seems to have wanted to preserve the idea of male cover or protection of women in marriage. She does not use any derivative of the word "equal." She suggests, as the traditional Blackstone doctrine does, that marriage is an institution ordained by God to afford women protection by men. Her statement that the law should "limit the power of the vicious and the Lawless to use us with cruelty and indignity with impunity" and that men should instead use "that power" for women's happiness seems to suggest that she is concerned not with voting rights but with a right not to be assaulted, so that "other women" out there with harsh husbands would have some legal recourse. And yet her statement that the male sex is so "naturally tyrannical" that it was indisputable suggests that she is not just talking about "other" harsh and vicious men, but *all* men. Combined with the statements about political obligation and representation, it suggests that the problem of male tyranny was systemic. A plausible interpretation is that while she clearly grasped the revolutionary argument on virtual representation and applied it to women and coverture, she needed to show that she still believed in marriage.

In the same letter, Abigail also reiterated her belief in universal natural rights. When Lord Dunmore, the royal governor of Virginia, carried out his threat to liberate the slaves to quash the revolutionary movement in the House of Burgesses, Abigail blamed the Virginians' defenselessness on their aristocratic values. The planters had been "duped" by Dunmore because their slaves were more dear to them than the cause of liberty: "I have sometimes been ready to think that the passion for liberty cannot be Eaqually Strong in the Breasts of those who have been accustomed to deprive their fellow Creatures of theirs." Abigail was much more liberal than Mercy Warren. Where Warren had declared Lord Dunmore "inhumane" for having armed the slaves against their masters, Abigail commented on the tragedy of slavery as an institution, taking into account the slaves' perspective. Slavery was wrong on two counts. It was anti-republican and it violated the Golden Rule. "Of this I am certain that it is not founded upon that generous and Christian principle of doing to others as we would that others should do unto us."[19]

The suggestion that Abigail was not serious in this letter probably stems from *her husband's* response, in which he trivialized the formal power of rights, and ridiculed his wife for seeking them:

> As to your Extraordinary Code of Laws, I cannot but laugh. We have been told that our struggle has loosened the bands of Government every-where. That Children and Apprentices were disobedient—that schools and colledges were grown turbulent.—that Indians slighted their guardians and Negroes grew insolent to their Masters. But your letter was the first Intimation that another Tribe more numerous and powerfull than all the rest were grown discontented.—This is rather too coarse a Compliment but you are so saucy, I wont blot it out.
>
> Depend upon it, we know better than to repeal our Masculine sys-tems. Altho they are in full Force, you know they are little more than Theory. We dare not exert our Power in its full Latitude. We are obliged to go fair, and softly, and in Practice you know We are the subjects. We have only the Name of Masters, and rather than give up this, which would compleatly subject Us to the Despotism of the Peticoat, I hope General Washington and all our brave Heroes would fight. I am sure every good Politician would plot, as long as he would against Despotism, Empire, Monarchy, Aristocracy, or Ochlocracy.[20]

John thought revolutionary rationality had gotten out of control. It was not meant to loosen the bands of government "everywhere." Not between Indians and their guardians, slaves and their masters, children and their parents or teachers, and certainly not between wives and hus-bands. The bottom line, after his bantering about the "despotism of the peticoat," was a firm *no*. They would not repeal their "masculine sys-tems," and indeed would fight against any ladies' rebellion.

Upon receiving this reply from John, Abigail took her ideas to Mercy Warren, recounting the exchange between herself and John almost verbatim. In this utopian moment, Abigail envisioned herself and Warren arguing for their rights before Congress:

I think I will get you to join me in a petition to Congress. I thought it was very probable our wise Statesmen would erect a New Government and form a new code of Laws. I venture[d] to speak a word in behalf of our Sex, who are rather hardly dealt with by the Laws of England which give such unlimited power to the Husband to use his wife Ill.

I requested that our Legislators would consider our case and as all men of Delicacy and Sentiment are averse to Exercising the power they possess, yet as there is a natural propensity in Humane nature to domination, I thought that most generous plan was to put it out of the power of the Arbitrary and tyranick to injure us with impunity by Establishing some Laws in our favour upon just and Liberal principals.

I believe I even threatned fomenting a Rebellion in case we were not considered, and assured him we would not hold ourselves bound by any Laws in which we had neither a voice, nor representation.

In return he tells me he cannot but Laugh at My Extraordinary Code of Laws. That he had heard their Struggle had loosned the bands of Government, that children and apprentices were dissabedient, that Schools and Colledges were grown turbulent, that Indians slighted their Guardians, and Negroes grew insolent to their Masters. But my Letter was the first intimation that another Tribe more numerous and powerfull than all the rest were grown discontented. . . .

So I have help'd the Sex abundantly, but I will tell him I have only been making trial of the Disintresstedness of his Virtue, and when weigh'd in the balance have found it wanting.[21]

Abigail was less inconsistent writing to Warren than to her husband. Rather than making a distinction between "liberal-minded" and "vicious" men, Abigail pointed out the theoretical implications of coverture on all women. To Warren, she argued that all human beings had a tendency toward self-interestedness, or "domination," and that the law buttressed this tendency in men by privileging them with a "tyrannic" power. Men's power, no less than the power of King George III, needed to be limited, through the establishment of "the most generous plan," which would afford women individual rights. Rights for women were the answer. Men were not disinterested, and the legal system supported their interests. John, in particular, lost the "trial" of disinterested virtue; when "weighed in the balance," Abigail "found it wanting."[22]

If John actually believed that coverture was justified because women ruled men informally, he certainly did not share this reasoning with his male colleagues in Congress. Six weeks after he had written Abigail about the despotism of the petticoat, John wrote James Sullivan a letter regarding the problem of universality in social contract theory.[23] If the "only moral Foundation of Government is the Consent of the People," he wrote:

> to what extent Shall we carry this Principle? . . . Shall we say that every Individual of the Community, old and young, male and female, as well as rich and poor must consent, expressly to every Act of Legislation? . . . Whence arises the Right of the Men to govern the Women, without their Consent? . . . Why exclude women?

He concluded that women could and should be excluded and governed "because their Delicacy renders them unfit for Practice and Experience, in the great Business of Life, and the hardy Enterprises of War, as well as the arduous Cares of State." Here John makes no mention of women's informal power, but recruits fair sex ideology to disqualify women from the franchise. The delicacy of the fair sex rendered its members unfit.

So did their ignorance and dependence. Like men "wholly destitute of Property," women were:

> too little acquainted with public affairs to form a Right Judgment, and too dependent upon other Men to have a Will of their own, for generally speaking, Women and Children have as good Judgment, and as independent Minds as those Men who are wholly destitute of Property: these last being to all Intents and Purposes as much dependent upon others, who will please to feed, cloath and employ them, as Women are upon their Husbands, or Children on their Parents.

Adams's letter to Sullivan was written only days after Adams's letter to Abigail telling her he had heard she was running the farm better than he had. Thus, it is difficult to believe that his use of fair sex ideology was anything but a pretext for keeping power concentrated in the hands of white men. He concludes by suggesting that female suffrage would inevitably lead to new claims by already excluded Others— "Lads," "every Man without a farthing," "Tories, Landjobbers, Trimmers, Bigots, Canadians, Indians, Negroes, Hanoverians, Hessians, Russions, Irish Roman Catholicks, [and] Scotch Renagadoes." The slippery slope of natural rights would "confound and destroy all Distinctions, and prostrate all Ranks, to one common Levell." In other words, racial, ethnic, gender, and class hierarchy needed to be preserved against claims of equality.[24]

John's refusal to share his thoughts that women were too dependent to have a will of their own, and similar to children and the poor with respect to an inferior rationality, signaled the breakdown of communicative rationality on gender issues with his wife. In this case, John was not being sincere with Abigail about his underlying objections to female suffrage. By raising with her only the objection that chaos would prevail, he did not give his wife an opportunity to confront his views on the lack of political competency in women.

Coping with Disillusionment

Having met with her husband's resistance, and lacking support from Mercy Warren,[25] Abigail retreated from her proposal for women's rights, and playfully appropriated fair sex ideology herself:

> I cannot . . . think you very generous to the Ladies, for whilst you are proclaiming peace and good will to Men, Emancipating all Nations, you insist upon retaining an absolute power over Wives. But you must remember that Arbitrary power is like most other things which are very hard, very liable to be broken—and notwithstanding all your wise Laws and Maxims we have it in our power not only to free ourselves but to subdue our Masters, and without violence throw both your natural and legal authority at our feet—/ Charm by accepting, by submitting sway/ Yet have our Humour most when we obey.[26]

The ladies would use their sexual power, such as it was, to subvert masculine power and oppression. Having been unsuccessful on the issue of woman suffrage, Abigail next took up the less radical proposal for female education. Without John's permission, Abigail arranged for their daughter to be tutored in Latin and Greek, just as her sons would be. When Abigail subsequently told John about this, he wrote the young Nabby in April 1776, begrudgingly consenting to her lessons, but warning her that she should not tell anyone because it was "scarcely reputable for young ladies to understand Latin and Greek." French would be more appropriate.[27]

Near the end of May, Abigail also made a move to solve her labor and cash flow problems on the farm. Although she had clearly understood the full implications of natural rights philosophy, especially as they applied to the issue of slavery, she did not fully apply the principles of equality.

Just six weeks after she wrote letters complaining of being overwhelmed by her responsibilities, she told John not to be anxious for her, for she was now making out much better than she had: "I have hired a Negroe fellow for 6 months, am to give him ten pounds which is much lower than I had any prospect of getting help, and Belcher [the white manager] is exceeding assiduous and I believe faithful in what he undertakes." Profiting by paying blacks less for the same work was a pragmatic solution to inflation and the high demand for labor. Whether she was influenced by her husband's complaint of too much disorder and the confounding of ranks or was blind to her own logic concerning her "fellow creatures" is unclear, but from this point forward, it appears that Abigail would never again raise the issue of racial injustice.[28]

She also toned down her rhetoric on issues of gender equality. In August of the same year, John complained to Abigail about the weak intellects of his countrymen—their provincial understandings, and their lack of art in presentation. To succeed as heroes, statesmen, and philosophers, they needed more than virtue; they needed to know how to present their knowledge strategically, including when to conceal it. In reply, Abigail noted her own lack of education. "I find myself soon out of my debth, and destitute and deficient in every part of Education." Daughters were even more neglected than sons when it came to education.[29] But she did not suggest that this was another aspect of male tyranny.

She took up John's rationale, and suggested later that month, "if we mean to have heroes, Statesmen, and Philosophers, we should have learned women." Obviously, if early education was as important as her husband and the great philosophers were saying, then those who typically took care of young children needed to be educated as well. Even in that suggestion, she feared that the world would "laugh at me, and accuse me of vanity," as her husband had done previously. But it seemed only reasonable to her that a "liberal plan might be laid and executed for the Benefit of the rising Generation," which would include the education of girls. She hoped that the new state constitution of Massachusetts would thus be "distinguished for Learning and Virtue."[30]

John wholeheartedly agreed that learned women benefitted men, but he showed no interest in establishing public education for girls. In the same month, he wrote Abigail, "your sentiments of the Importance of Education in Women, are exactly agreeable to my own." But he frowned on "Femmes Scavans [savantes?]" and "Pedants" as contemptible characters. History taught that every great character, whether a general, statesman, or philosopher, was supported by "some female about him either in the character of a Mother, Wife, or Sister," with "Knowledge and Ambition above the ordinary Level of Women, and that much of his Emminence" was owed "to her Precepts, Example, or Instigation, in some shape or other."[31]

The proper role for a talented woman was not on center stage, but behind the curtain in support of her husband or other men. "Aspasia the wife of Pericles," for example, taught her husband "his refind Maxims of Policy, his lofty imperial Eloquence; nay, even composed the Speeches, on which so great a Share of his Reputation was founded." So extraordinary was this lady that:

> [t]he best Men in Athens frequented her House, and brought their Wives to receive Lessons from her oeconomy and right Deportment. Socrates himself was her Pupil in Eloquence and gives her the Honour of that funeral Oration which he delivers in the Menexensu of Plato.

John praised exceptional women who had learned despite the bans against them. He also had the nerve to suggest that such women did not exist in America: "I wish some of our great Men had such Wives."[32]

In April 1778, after he had been in France a few weeks, John boasted of the "exceedingly brilliant accomplishments" of "well educated" French women.[33] Abigail replied that she could hear about their accomplishments and rejoice in the liberal sentiment that acknowledged them. She lamented once again the "trifling narrow contracted education of Females in [her] own country," and the American tendency to "ridicule Female learning." She found support in an unnamed male author, who suggested that the denial of education to women was evidence of a power struggle, where the balance was already tipped to one side. If women were the enemies, he argued, then it would be "an

Ignoble Cowardice thus to disarm them and not allow them the same weapons we use ourselves." But if women were men's friends, it would be "an inhumane Tyranny to debar them of privileges of ingenious Education which would also render their friendship so much more delightfull to themselves and us." Abigail reiterated this fair sex ideology. With an "ingenious" education, "what polite and charming creatures would they prove whilst their external Beauty does the office of a Crystal to the Lamp not shrowding but discloseing their Brighter intellects." Women's beauty would no longer be merely skin deep. Nor need men fear losing their "Empire" over women, since "where there is most Learning, Sence and knowledge there is always observed to be the most modesty and Rectitude of manners."[34] In short, men would benefit because women would develop finer characters, and use them to refine and civilize mankind.

Abigail was much more direct about the issue of female education with John Thaxter. In February 1778, just two days after her husband left for France, she wrote Thaxter that she found it "mortifying" that females with a "common share of understanding" were not given equal educational opportunities. "Every assistance and advantage which can be procured is afforded to the sons, whilst the daughters are totally neglected in point of Literature. Writing and Arithmatick comprise all their Learning." She did not understand why fathers would wish to deprive their daughters or husbands would wish to deprive their wives of equal education and respect. "Why should not the Females who have a part to act upon the great Theater" as mothers, "a part no less important to society," be "suitably qualified for the Trust, Especially when we consider that families compose communities, and individuals make up the sum total[?]" And why would men "wish for such a disparity in those whom they one day intend for companions and associates[?]" Abigail could not avoid the conclusion that men opposed the education of women because they wanted to maintain their dominance over them in the new Republic. She suspected that "the Neglect arises in some measure from an ungenerous jealousy of rivals near the throne."[35]

Thaxter validated Abigail's views:

> After mentioning that our sex wish a disparity, you subjoin a suspicion that Jealousy of rivalship is the foundation of the neglect of your sex. Madam, I am positive it is too often the case. It is an "ungenerous Jealousy" as you justly term it.

Abigail looked forward to letters from Thaxter, who validated her more radical views and knew how to blend important news with appropriate affection. "Continue to write by every opportunity," she asked him, "I love to know what is passing in the world tho excluded from it."[36]

John and Abigail had about a month together in the late summer of 1779, when John returned from his first trip abroad in August. Soon after he arrived, he was busily engaged as the sole drafter of the Massachusetts constitution. In late October, he left once again for France in hopes of working out a peace treaty with Great Britain through the French Court. He took along his two sons, John Quincy and Charles, as well as Thaxter. The separation was difficult on Abigail, who viewed it a "cruel torture," especially since John had just been to Europe, and she had counted on being able to see him in Boston on the weekends. Thus began the warm epistolary relationships with Lovell and Thaxter, and Mrs. Adams's access to the annals of Congress. Abigail continued to inform John, and continued to import goods for resale.

Early in 1780, Abigail had heard about Mercy Warren's letter to her son criticizing Lord Chesterfield's letters. Chesterfield was a bachelor who fathered a child with his mistress, and his letters to this only son were admired by Mercy's son Winslow. Mercy wrote an epistolary essay to her son in which she praised Chesterfield's elegant command of the English language, but criticized his corrupt morals and his incitements to passion and sexual desires. In the letter, she took issue with Chesterfield's asperity toward women, especially his tendency to lay blame for social vices on them. She retorted that she ever considered "human nature as the same in both sexes." Either sex could be virtuous or depraved, because virtue and vices were characteristics of the human soul. The soul was genderless—equally susceptible to "the foibles, the passions, the vices and the virtues," whether in the "vehicle" of a male or female body.

Abigail had read enough of Chesterfield's letters to think of him as a "polished libertine." In February and again in September 1780, Abigail requested a copy of the critical letter from Mercy Warren. On December 21, Mercy wrote Abigail to ask what she had done with the letter, and to return it if she was done with it. Shortly thereafter, Abigail sent it to the editor of the Boston *Independent Chronicle*. The letter was finally published anonymously therein on January 18, 1781.[37]

After this effort, Abigail's interest in pursuing issues of equity for women waned; nevertheless, she remained interested in other political issues and events. In July 1780, there was a gubernatorial election, and Adams observed and discussed it with her husband: "The man who from Merrit, fortune and abilities ought to be our *Chief* is not *popular*, and tho he will have the votes of the sensible judicious part of the State, he will be more than out Numberd by the lovers of the tinkleling cymball." Her man of merit was James Bodoin, the tinkling cymbal, John Hancock. Aware of the irony of a woman's following elections, she exclaimed to her husband: "What a politician you have made of me? If I cannot be a voter upon this occasion, I will be a writer of votes. I can do something that way but fear I shall have the mortification of a defeat."[38]

Later that year, Abigail had a difficult time. She had been sick in the fall, and the British Navy had overtaken Charleston. She lost faith in the army, and said that too many of the soldiers lacked the requisite virtue to get the job done. Peace seemed further away than ever before. As the holidays rolled around, she became depressed. She received far fewer letters from her husband than she had sent, in part because most were lost at sea or confiscated, and the only one she received between June and December was cold and dry. On Christmas she wrote John about feeling "alone in the wide world, without anyone tenderly to take care of me, or lend an assisting hand through the difficulties."[39]

Reflecting on her pain, and her husband's apparent lack of it, she suggested that women were more emotional than men, and that was why she grieved over the separation more than her husband did. She resorted to fair sex ideology. "Man is active resolute and bold/ Woman is fashioned in a different mold." Never mind that she had requested permission from John to cross the Atlantic to be with him. He had refused her. She thought that perhaps he did not need her as badly as she needed him. Men were "[m]ore independent by Nature," scarcely able to "realize all those ties which bind our sex to his." She now supposed that it was "natural" that as women's dependence was greater, their attachment to others was also stronger.[40] Whether she meant that women were more relational than men because they were forced into dependency or that both were part of women's nature is unclear. But the winter of 1780 marked a turning point at which Adams no longer desired or cared about gender equality, wanting only peace and a reunion with her husband.

John was experiencing difficulties that Abigail would only find out about the following June. Just a day after Christmas in 1780, a committee of Congress was studying a packet of correspondence between Mr. Adams and Vergennes, the French foreign minister. When John was sent to France, he was commissioned to work out a commercial treaty with Great Britain under the guidance of the French, who had provided early support for American independence. Franklin had already been in France for several years, but had failed to make headway on commercial treaties. Adams had suspected that progress in the negotiations was stalled because the French had their own interests to pursue and were not ready to abate their hostilities with England.

Frustrated, Adams wrote a series of letters to Vergennes, and finally requested leave from the French government to go to Britain and announce that he was the minister from the United States empowered to negotiate the treaty. In July, Vergennes basically threatened to expose Adams as a maverick, which he did, by sending all of the recent correspondence between himself and Adams to Benjamin Franklin. Franklin, who had ingratiated himself with the French by wining and dining with them and frequenting the salons, was happy to tattle on his more programmatic and unpopular colleague. Franklin sent the entire packet with a note of his own to Congress that August, and it was received by Christmas.

The first order of congressional business in January 1781 was thus what to do with the American politician who had angered the United State's only firm ally. A committee was formed to study the letters and make its report. That spring, La Luzerne, the French minister to the United States, lobbied members of Congress in Philadelphia to censure Adams and curb his diplomatic powers as Vergennes had recommended. In June, the committee recommended transferring Adams's powers to five newly named commissioners, but the recommendation failed to pass. On July 12, however, James Madison headed the effort to revoke Adams's powers, and this time it passed by a large majority. John could not even count on the support of his Massachusetts colleagues, who were split on the matter. James Lovell was one of the men who voted in favor of the censure.

When Abigail found out, she took it poorly. Her letters expressed so much venom that her grandchild, Charles Francis Adams, excluded them in his original publication of the family correspondence. Whatever pleasure she had from Lovell's attentions, and however useful he was in providing her with information, these things could not restrain her pen. "I want to ask you a hundred Questions and to have them fully and explicitly answerd. You will send me by the first opportunity the whole of this dark prosess." It wasn't the first time that Abigail got involved in her husband's dealings with Congress, or tried to protect his reputation;[41] but it was the first time that she made angry demands of a man.

Thenceforward, she expressed a continual preoccupation with her husband's reputation. In her letter to Lovell of June 30, she viewed the censure of Mr. Adams as a conspiratorial indictment of John's character:

> Was the Man a Gallant I should think he had been more monopolising the Women from the enchanter. Was he a Modern Courtier I should think he had outwitted him in court intrigue. Was He a selfish avaritious designing deceitfull Villan I should think he had encroached upon the old Gentlemans perogatives.[42]

The "enchanter" and "old Gentleman" was Franklin, and Abigail thought everyone in the Continental Congress was duped by him.

Lovell did answer Mrs. Adams, explaining that his vote had nothing to do with John's character; Congress's hands were simply tied by the French, on whom they depended. Abigail's response was that vulnerability to such "parissian influence" was shameful. "It bears a striking likeness of a servility to a court that ought not to have so undue an influence upon an Independent Nation." She expressed a similar thought to Elbridge Gerry, complaining that the plan that appeared to be adopted both at home and abroad was "a servile adulation and complasance" to the French Court, which would be costly for American interests. Her husband was to be respected, Franklin reviled: "The Independent Spirit of your Friend, abroad, does not coinside with the selfish views and inordinate ambition of your Minister, who in consequence of it, is determined upon his destruction."[43]

The question here is not whether Abigail was correct in her assessment of the situation or of her husband's character. John was at this time in pursuit of a decisive alliance with the Netherlands, completely unbeknownst to his wife. More pertinent to the theme of this inquiry, a subtle shift was occurring in Abigail's political thought. She had long ago realized that her fate was tied to her husband's by law, custom, and her own desires, and now she seemed to be totally absorbed in a vicarious ambition for his career. In fact, her political voice became stronger as she adopted this role. Although she could not prevail upon him to take her side on the political issues that were dear to her, she could not have been unaware that if John fell from grace, she would fall with him. If his career suffered, the deference that she had become accustomed to would not be ensured.

By August 20, 1781, Congress restored Adams's diplomatic power, naming him sole minister plenipotentiary to negotiate an alliance with Holland, France, and possibly Spain.[44] Abigail continued to show concern for John's reputation in letters to Lovell, who repeatedly attempted to reassure her by telling her that the Congress had a high opinion of him.

Turning to Fair Sex Ideology

The shift in Abigail's thinking on gender was clearly marked in September 1781, when she wrote to Lovell, "[f]or myself I have little ambition or pride—for my Husband I freely own I have much." To Lovell, it was merely an excuse for her regular inquiries about John's reputation in Congress. But her statement indicated the end of her utopianism. She distanced herself from ambition as soon as she acknowledged it. Her desires were now simply for a private life of virtue and harmony with John in their "rustick cottage." Her involvement in his career was not self-interested in any way, she suggested; it was evidence of her commitment to the public good. The great theater had called forth her husband as a principal actor upon the stage, and her ambition was for his character—so that he could "do Honour to his country whilst he secures it to Freedom, independence, and fame." From this point on, she would play the role of the supportive wife behind the scenes in keeping with fair sex ideology.[45]

Abigail's renunciation was really a renunciation of ambition for the ladies, whom she had deemed more severely oppressed by the laws of England than the men had been. She was less likely to examine her situation as a woman through a critique of the political machinations of men. By April 10, 1782, with John still gone, Abigail turned to the Bible to help her cope with the separation. "Desire and Sorrow were denounced upon our Sex: as punishment for the transgression of Eve." This explained why women were "formed to experience more exquisite Sensations" than men. "More tender and susceptible by Nature of those impression[s] which create happiness or misiry, we Suffer and enjoy in a higher degree."[46]

She had just received two letters from John, written October 9 and December 18 of the previous year. For the second half of 1781 and the first quarter of 1782, Abigail received no letters from her husband. She had not heard from him from July 1781 to that day in April, excepting one letter he had written to her son Charles in November, which she read in January. Although she was very happy to have finally received the two letters, they were insufficient to cure her melancholy. She told him that the romance of their relationship had long ago passed, but the affection remained strong, and there was nothing in the world that could compensate her for the loss of him. Having been unsuccessful in persuading John to come home, or gaining his consent for her to go abroad, she was stuck with unresolved feelings. She could blame him for his ambition, but she fundamentally believed in the cause he was serving. She blamed herself for weakness instead. "I never wonderd at the philosopher who thanked the Gods that he was created a Man rather than a Woman."[47]

John had won a formal declaration by the Netherlands to respect the United States as an independent nation on April 19, 1782, but Abigail did not receive John's letter telling her the news, and thus was informed about the event only through the newspapers in July 1782. By the end of July, John had also managed to secure a $5 million loan from the Dutch, which pretty much ensured the subsequent surrender of the British that would follow in the fall of the next year. By mid-June, however, she had received letters that John had written only up to the last week of March.

She was relieved to hear that he had made a favorable impression in Holland. At this time, she consented to his continued absence, stating that a peace treaty could be accepted only upon "the most liberal foundation," that is, with Britain's recognition of U.S. independence. Abigail had already been apart from her husband without once seeing him once since the fall of 1779. She did not at this time know that she would have to wait out two additional years of separation. Her support for her husband's work prompted a backward reflection on the inequality of the sexes in the American polity: "Patriotism in the female Sex is the most disinterested of all virtues. Excluded from honours and from offices, we cannot attach ourselves to the State or Government from having held a place of Eminence." She quoted Thomas Paine's

"Occasional Letter on the Female Sex": "Even in the freest countrys our property is subject to the controul and disposal of our partners, to whom the Laws have given a sovereign Authority." And she added, "[d]eprived of a voice in Legislation, obliged to submit to those Laws which are imposed upon us, is it not sufficient to make us indifferent to the publick Welfare?"[48] In addition to their wartime efforts, women gave their sons and their husbands to the public cause, but were not considered virtuous enough to be rewarded with political rights. Abigail would never bring up women's deprivation under the law again.

On the very same day, she wrote John Thaxter a personal letter to update him on the singles scene back home. Thaxter was single and longed for a wife. He shared his longing with Abigail, who became a confidante. Abigail noted that "licentiousness and freedom of manners" seemed to predominate in the men and women that she observed. She now looked to Rousseau and Fordyce for guidance on gender issues, and began to consider their ideas on the particular importance of female virtue: "Rousseau observes, that the manner of thinking among Men in a great measure depends upon the taste of the Ladies. If this is true, the manners of the present day are no complement on the fair sex."[49] Abigail thought rather that the manners of the two sexes kept pace with each other; "in proportion as the Men grow regardless of character, the women neglect the Duties of their Sex." Women looked to luxury and fancy dress to impress men whose interest in women's beauty was skin deep. She cited Fordyce, "to whom our Sex are much indebted for the justice he has done them," for his comments on the virtuous influence that women could have on men. Virtuous and "well-bred women" provided the

> best School for Learning the most proper demeanor, the easiest turn of thought and expression and right habits of the best kind, that the most honorable the most Moral the most conscientious Men, are in general those who have the greatest regard for women of reputation and talents.[50]

This sort of thinking was a subtle but not insignificant step away from women's equality. The Chesterfield point could also be made simply by an inverse corollary. If women could be credited for the manners and morals of men, they might also be blamed for their vices. White women certainly were indebted to Fordyce, for his *Sermons for Young Women* helped to put meat and substance into the term "fair sex." His sermons provide a list of dos and don'ts for proper Anglo-American woman-hood, reading like a manual for anyone who would call herself a lady. The basic message in his sermons was that female delicacy required a strict observance of separate spheres and male superiority. A lady should be educated, but only in such a way as to make herself fond of and fit for domestic employments, not to become a masculinized "learned lady."

Fordyce's arguments blatantly reinforced the idea of women's infe-rior mental capacities and their primary role to be agreeable and useful to men. Women had a "defect in point of depth and force," but enjoyed a refined "sentiment" and more insight into human character. Thus he recommended that women narrow their interests to "refined" rather than "profound" subjects.[51] This was hardly in line with Abigail's ear-lier proposal for an "ingenious" education, which emphasized the *pub-lic* aspect of women's mothering, as equally important actors in the great theater of society. And yet, Fordyce's proscriptions against women who disgustingly flaunted their knowledge or literary talents may well have been taken to heart, for Adams refrained her whole life from ever flaunting her knowledge or talents.

Abigail now settled for the identification of woman as noncitizen, one who was formally ruled without the chance to take part in ruling. Even with John Thaxter she dropped her critique of male tyranny, and con-tended for ladies only the private duty to soften men through their purity and virtue. "It is in the company of the virtuous Fair that Rusticity and asperity are softened and refined into Benevolence and philanthropy. There the Graces may be acquired without sacrificing the virtues."[52]

Interestingly, Mrs. Adams's accession to fair sex ideology did not prevent independent or bold action. Indeed, paying lip service to the notion of the domesticated fair sex may have allowed her to subvert its norms. In the last week of April 1782, she informed her husband of her plan to purchase over 1,200 acres in Vermont. Farmers were losing their lands to foreclosure because of their inability to pay taxes, but Abigail had cash to invest. People she spoke to told her the land was good and would only go up in value. She sought John's approval, but by mid-July had received letters from him dated only to March 29. Seizing the opportunity before her, she went forward with her plan, and purchased 5 lots of 330 acres apiece, paying outright for four of them while financing the fifth. Everyone in the family would have his or her name attached to a plot, except for Abigail herself. She also footed the bill for their son Charles's passage from Europe to Boston, leaving herself financially tight. Despite Abigail's effort to please him, John appeared disappointed, as he told his wife a little too late not to "meddle" any more in Vermont, and told James Warren that he would not go to Vermont.[53]

As she purchased the land, she continued the practice that enabled her to buy it in the first place. Still committed not to draw any bills from John's account, Abigail asked him to have merchants send her "black and white Gauze and Gauze handkerchiefs" in addition to scarlet satin and broadcloth. She acknowledged that her retail practice "may not be to the credit of my country, but it is a certain fact, that no articles are so vendible or yeald a greater profit."

At the same time, Abigail was beginning to find Mercy Warren a bit of an irritation. Mercy often requested information, but had none to offer, as she and her husband were far removed from politics and urban life. And now she wanted Abigail to procure for her an entire set of china, at a price that Abigail thought was unrealistically low.[54]

Peace was secured in September 1783, when John signed an official treaty with the powers of Great Britain in Paris. He would be staying in Europe for one purpose only: to carry out the original mission to negotiate a commercial treaty with Great Britain. On September 7, he received word from Congress of its resolution to appoint him for that purpose, as head of a three-man delegation that included John Jay and Benjamin Franklin. Adams immediately asked his wife and daughter to join him in France. Abigail handed the farm over to her uncle, Dr. Cotton Tufts, and left for London with Nabby in June 1784. In England, they were greeted by John Quincy. John Adams joined them in London on August 7, marking the date of their reunion about three months short of five years. By August 17, the family had taken residence at Auteil, where John had been living.

The physical reunion of Abigail and John also reinforced the conservative terms of the marriage contract. Once Abigail joined her husband, her individual political existence gradually diminished. Of course there was no longer a need to keep her husband abreast of politics as she had done; and Abigail would have had to be careful about what she reported to her friends and relatives back home, in order to avoid inappropriately divulging anything about John or their life together in his official capacity.

Perhaps Abigail pragmatically avoided writing details of political developments because it was important for her not to outshine her husband as he was in the process of attaining a commercial treaty with Britain. The loss of political independence was not a question of time, because without the farm to manage, and with nine servants to attend to the cooking, cleaning, and entertaining, Abigail enjoyed more leisure and relaxation than she had known in years. In December 1784, she complained to her sister about becoming lethargic. "My domestick business is so different and my family cares so lessned that unless I ride I have no exercise. The cooks department relieves me from every care of that kind, and cleaning house is performed by Men Servants."[55]

In France, Abigail and her daughter met renowned women, including Madame Helvetius, the intimate friend of Benjamin Franklin and wife of Claude Helvetius, the deceased French philosopher; Adrienne Noailles, the Marquise de Lafayette; and Anne-Catherine, Comtesse de Lignivielle d'Autricourt. Of these, only Noailles impressed her favorably. Madame Helvetius disgusted Abigail in her appearance, wearing decayed tiffany and gauze, and letting her hair dangle unkempt from a dirty old hat. Probably more disgusting was the liberty she took to sit between Dr. Franklin and Mr. Adams at the dining table, dominating the conversation, and throwing her arms around each of their chairs, periodically putting her arm around Franklin's neck. By contrast, Abigail admired the Marquise de Lafayette for her propriety. "I should always take pleasure in her company. She is a good and amiable Lady, exceedingly fond of her Children and attentive to their education, passionatly attached to her Husband!!! A French Lady and fond of her Husband!!!"[56]

Abigail's most important acquaintance in France turned out to be Thomas Jefferson, who had arrived in Europe at about the same time she did, as Franklin's replacement. In Jefferson she found intelligence, gentility, and appreciation for American values and manners. When John was named the first U.S. minister at the Court of St. James in April 1785, Abigail was thrilled to join him; but she hated to leave Jefferson. The family moved to London in the summer in pursuit of a commercial treaty with Britain. As they departed France, John, Abigail, and 20-year-old Nabby took Jefferson's *Notes on the State of Virginia* as their "Meditation all the Day long."[57]

John wrote a letter to Jefferson, praising him lavishly. He especially liked the "passages upon slavery." He told Jefferson that they were "worth Diamonds," and would have "more effect than Volumes written by mere Philosophers." Of course, Jefferson's passages on slavery ruminated the "natural" differences of the races, one being that blacks were mentally inferior to whites by nature, and another that Negro men were too sexually "ardent" to comprehend the tender affections of romantic love. In any case, it is interesting that there appears to have been no dissent among the ladies, whom John reports as commenting only on his depictions of American talent and his failure to mention West and Copley among America's geniuses.[58]

Soon after the Adamses settled in England, Abigail developed a correspondence with Jefferson. At first it was perfectly polite and restrained, an exchange between two displaced Americans who needed to show gratitude for each other's acquaintance in France. Then the Adamses requested wine from France, and Jefferson desired linens from England. An intricate balance sheet between Abigail and Jefferson soon developed, providing fodder for friendly banter about who was indebted to whom after any given shipment. And like anyone who had ever received a letter from Abigail, he became attached to her favors, which had increasingly become important vehicles of political information. Indeed, he preferred to get his facts from her over her husband: "You referred me to Mr. Adams for news; but he gives me none; so that I hope you will be so good as to keep that office in your own hands. I get little from any other quarter since the derangement of the French packets."[59]

Abigail Assents to Class, Race, and Gender Hierarchy

When Jefferson received the news about Shays's Rebellion the previous August and September in Massachusetts, he wrote Abigail to confirm the news about her home state. She wrote back that it was indeed true: "Ignorant, wrestless desperadoes without conscience or principals, have led a deluded multitude to follow their standard, under pretense of grievances which have not existence but in their imaginations." Abigail sounded the alarm of the mercantile interests in Massachusetts:

> Some of them were crying out for a paper currency, some for an equal distribution of property, some for annihilating all debts, others complaining that the Senate was a useless Branch of Government, that the Court of common pleas was unnecessary, and that the sitting of the General Court in Boston was a grieveance.[60]

Abigail, who had been introduced to the King of England with her husband and daughter and become accustomed to the order and civility of England, was alarmed and embarrassed by the rebellion. She advocated "the most vigorous measures to quell and suppress it." In fact, the farmers had organized county conventions to seek a restructuring of debt so that they would not lose their only means of income, either through foreclosure or debtors' prison. When Jefferson suggested to her that the rebels displayed a "laudable spirit" in defense of their liberties, Abigail took offense. From her perspective, liberty was now defined through *order*, not dissent or protest. These were "mobbish insurgents" sapping the foundation of liberty and destroying the nation.[61] The sea change in Abigail's political ideology thus went far beyond the issues of gender, to a wholesale conservatism that clamored for obedience and social hierarchy.

Abigail took satisfaction knowing that Shays's Rebellion and its forceful suppression would prompt an investigation into the root causes of the problem, which she considered to be the vices of the people. The uncontrolled desire for luxury was to blame here.

> Luxury and extravagance both in furniture and dress had pervaded all orders of our Countrymen and women, and was hastening fast to sap their independence by involving every class of citizens in distress, and accumulating debts upon them which they were unable to discharge.

It was all a matter of vanity becoming a more powerful principle than patriotism. When the "lower order of the community" were "prest for taxes," they refused to sell their land to pay; and those who had money would not lend it, fearful that the Legislature might be forced to make a motion for the annihilation of debts.[62]

Abigail was not interested in the farmers' perspectives, and she did not care that over 20 persons would die in the squalid conditions of the debtors' prisons in her own state. The farmers had claimed in county conventions that the higher taxes on land to pay war debts had a disparate impact on farmers as compared to merchants, whose assets were tied up in stocks. She completely disregarded the farmers' problem of being forced to trade in a cash economy. Just a few years earlier, the same farming families survived through subsistence agriculture supplemented by bartering in labor or grain, to purchase items such as iron tools or medicine. In addition to the tax burden, the inland general store merchants now demanded cash, as their credit was cut off by coastal merchants, whose credit was no longer good in Europe. To the extent that the rebellion in any way resulted from an uncontrolled appetite for luxury among the lower classes, Adams certainly took no responsibility for peddling the very sort of items that helped her stay ahead of her own tax burden. Her attitude was rather that because she had paid her own taxes, everyone else ought to pay theirs as well. Never mind their disadvantage in not having a special direct connection to European traders who extended orders on credit.

While Abigail took her profits and invested them in additional property in Vermont, which was not yet a state and would not levy property taxes for some time, other ordinary people lost their property. James and Mercy Warren were one couple who lost prized family property in the credit crisis. They had lived in a large and notable house in Milton, near Boston, but had to sell their place and move to an old family farm, leaving them quite isolated from politics, but able to meet their tax burden. Their son Winslow was pursued by creditors he couldn't pay, and eventually landed in debtors' prison. The Warrens had written to the Adamses to warn them of the tumults in the state from the fall of 1785 through the spring of 1786.

But John did not take them seriously. Of course, he could not totally trust their view of the world, because it was clear that each of them had an agenda for personal gain when they wrote him. Mercy wrote preachy letters to John, indirectly suggesting that he was becoming elitist and possibly tainted by the courts of Europe, because he seemed so out of touch with the economic crisis in his own country. John had probably offended Mercy by not responding to all of her letters. Both she and her husband asked John to help their son Winslow get a job in Lisbon. James asked Adams to use his influence with Jefferson to urge him to make a trading alliance with Portugal. Warren had in mind the establishment of a U.S. consulate there, preferably manned by his son Winslow, to facilitate the "fishery" trade with the United States and to enable his son to pay back creditors at the same time. This did not come to pass, and things for the Warrens, as well as their countrymen, got worse.[63]

Abigail's anger about Shays's Rebellion and her joy and satisfaction in its suppression revealed a fundamental difference between her and her husband and Mr. Jefferson. When Abigail happily reported that some of the rebels had been jailed, Jefferson hoped that they would be pardoned. "The spirit of resistance to government is so valuable on certain occasions, that I wish it to be always kept alive. It will often be exercised when wrong, but better so than not to be exercised at all."[64] Jefferson was much less sure of the establishment than Abigail, and much more willing to see two sides of an issue. Abigail was becoming extremely partisan in her views of politics. Or, more to the point, her views mirrored those of her husband. It became impossible, after the two were reunited, to distinguish their political positions. On some issues, Abigail was more extremist than her husband, but her politics always supported the goal of protecting his power, authority, and reputation.

This trend intensified after John was elected vice president and then president of the United States. John's efforts to restore trade relations with Great Britain were largely unsuccessful, as Britain was in no mood to support the development of the independent nation. While the Federalists were campaigning for the ratification of the U.S. Constitution at home, Jefferson and Adams secured a new loan in Amsterdam; both of these men agreed that the Constitution's delegation of power to the U.S. Congress to regulate interstate commerce was a huge improvement over the Articles of Confederation.

The Adamses returned to Boston in the middle of June 1788. After the Constitution was ratified in 1789, John was elected the first vice president, in the Federalist administration. Abigail suspected that James and Mercy Warren were Antifederalists, given their previous sympathy with those who created anarchy in Massachusetts in the fall of 1786. Abigail suspected that Mercy had a secret correspondence with Elbridge Gerry. She wrote her sister Mary Cranch, "there is not a member [of Congress] whose sentiments clash more with my Ideas of things than Mr. G[err]y." Abigail detested Elbridge Gerry, a known Antifederalist and the only delegate from Massachusetts who went to the Constitutional Convention and refused to sign. In Abigail's mind, he was a provincial politician who failed to "comprehend the Great National System which must Render us respectable abroad & energetick at Home." He and the Warrens were now "jealous partizans." Abigail was appalled by the "ambition" of Mercy Warren—asking John to give patronage jobs to the men in her family, especially after siding with the Antifederalists, who criticized the Federalists as self-interested aristocrats.[65] The conflict over ratification of the Constitution effectively ended the eroding friendship between Mercy and Abigail.

John took office in the autumn of 1789. Abigail's main task was to entertain politicians and others who came to call on them. Abigail complained that the help she found was so indifferent compared to the help she enjoyed in England: "I cannot find a cook in the whole city but what will get drunk, and as to the Negroes, I am most sincerely sick of them." She could get "hands" but no "head," and their chief objective, other than getting drunk, was to "be as expensive as possible."[66] But by the following April, Abigail had changed her tune. No longer sick of blacks, she now preferred them. "The chief of the servants here who are good for anything are Negroes who are slaves. The white ones are all foreigners & chiefly vagabounds." Although the slaves were better than the indentured or free white servants, they couldn't come near the service she had experienced in England. "I really know now more than ever how to Prize my English servants," Abigail lamented to her sister.[67]

The pragmatic Abigail adapted to her context once again. In this country, she found that the best servants were slaves, but when she could not get them, she would settle for the help of free blacks. In the summer of 1791, she wrote her sister Mary again:

> You wrote me in your Letter of January 25th of a Negro Man and woman whom you thought would answer for me this summer. If she is cleanly and a tolerable cook I wish you would engage her for me. I had rather have black than white help, as they will be more likely to agree with those I bring. I have a very clever black boy of 15 who has lived with me a year and is bound to me until he is 21. My coachman will not allow that he is a Negro, but he will pass for one with us.[68]

Abigail had obviously taken advantage of the prolonged slavery in the state of New York, which was home to the first capital of the first administration.

With her reversal on racial slavery, Abigail's signature to racial patriarchy was complete. Her attachment to her husband had led her to abandon the idea of women's rights and transfer her ambition to his career. His career required order, stability, and the protection of his reputation. Order required hierarchy, the submission of the lower to the higher. Men ruled women; government ruled the people; whites ruled blacks; and savages were to be conquered.[69]

In the years that followed, Abigail's views were indistinguishable from those of her husband. In the second presidential election (1792), there was no opposition to George Washington; however, the emerging Democratic-Republican Party put up George Clinton, governor of New York, against John Adams. They represented John Adams as a friend of monarchy, which Abigail resented. She loathed the Democratic-Republicans for their radical ideology, the same ideology that she had adopted for herself in 1776. "The cry of rights of man, liberty and equality were popular themes," she wrote to her daughter.[70]

Tom Paine was once again in fashion for many, as Jefferson published his *Rights of Man* in America. But Abigail, who had approvingly quoted Paine's *Common Sense* in 1780, was now just as conservative as John in his view that Paine's ideas were dangerous. Of course, the real target of the Democratic-Republicans had been Hamilton and his finance system. Both of the Adamses supported Hamilton's plan for the federal adoption of states' debt and the establishment of a national bank. Yet Abigail was troubled more by the lack of respect due her husband and the government than by a populace that had a genuine disagreement about policy.

Vicarious Citizenship and Statesmanship

After John Adams was elected president in 1796, Abigail became even more conservative. She became hawkish in her attitude toward France, whose Jacobins had certainly gravitated toward anarchy themselves, and who seemed to infect the United States. As First Lady, Abigail continued her critique of the Republicans, whom she and other Federalists now referred to as "Jacobins" for their support of the rights of man and the French Revolution. Pro-French Republicans, especially Benjamin Franklin Bache, publisher of the Philadelphia *Aurora*, continued "libelling" the president; they called him a "monarchist" for his pro-British sympathies and his eventual preparation to aid the British militarily.

This "calumny" made the First Lady increasingly angry. She was especially infuriated with members of the opposition for criticizing the president's choice of envoys in the mission to France to try to stem the hostilities that were developing toward the United States in France's war with England. The Republicans accused the president of choosing envoys for the "XYZ affair" from Federalist ranks who would be hostile to the French on a mission of purported reconciliation; the First Lady defended her husband's choices of men who were, in her view, "honorable," "truly American" and "professional." She never revealed that in fact she was in favor of war with France, despite her husband's choice of peacemaking envoys. And when the papers of the mission were exposed, proving that the French were hostile to the American envoys, who in turn acted in good faith to avert war but were not accepted by Talleyrand, Adams rejoiced in the vindication of her husband's character, not in the actual aversion of an all-out war.[71]

The First Lady's concern for her husband's reputation colored all of her political writings. Every contest would now be evaluated in terms of its potential or actual threat to the established government, or John's reputation and power. Congressional debate on the Foreign Intercourse Bill of 1798, for example, was worthy of discussion not on the merits, but for the power relations that it unveiled. Abigail wrote her sister, "You will see by the papers I send you the debate continued by Congress for 15 days and yet undetermined, upon the Foreign Intercourse Bill." The papers were supposed to give her a "clue" of "the full system of the Minority, which is to usurp the Executive Authority into their own Hands."[72]

Mrs. Adams was more hawkish than her husband. The United States had tried to maintain neutrality with respect to the war between France and England. When the French privateers began to capture unarmed American ships within American territorial waters, the Hamiltonian Federalists urged preparation for war. The president was ambivalent about actually going to war, as most of the American Republic were reluctant to be involved in anything but a *defensive* war; the Republicans, led by Vice President Jefferson, feared that England posed a greater threat to the United States than France, and were positively opposed to a declaration of war on America's old ally.

In 1799, after John Adams decided to accept the olive branch that Talleyrand had extended by sending a minister plenipotentiary to France, he wrote his (then ill) wife that the Hamiltonians missed her because she was more hawkish than he:

> I have instituted a new mission, which is kept in the dark, but when it comes to be understood it will be approved. O how they lament Mrs. Adams's absence! She is a good counsellor! If she had been here Murray would never have been named nor his mission instituted! This ought to gratify your vanity enough to cure you.[73]

The First Lady was also a strong supporter of the Sedition Act. To tighten national security, the Congress had passed a sedition law in the summer of 1798. The sedition law provided for the punishment of any persons who unlawfully combined or conspired together to oppose any measure or measures of the U.S. government. It was a broad net that caught many dissenters. Republicans printed falsehoods about Adams and his administration, and the Federalists printed lies about Vice President Thomas Jefferson and his allies in Congress. Yet only calumnious *Republicans* were punished under that law.[74] The Federalist administration brought 15 indictments under the Act, 10 of which resulted in conviction. The conviction and imprisonment of James Callender was particularly important to Abigail Adams, for when Thomas Jefferson, as president, had Callender released from custody, she regarded the gesture as one that severed her friendship with Jefferson. Mrs. Adams blamed President Jefferson for having practiced the "blackest calumny" and "foulest falsehoods" to defame her husband and win the election. And then, once in office, he liberated a

> wretch [James Callender] who was suffering the just punishment of the Law due to his crimes for writing and publishing the basest libel, the lowest and vilest Slander, which malice could invent, or calumny exhibit against the Character and reputation of your predecessor, of him for whom you profest the highest esteem and Friendship, and whom you certainly knew incapable of such complicated baseness.[75]

In Mrs. Adams's opinion, President Jefferson's release of Callender signaled the reign of vice and the downfall of the Republic. Letting Callender go was "a public approbation of his conduct." The chief magistrate had opened the floodgates of vice by approving the conduct of a "base Calumniater." He had permitted his "public conduct to be influenced by private resentment." In releasing the liar from his sense of shame, "the last restraint of vice," President Jefferson set a bad example "upon the manners and morals of the community," opening the floodgates for vice throughout the nation. Thus, in addition to "stabbing" her with this "personal injury," he had contributed to the degeneration of the Republic.[76]

Jefferson defended himself against Adams's criticisms. First, the reason he discharged every person punished by the Sedition Act was that he viewed the law unconstitutional—"a nullity as absolute and palpable as if Congress had ordered us to fall down to worship a golden image." It violated the First Amendment because it coerced the people to worship their government officials, almost as a religion, and violated their right to free expression. It was the law, not the person, that received his attention. His motivation was not to reward slander but to "inspire ordinary charities to objects of distress, meritorious or not," and his "obligation . . . to protect the constitution," which was "violated by an unauthorized act of Congress."[77]

Mrs. Adams objected to Jefferson's constitutional theory. Jefferson's mistake was to assume that the president could nullify a law rather than the "Supreem Judges of the Nation" on the Supreme Court. Thus, like other Federalists, she accepted Justice Marshall's theory of judicial review articulated in *Marbury v. Madison* (1803). Further, only Congress could *repeal* its own law; if the executive had the power to repeal laws, then the separation of powers doctrine would be violated. If "a Chief Magistrate can by his will annul a Law, where is the difference between a republican, and a despotic Government?"

The Sedition Act was lawful in Abigail's view because all civilized nations had agreed that "some restraint should be lain upon the asassin, who stabs reputation." If the injured could not resort to the law for reparation, then they would take the law into their own hands. Man would "become the judge and avenger of his own wrongs," the "sword and pistol" deciding the contest. Once men who had been injured, like her husband, began retaliating outside the law, then "[a]ll the Christian and social virtues will be banished from the land."[78] The real injury, however, was more personal than constitutional. Here she did invoke the Lockean notion that government was instituted to prevent the problems associated with men being both party and judge to their own cases. However, her overriding concern was for her husband's reputation rather than legal principles.[79] She was not concerned with libelous remarks about the opposition.

In the same letter, she criticized President Jefferson for another "intentional act of unkindness," the removal of her son from office when Jefferson assumed the presidency.[80] It appears that Abigail was about as ambitious as she had accused Mercy Warren of being. Jefferson replied that he never knew her son was commissioner of bankruptcy, and that he made the changes in the federal judiciary because Congress had requested him to remove some Federalists from office and replace them with Republicans, according to the parties' representation among the population.[81] Jefferson then proceeded to defend a constitutional theory that granted the president the power to declare the Sedition Act invalid, contesting the power of judicial review: "You seem to think it devolved upon the judges to decide on the validity of the sedition law. But nothing in the constitution has given them a right to decide for the executive, more than to the Executive to decide for them."

Jefferson's constitutional interpretation held that the judiciary was obligated to issue fines and imprisonments according to acts of Congress, but the president "was bound to remit the execution" of a law he considered unconstitutional as part of his obligation to protect the Constitution.[82] This distribution of power made the presidency and judiciary "checks" on each other; "[b]ut the opinion which gives to the judges the right to decide what laws are constitutional, and what not . . . would make the judiciary a despotic branch." Further, while the U.S. Congress could make no law abridging the freedom of the press, the "power to do that is fully possessed by the state legislatures."[83]

Adams could not agree. She continued to defend the Federalist policy on the grounds of national self-defense. To her it was a perversion of republicanism to suppose that "the constitution ever meant to withhold from the National Government the power of self-defense, or that it could be considered an infringement of the Liberty of the Press, to punish the licentiousness of it."[84]

Abigail Adams's identification with her husband and Federalist philosophy followed her acceptance of fair sex ideology. Especially in assuming her role as First Lady, Adams could now refer to the franchise and women's exclusion from it with levity, while endorsing the ideology of separate spheres. She wrote her sister Mary: "Present my compliment[s] to Mr. Whitman, & tell him if our State constitution had been equally liberal with that of new Jersey and admitted the females to a vote, I should certainly have exercised it in his behalf."[85] During the same period, she wrote her son that:

> [h]owever brilliant a woman's talents may be, she ought never to shine at the expence of her Husband. Government of States and Kingdom, tho' God knows badly enough managed, I am willing should be solely administered by the lords of the creation. I should only contend for Domestic government, and think that best administered by the female.[86]

No longer pressing for woman citizenship, or for women's property rights in marriage, she subscribed to the idea that the fair sex belonged in a domestic "orbit" outside of public affairs: "I will never consent to have our sex considered in an inferiour point of light. Let each planet shine in their own orbit. God and nature designd it so—if man is Lord, woman is Lordess—that is what I contend for."[87]

Signing on to Racial Patriarchy

The question of *how* Abigail came to sign on to racial patriarchy would seem to be answered by political pragmatism. It happened gradually, as a series of pragmatic responses to a lifetime of events that shaped the limits of what she reasonably could bargain for and not do damage to herself or the country at large, at least from her own perspective. When she encountered resistance from her husband on the issue of women's rights, and received no support from her closest female friend Mercy Warren, she changed tactics and focused on the milder goal of systemic female education. When John expressed disapproval of female pedants and praised the intelligent woman behind the powerful man, Abigail adjusted her behavior to play exactly that role; even though she knew and perhaps resented that men including her husband refused women access to serious education to maintain power over them.

And on racial issues, Abigail had been more progressive than John, but appears to have been influenced by his steadfast preference for hierarchy. When Abigail expressed to John in the 1770s that she thought slavery was wrong, he let her know that the Revolution was not supposed to go that far. He lamented that Negroes had grown "insolent" to their masters. Of course, even abolitionists often demonstrated white supremacy. When Abigail profited by paying her black farm hand less than the going rate for whites, she partook of white privileges. But she took a definite step backward when she began to use slave labor in the 1790s, as John became vice president in the first administration. Clearly, this action indicated a complete reversal of her earlier radicalism.

When John resisted Abigail's radical ideas in 1776, Abigail went along with him, but joked that he should beware, because she would gain power over him despite the masculinist system. The fair sex would "charm by accepting, by submitting sway," yet have their humour most when they obeyed.[88] Abigail *was* obedient and charming, as well as sharp and savvy. Her life seems to support the rewards thesis of racial patriarchy. She adapted to and lived within the limits of fair sex ideology, and was handsomely rewarded by the dominant culture. In fact, she was able to supercede gender restrictions and have a political voice in ways that other disfranchised persons could not. One need only remember the costs that Mercy paid as an author and an "ambitious" woman to appreciate Abigail's prudence.

An interpretation of *why* Abigail signed on to racial patriarchy is a much more delicate matter. Interestingly, Abigail's acceptance of racial privileges seemed to have followed her retreat on the issue of women's rights. It is possible that in signing on to the sexual contract and the racial contract, her intentions were to do only what she believed to be her duty, as a wife and a patriot. That is certainly how she interpreted her own actions. It is not my purpose here to judge Abigail as having "sold out" for personal gain, but to show just how easy and insidious it was to sign on to the terms of racial patriarchy.

Abigail had more choices than most women, but they were still limited. It is not clear that she or anyone had anything concrete to gain by an unwavering demand for women's rights, or the principles of abolition, when most of the established powers including her husband seemed uninterested in them. With four children to care for and no income except through her own labor, Abigail might have done harm to herself, her family, and possibly even national development by arguing with John, or continuing to press the issues of equality. Had she demanded that he curtail his activities, especially during the second trip to Europe, things might have turned out very differently indeed.

Still, one looks in vain for the tiniest act of resistance to or subversion of her accession to racism and patriarchy. One must be satisfied with a single attempt to get Mercy Warren interested in women's rights, and her initiative to enroll her daughter in classical studies. There is no evidence that she attempted to pay her black workers and her white workers equal wages; there appears to have been no loan to neighbors in need who stood to lose property when she was doing so well with her profits. She expressed no great compunction about having sold the luxuries she understood to be the cause of destruction among the "lower classes." The evidence shows no attempt in New York to teach her enslaved boy how to read, nor any discussion with Jefferson, Lovell, Gerry, Thaxter, or any of the powerful men who read her letters, about woman suffrage or abolitionism.

Any attempt to explain Abigail's political choices must take into account her complete reversal on universal natural rights and woman suffrage. And any serious attempt to explain that reversal cannot ignore

Abigail's own interests and ambitions. It may well have been the case that the disadvantages she suffered as a woman in a masculine political system were more than offset by the advantages she secured as a *white* woman who shared class privileges with her elite husband. By publicly and privately touting the ethics of the fair sex, Abigail may have "sold out" and complied with her own sense of oppression.

But she also exercised power over others. She found her subjectivity through her intermediate position. Granted, she could not vote, but she had total liberty to direct her slaves and lower-class servants. She could not run for office, but by supporting her husband's career, she availed herself of access to male politicians who might not otherwise have been interested in her. We cannot avoid the uncomfortable truth that Abigail's choices resulted in race and class privileges for herself that probably exceeded anything she had to gain by refusing to sign on to racial patriarchy.

6

Gleaning a Self between the Lines

Judith Sargent Murray and the American Enlightenment

If an able writer who has a clear mind and a perfect knowledge of the orthodox view and all its ramifications contradicts surreptitiously . . . one of its necessary propositions or consequences which [she] explicitly recognizes and maintains everywhere else, we can reasonably suspect that [she] was opposed to the orthodox system as such and—we must study [her] book all over again.
—Leo Strauss, *Persecution and the Art of Writing*, 1947

And this fact, that women participate in their own submission, has often embarrassed critics of psychoanalytic theory.
—Jessica Benjamin, *The Bonds of Love*, 1988

Feminism, Selectivity, and Exoteric Writing

Does Judith Sargent Murray reproduce the orthodoxy of fair sex ideology for mass consumption, to avoid persecution for her radicalism? Or does she do it because ultimately, she desires domination? Can we even speak of Murray as a unified self with a coherent political strategy? Who *was* Judith Sargent Murray, and why have her writings been so indeterminate with respect to feminism?

First, let us begin by reviewing Judith's life from Vena Bernadette Field's biography.[1] Judith was born into the elite Sargent family of Gloucester, Massachusetts, in 1751. Her father, Winthrop Sargent, was distinguished in Gloucester as a ship owner, sea captain, and successful merchant. He also served the state government. During the Revolutionary War, he worked in a government agency, and during the ratification of the U.S. Constitution, he was selected as a delegate to the Massachusetts convention. Judith's mother, Judith Saunders Sargent, bore eight children. Three of her children achieved distinction: her daughter Judith and her two sons Fitz William and Winthrop Junior. Fitz William founded the India Company. Winthrop Junior served in the Revolutionary army, was named Secretary of the Northwest Territory in 1787, and was appointed by President John Adams to be the first governor of the Mississippi Territory in 1798. Later generations of Sargents were also distinguished as artists, painters, writers, soldiers, and scientists.

As a girl, Judith enjoyed the best education afforded to a young person. She was tutored by local clergy alongside her younger brother Winthrop, and thus may have learned some Latin and Greek. Of course, as a female she could not attend Harvard, as Winthrop did. At age 18, she married John Stevens, a sea captain, like her father.

During the marriage, Judith and John befriended a minister named John Murray, who had come to the United States from England to preach the doctrine of universal salvation. On Murray's first visit to Gloucester in 1770, he was hosted by Judith's parents. Judith and John later hosted Murray themselves, and converted to his church of the Independent Christian Universalists.

Judith and John Stevens were married for 17 years. Over the years, Murray and Mrs. Stevens developed a close friendship. Judith took an interest in his religious ideas, and Murray encouraged her literary talents. While married to Stevens, Judith had not published anything until 1784, when she published an essay, "Encouraging a Degree of Self-Complacency, Especially in Female Bosoms." Shortly thereafter, in 1786, her marriage to Stevens ended. In the postwar economic crisis her husband suffered a reversal of fortune, like so many Americans, and fled the country to escape creditors. He died of illness in the West Indies.

About two years later, in 1788, Judith and the Reverend John Murray were married. This marriage provided fertile ground from which both persons cultivated professional success. Murray became famous as the founder of Universalism in the United States, the root of today's Unitarian Church, and Judith produced many writings as well as a daughter. In 1790, at age 40, she published her 1779 essay entitled "On the Equality of the Sexes." In 1791, she gave birth to her only child to survive to adulthood, Julia Maria Murray. The next year, Judith wrote the prologues and epilogues for each of four plays that were introduced in Gloucester. From 1792 to 1794, she also wrote two columns for the *Massachusetts Magazine*: a fictional column called "The Gleaner" and a religious or spiritual column called "The Repository."

Sometime in this same period, she also wrote her first play, *The Medium; or, Virtue Triumphant. The Medium* was produced in Boston in 1795, and was thereby distinguished as the first American-authored play to have been performed in that city. Although the production flopped, Judith persisted in her writing career. The following year she wrote another play, *The Traveller Returned*, which was also performed at the Federal Street Theater in Boston.

By the late 1790s, John Murray's health was beginning to decline. He wrote a friend that he ventured to persuade his wife to republish her articles in book volumes to earn money. Judith compiled articles from her Gleaner column with other writings for a three-volume work entitled *The Gleaner: A Miscellany*, published in 1798. As John continued his preaching tours along the East Coast, he solicited orders for his wife's book. Together, they secured 824 orders, which brought a dollar per volume.

The relationship between Mr. and Mrs. Murray seems to have been happy and mutually beneficial. Judith wrote well of her husband in letters, and took pleasure accompanying him on his travels to preach in New York, Philadelphia, and Washington, D.C. Between 1788 and 1790, John's notoriety won invitations for the couple to visit the homes of elite founders, including George Washington, John Adams, Benjamin Rush, and Benjamin Franklin. These visits facilitated Judith's career. She later secured subscriptions to *The Gleaner* by the first two presidents of the United States.

Judith Sargent Murray also contributed to her husband's writings. When Mr. Murray became too old or too ill to write, she finished his three-volume work entitled *Letters and Sketches of Sermons*, and then had it published in Boston in 1812 and 1813. Mr. Murray died in 1815. The next year, Judith completed and published her husband's autobiography. In 1818, she went to live with her daughter Julia and her husband, Adam Bingaman, and their two daughters. Two years later, at age 69, Judith Sargent Murray died. With little public notice, she was buried at the Bingaman family cemetery on a plantation called Fatherland.

With the rise of women's studies in the past three decades, Murray has been revived from obscurity as an important female author of the United States in the late eighteenth century.[2] Murray wrote and produced three plays and published several poems and essays, as well as the three-volume book of writings called *The Gleaner*.[3] Curiously, Vena Bernadette Field, her first biographer, made little mention of the essays that women's studies scholars find most interesting today as evidence of eighteenth-century feminism. Field's failure to analyze Murray's radical thought on gender can perhaps be explained by her own historical context. Writing in the early 1930s, women were not encouraged to consider themselves equal to men, or to work outside the home.[4] It is possible that addressing such issues in her 1931 master's thesis may have created tension for Field herself.

But we cannot ignore the possibility that Field's lack of interest in Murray's "feminist" essays may be attributable to their thin representation in Murray's published corpus of writings. To put it bluntly, a strong argument can be made that Murray was no feminist at all—that she accepted the separate spheres that would define modern patriarchy in the United States, as well as her ascribed role as a female within that overall system. Consider Murray's "feminist" thought in several essays—"On the Equality of the Sexes" (1790), "Desultory Thoughts upon the Utility of Encouraging a Degree of Self-Complacency, especially in Female Bosoms" (1784), and "Observations on Female Abilities"—as Sheila Skemp, her most recent biographer, does. Even if we add to these another essay, "Industry, with the Independence Which It Confers," we must concede that Murray's "feminist" writings are represented in only about 50 out of more than 800 pages, less than 7 percent of her total published writing. The bulk of her oeuvre is either decidedly conservative on gender relations, or fails to discuss them at all. By conservative, I mean they repeat and uphold the public/private split of modern patriarchal relations, including enforced domesticity, coverture, disfranchisement, and stereotypical notions of woman as the tender, fair sex.

Despite the apparent conservatism in her writings, I will argue that Judith Sargent Murray was the founder of liberal feminist thought in the United States. Because the word "feminism" was not in usage during Murray's lifetime, the term is bracketed here. By "feminist," I mean one who conscientiously identifies, challenges, and resists the system of male privilege of her time, as well as one who proposes utopian alternatives from a female perspective. On the level of philosophical foundations, the core holding of Western liberal feminist thinkers has been—from the late eighteenth to the late twentieth century—that "women" should be included in the philosophy of the subject as bearers of reason, just as "men" have been. In other words, if the grand dictum of the Enlightenment was, as Kant put it, to think for oneself, then women should also be considered rational creatures with the capacity for judgment, choice, and intellectual and moral progress through education.[5] We also understand by liberal feminism that body of thought that has deployed the universal "woman" or "women" for strategic purposes, when what is really meant is the advancement of a specific grouping of females qualified for "equality" with a specific grouping of men, with whom they identify based on similar race and class privileges.[6]

The argument will be made by reading selectively, as others have done. It will prove heuristic to treat Murray as an "exoteric writer" in the Straussian sense, as one who holds a truth (or belief) that must be concealed to avoid persecution by the "nonphilosophic majority," or more precisely, the patriarchal majority of post-revolutionary America. According to Strauss, when there is not perfect freedom of expression, the truly independent thinkers will find a way to express their truths and avoid persecution. Such masters of writing fill the bulk of their published pages with the "party line" or the accepted political logic of the day, expressing their own truths "between the lines." Their independent and threatening ideas come out in slippages and inconsistencies, or in careful restatements of the view that one is putatively undermining or criticizing.[7] Murray's political thought is laden with inconsistencies. The inconsistencies are so deep, one can hardly call her a political theorist. And yet, I would urge we do just that, because the inconsistencies themselves would seem to fit within a comprehensible, if frustrated, strategy for female and personal emancipation.

There are two main types of inconsistencies in Murray's feminist and political thought. At the foundational level, Murray posits a universal rational human nature through a concept of the immortal soul, which turns out to apply only to white men and white women. The argument that reason originates in a soul distinct from the body is useful for Murray's attempt to free rationality from the constraints of gender; but she fails to universalize this logic to apply to the hierarchies of race or class. As we shall see, Murray interrogates the concept of "natural" rational inequality only when it applies to gender within the European American community. By contrast, all other kinds of social inequality seem to be in keeping with Murray's concept of natural order and appropriate hierarchy.

The second type of inconsistency may be found in Murray's politics. Accepting provisionally her feminist arguments on the genderless soul and the equal capacity of men and women for moral and intellectual reasoning, we are then confounded by Murray's conservative political prescriptions. After advocating sexual equality that serves to justify education rights for women, she moves toward prescriptions that would disrupt the public man/private woman binary. As we shall see, examples include women who act like men in the world, and are systematically praised for their virtues. In the end, however, Murray withdraws, reverses, or denies these radical gestures, suggesting that all she ever contended for was completely harmonious with the separate spheres of modern patriarchy. This political inconsistency—the failure to contest the masculine state and family patriarchy—then grounds Murray's reversion to sexual difference and fair sex ideology, despite her obvious attempts to supercede both. We are then left to consider whether Murray reverted to the sexual contract to save her herself from persecution, or freely chose to revert, participating in her own submission.

The purpose of this chapter is to provide possible interpretations of Murray's inconsistencies and reversals. I begin by reconstructing the elements of Murray's radical arguments on gender to demonstrate that Murray qualifies as the founder of liberal feminism in the United States. I then reexamine the foundations of gender equality in universal reason, to demonstrate that her use of the universals is strategic, since it is actually quite limited in its application to the equality of white men and white women of a very specific social class. Murray ignores the problem of inequality between whites and blacks (slave or free) and seems to be quite content with the inequality of economic classes. After examining the boundaries of race and class, I turn to the reversals on gender equality. The chapter concludes by considering Murray's inconsistencies and reversals in light of the three questions originally posed concerning identity and political strategy. I argue that these cannot be explained simply through exoteric writing or a conversion to fair sex ideology because both assume a unified self that seems unsupportable by the evidence. I find Jessica Benjamin's theory of masochism compelling and useful to explain Murray's fragmentations as part of her survival strategy as a "woman" in patriarchal culture.

Murray as the Founder of Liberal Feminist Thought in the United States

The foundations of Murray's feminist theory can be found in the Enlightenment premise that human beings are universally endowed with reason, and the universalist premise that all are equally capable of knowing God through their reason. Like other Enlightenment thinkers, Murray locates the source of rationality in the mind or soul, which is viewed as distinct from the body. The soul is privileged above the body.[8] It is "preeminent," "independent," and "immortal," whereas the body is but a "decayed instrument" for the soul's expression.[9]

This mind-body dualism functions within feminist theory the same way as it does within liberalism: It provides the foundation for government by consent. Murray echoed Locke in emphasizing that reason, not might, justifies political obligation and the coercive power of government. Reason privileges human beings over other animals, and constitutes the essence of humanity. According to Locke, differences in physical strength have no bearing on men's natural equality as human beings. Such differences cannot justify the subordination of one human being to another. Nevertheless, when considering the relation of men and women in conjugal society, Locke grants men a natural ruling power in matters of dispute by viewing them as "the abler and stronger."[10]

Murray argues that this is slippage. If bodily strength were a basis for social and political authority, two corollaries necessarily follow. First, men of learning would have to yield to the governance of "brute creation," their "brethren of the field." Second, "robust masculine ladies" would have to be granted cultural dominance over "effeminate gentlemen."[11] This *reductio ad absurdum* implies that sexual difference resides in the body, not the soul. The feminine body has no bearing on rationality. To deem women inferior rational beings on account of their bodies is to confound first principles. Murray makes the point that women are rational creatures just like men; however, she stops just short of the logical implications of the argument, that is, if universal reason and human agreement are the only just underlying principles for government, then women too must consent to be governed.

Murray takes pains to prove that women are in fact modern rational subjects. No doubt women are socially inferior, but this inferiority, she argues, is culturally imposed rather than inherent. In "On the Equality of the Sexes," Murray claims that the fair sex is labeled the weaker sex arbitrarily. Nature distinguishes in ability, she concedes:

> Yet cannot I their sentiments imbibe,
> Who this distinction to the sex ascribe,
> As if a woman's form must needs enrol,
> A weak, a servile, an inferiour soul;
> And that the guise of man must still proclaim,
> Greatness of mind, and him, to be the same:
> Yet as the hours revolve fair proofs arise,
> Which the bright wreath of growing fame supplies;
> And in past times some men have *sunk* so *low*,
> that female records nothing *less* can show.

Although all human beings are rational by nature, not all possess equal talent and ability. Murray accepts that those with greater mental abilities should have the greater share of ruling power. Using this meritocratic principle, she argues that it is unjust to grant inferior men privileges that intellectually superior women are denied. Continuing, she suggests that there is a kind of conspiracy or system to deny women equal access to power and privileges:

> But imbecility is still confin'd,
> And by the lordly sex to us consign'd;
> they rob us of the power t'improve,
> And then declare we only trifles love;
> Yet haste the era, when the world shall know,
> that such distinctions only dwell below.

In the essay following her introductory verses, Murray argues that culture, not nature, constructs woman as "naturally" inferior to man. Like Mary Astell a century earlier and her senior, Mercy Warren, Murray argues that the vices typically associated with women result from oppression. They are the debris of a silly education or none at all.[12] Preoccupation with fashion and trifles and the tendency of women to gossip are evidence of female talent distorted through confinement.

Yes, women engaged in inventive slander, gossip, innuendo, and double entendres, but these vices of "woman's speech" were the result of social prescriptions against female rationality and intellectualism. The image of oppression repeatedly offered is that of the home as a cage for the naturally intelligent woman. "Is the needle and kitchen sufficient to employ the operations of soul thus organized?" No; those occupations left "the intelligent principle vacant, and at liberty for speculation."

Systematic denial of the female intellect began in families. At two years old, girls were generally more mentally developed than boys of the same age. Yet not long after that, girls would be "wholly domesticated," while their brothers would be "led by the hand through all the flowery paths of science." Education of males explained their apparent superiority, while neglect of education for girls explained female vice. This neglect of daughters set them up for lives of emptiness, boredom, and rage:

> At length arrived at womanhood, the uncultivated fair one feels a void, which the employments allotted her are by no means capable of filling. What can she do? To books she may not apply; or if she doth, *to those only of the novel kind*, lest she merit the appellation of a *learned lady*; and what ideas have been affixed to this term, the observation of many can testify.

The ideas affixed to the appellation "learned lady" were negative. In republicanism, one could not be both "woman" and "independent intellectual" because the culture viewed women essentially as wives and mothers, categories which were viewed in opposition to citizenship, intellectualism, and individuality. As Rousseau made plain, "a brilliant wife is a plague to her husband, her children, her valets, everyone."[13] American authors agreed. Even curiosity was considered a vice in females, since it could threaten proper subordination. As she did with the "vices" of gossip and fashion sense, Murray validated curiosity as evidence of virtue. Curiosity, she argued, was essential to scientific inquiry. Without it, the discoveries of the "sublime genius of a Newton" would not have been possible. Those who deemed female curiosity a vice were "levellers of female abilities."[14]

Murray took her critique a step further in the second segment of "On the Equality of the Sexes" (April 1790). She identified the roots of hostility toward the female intellect in popularized interpretations of Eve in the Garden of Eden. She criticized the notion of woman as the "fallen sex," as presented in John Milton's *Paradise Lost*. Her basic argument here is that Adam was rationally inferior to Eve. Eve was *deceived* by the serpent who appeared as an angel to eat the apple from the tree of knowledge. Her "sin" was actually a virtue—intellectual curiosity. She craved knowledge; "ambition fired her soul." But as a witness to Eve's fall from grace, Adam was in position to make a sound judgment and failed: "His gentle partner stood before him, a melancholy instance of the direful effects of disobedience; he saw her not possessed of that wisdom which she had fondly hoped to obtain." Rather, his "bare pusillanimous attachment to a woman" led him to abandon his reason and eat the fruit with Eve:

> Thus . . . all the arts of the grand deceiver [the devil] . . . were requisite to mislead our general mother, while the father of mankind forfeited his own, and relinquished the happiness of posterity, merely in compliance with the blandishment of a female.[15]

Reversing Milton's lesson, Murray contended that we ought not uphold men as closer to God, since Adam proved to have been morally weaker than Eve.

The idea of woman as morally inferior to man was simply not supportable on Murray's re-reading of the Bible. Not only Adam but also David and Job were morally weak; thus one could not take the Bible literally and use it as a foundation for the claim that women were by nature morally inferior to men. Taking the Bible literally would compel the conclusion that many of its enshrined male characters displayed many vices for which women were peculiarly blamed:

> Thus David was a man after God's own heart, but see him enervated by his licentious passions! behold him following Uriah to the death, and show me wherein could consent the immaculate Beings complacency. Listen to the curses which Job bestoweth upon the day of his nativity, and tell me where is his perfection, where his patience—*literally* it existed not. David and Job were types of him who was to come; and the superiority of man as exhibited in scripture, being also emblematical, all arguments deduced from thence, of course, fall to the ground.[16]

One could ascertain that David was effeminate, "enervated by his passions"; and Job was impatient and irreverent, cursing the day he was born. Murray's effort to rescue the Bible from eighteenth-century sexism enabled her to argue against all of the social and political arguments of female inferiority that flowed therefrom. Women's minds were by nature neither intellectually nor morally inferior to those of men.

Patriarchal culture stunted the development of rationality and individual ambition through deprivation, confinement, ignorance, objectification, and a romance ideology that defined marriage as the ultimate goal of a female's life. In "Desultory Thoughts Upon the Utility of Encouraging a Degree of Self-Complacency, Especially in Female Bosoms," Murray describes this patriarchal culture's hostility to women's development. She calls the female psyche a makeshift ocean vessel, "rudely tossed" in an unwelcome sea. In this sea, she is lost with neither compass nor helm to guide her; nor can she drop anchor, for she is tossed about amid contending waves. She hits unforgiving rocks and dangerous quicksands, "[t]ill dash'd in pieces, or till found'ring we / One common wreck of all our prospects see!" Yet women do not even mourn for being "lost to fame," or having never reached a "towring name," because they were never taught to "rev'rence self" in the first place. In a sense, Murray's argument here calls to mind Rousseau's admonition that all healthy young boys must have amour-de-soi, that self-love which is necessary for self-preservation.[17] Deprived of education and encouragement, girls were excluded from the narcissistic experience of being engaged as full, intact subjects of reason.

Yet Murray wants more than mere self-preservation for women. As a modernist, she embraces *ambition* as a virtue:

> Our bosoms never caught ambition's fire;
> An indolence of virtue still prevail'd,
> Nor the sweet gale of praise was e'er inhal'd;
> Roused by a new stimulus, no kindling glow.
> No soothing emulations gentle flow, . . .

Woman was then judged to be of inferior make, unfit for the sea, and thereafter landlocked in domesticity:

> In narrow bounds, our progress had cofin'd,
> And, that our forms, to say the very best
> Only, not frightful, were by all confest.[18]

Instead of encouraging self-love and rationality, daughters were fed romance novels and objectified through ornamentation. At the ripe age of 15, they were presented to the world decked out in "ribbons, and other gewgaws" to attract a suitor, not unlike the preparation of "ancient victims previous to a sacrifice."[19]

Courtship was sexual "warfare" in which men held all the weapons. Rendered weak and lacking in self-confidence, a young woman was susceptible to flattery. Her servile and neglected condition made any praise seem "sweet" and "intoxicating," but considered the sinful descendant of Eve, she was expected to be more restrained and "triumph over the machinations of the most artful." A woman must be constantly upon her guard: "prudence and discretion must be our characteristics; as we must rise superiour to, and obtain a complete victory over those who have been long adding to the native strength of their minds by an unremitted study of men and books." The end of this war was marriage, which Murray likened to a ritualized death march. Having been long taught to value her exterior more than her mind, the bride was a "polished casket," or "beautiful gem" "highly finished, and calculated for advantage, as well as ornament." Neither could we count on her husband to awaken her dying soul, since the beautiful young woman with low self-esteem was unable to distinguish "real worth" from "worthless characters." The whole system promoted women to attract "flatterers" and "artful betrayers" with "interested views" and "deep-laid schemes," who "smile at your undoing."[20] The marriage contract here appears as an exchange of sex for romance and shallow admiration. For women it was a rotten deal; the real contract traded a woman's soul for a man's financial support, and thereby produced the finished American woman as a rationally inferior economic dependant.

Murray's feminist theory not only critiqued oppressive institutions and practices; it also provided a utopian vision with prescriptions for change. Girls should be raised and educated like boys. They should be taught to aspire. They should be taught that "everything in the compass of mortality was placed within their grasp, and that . . . the intenseness of study, were only requisite to endow them with every external grace, and mental accomplishment." To teach girls to aspire would require first that they "know their truth" and not objectify themselves. Parents must treat girls as rational creatures. Girls should be taught that they *are* pretty, but that their true value came from the intellect, not the body. "Rev'rencing" the self was thus intimately bound with reason and reflection. The ability to distinguish true worth in others necessitated proper value of the self. And self-love in females required appropriate nurturing and education.[21]

Clearly, Murray's insistence that girls aspire to "everything in the compass of mortality" suggested that females should aspire to become and do anything that males have done. This would require "serious study of men and books." However, just as romance novels could warp the female mind into fantasy, "serious" literature could also damage a girl's psyche. Many esteemed male writers had "a most contemptible opinion of the sex," and propagated images of women as "loose characters."[22] Unguarded, female readers risked the internalization of a negative alterity.

Girls should also be taught to consider marriage an option rather than a requirement. "Marriage should not be represented as their *sumum bonum,* or as a certain, or even necessary event." Instead, girls should be reared and educated to "administer to their own efforts." They should resist entering the corrupted marriage contract, and learn to respect the "single life," for spinsterhood was preferable to the death of the soul. With education and economic independence, they could develop their judgment and meet men on level ground in the marriage market, or not at all. Sexual warfare and spiritual death would be transformed by beginning with independent selfhood and then proceeding to rational friendship and/or a companionate marriage.[23]

All of the foregoing suggests that to be a human being meant that one should seek to define oneself; and for women self-definition required aspirations beyond the limiting roles of wife and mother. The transcendence of domesticity is further developed in *The Gleaner,* in Murray's four-part essay "Observations on Female Abilities." Continuing from the arguments made in "On the Equality of the Sexes," and "improving on the opinions of a Wollstonecraft," Murray boldly proclaimed that in this new world, "the Rights of Women" would begin to be understood. There would be a "new era in female history," as the Republic would "do justice to the sex," "improving on the opinions of a Wollstonecraft" by contending for "the *quantity, as well as the quality* of mind."[24]

In this new enlightened age, the very idea of "the incapability of women" would be "totally inadmissible." Note the universal language: the "full blessings of equality" would now "remove every obstacle to their advancement."[25] "Our object is to prove, by examples, that the minds of women are *naturally* as susceptible of every improvement, as those of men."[26] Here she offered historical examples of women who had demonstrated excellence in several virtues that were characteristically deemed masculine. In so doing, she created a kind of canon of women whose virtues should be remembered and emulated by the young. Their virtues included endurance, ingeniousness, fortitude, heroism, bravery (including military bravery), patriotism, influence, energy, eloquence, commitment, fidelity in preserving attachments, the ability to govern, and intellectualism. Clearly, the list extended beyond the virtues assigned to white women in late eighteenth century fair sex ideology.

Murray named names where she could, and where she had none, she offered what details were available to her. That women endured hardships men could never know was evident in the case of objectification and rape, which was as wrong as it was ubiquitous.

> [W]e need not take a voyage to Brittany, nor penetrate the haunts of savages, to prove that women are capable of suffering. They are the *enduring sexy*; and by the irreversible constitution of nature, they are subjected to agonies unknown to manhood.

Rape and survival exemplified "masculine weakness and feminine vigour." On top of this universal sexual hardship, women also suffered other "calamities incident to humanity."[27]

Female ingenuity and resourcefulness were exemplified by an unnamed historical queen who had to manipulate her tyrant husband to tend to the agricultural needs of his people rather than allow them to starve as he amassed wealth by forcing his subjects to labor in the mines. Unable to confront the king directly, she commissioned an artist to paint a still life of the king's favorite foods; fish and fowl, bread and fruits were now displayed before him, awakening his hunger. Subsequently he "dispeopled" the mines and ordered the laborers once again to attend to agriculture.[28]

Fortitude and heroism were demonstrated by the classical ladies of Sparta and Rome, who chose death over servitude when captured in war. In more recent times, the Lady Jane Gray of Britain, who became adept in both Greek and Latin, and at age sixteen found Plato "a more pleasing entertainment . . . than all those enchanting pleasures usually so captivating to the unexperienced mind." Preferring intellectual pursuits to her "imposed queenship," she was called to the scaffold only 10 days after assuming the throne. Her fortitude lay in her refusal to rule, and then in refusing to see her husband for a last exchange before her death.[29]

Women were as brave as men. Faced with the death of her father in battle with the Turks, a young woman of the Greek Island Lemnos seized the sword and shield herself, and roused the soldiers to bravely oppose the Turks. Jane of Flanders also led her warriors during the imprisonment of her husband; and Margaret of Anjou directed the armies which her pusillanimous and imbecilic husband could not. As general and soldier she fought "twelve decisive battles."[30]

Women were also equally patriotic. Women of classical Greece prized the appellation "Citizen" more than the endearing ones of "Wife and Mother." Though their examples proved an unsurpassed patriotic zeal, most women could not be both mothers and citizens: "[S]exual occupations frequently humiliating, and generally far removed from whatever has a tendency to elevate the mind, may rationally be supposed to chill, in the female bosom, the fine fervours of *amour patriae*."[31] For Murray, domesticity degraded the mind and made women perhaps too partial and weak to embrace nationalistic pride.

Women were as influential as men; instances abounded in which they "bent to their purposes the strongest masculine understanding."[32] They were equally energetic and eloquent. "Aspasia of Miletus" taught rhetoric and politics to Socrates; "Hortensia" was a "voluntary advocate for her sex" who pleaded on behalf of Roman matrons oppressed under the cruelty of the second Triumvirate. Women were as faithful as men in preserving their attachments. Murray pointed to the degraded wife who stayed with an unfaithful husband, though if roles were reversed, he would have left her to suffer through divorce and loss of reputation:

> Repeatedly I have seen the faithfully attached female, firmly persevering in that affection which was first implanted in the soil of innocence, and fondly watching with tender anxiety every symptom of the diseased man: with patient assiduity she hath hung over the couch, and fought to mitigate the pangs of him whose licentious conduct had brought ruin on herself and her unoffending children.[33]

Several queens proved that women could govern as well as men: Artemisia, queen of Caria; Amalansuntha, Zenobia, Elizabeth of England; Isabella of Spain; and Christina of Sweden. And many, many others proved that women were equally capable of literary acquirement:

Sappho, the lesbian poetess; Hypatia, who presided over the Platonic school at Alexandria; and Sulpicia, "the Roman Sappho." Among more modern literary women, Murray included Margaret Cavandish, the Dutchess of Newcastle; Mary Astell; Lady Mary Chudleigh; Anne Finch, Countess of Winchilsea; Lady Mary Wortley Montague; Catherine Macaulay; Mary Wollstonecraft; Sarah Wentworth (Philenia); and Mercy Warren. The list reads a little bit like the table of contents of today's *Norton Anthology of Literature by Women*.[34]

For women to revere themselves, they had to stop viewing themselves through the male gaze. A key part of the strategy was to learn from other women. The history of women had been silenced. Women who had excelled despite oppression against them as women had not been sufficiently valorized in the past, but with the *Gleaner's* canon, they could begin to correct the distortions of patriarchal learning. From now on, "the equality of the female intellect to that of their brethren, who have so long usurped an unmanly and unfounded superiority, will never, in this younger world, be left without a witness."[35] Women could now determine their own destinies, and depend on themselves for an establishment in life, regarding marriage with proper "indifference."[36]

Murray offered two vignettes of contemporary women who embodied her vision of equality, economic independence, and fame. Writing in the male persona of the Gleaner, she described a female farmer from her own state, and a businesswoman from Europe. The farmer was raised without formal education, and was permitted to roam about freely in the fields. Echoing Wollstonecraft, Murray praised the physical freedom that made the girl develop long, strong limbs, so that by adulthood she was unusually strong and tall, even "athletic," and "not corpulent." Painfully aware of the education she missed as a girl, this woman read everything she could, and acquired great proficiency in math and writing. Through her own efforts she became knowledgeable about the science of agriculture, which she applied to improve a few acres her father had given her. "She is mistress of agricolation, . . . and at once a botanist and a florist." She studied the science of soils and manure, and their relation to the various fruits of the earth. She was an expert tree trimmer. She became an authority among the farmers in her vicinity, so that when they cleared and planted their own grounds, they consulted her as an "oracle." Tourists came to view her spectacular gardens.

She was a "complete husbandwoman." Her knowledge was so vast and her manner so generous that villagers consulted with her on "every perplexing emergency." Nor was she particularly masculine. She was "affectionate," "attentive," "faithful," and "sympathetic," even tending to the sick with special herbal concoctions. Yet she almost never yielded to illness herself. Her health was maintained by tireless work and plenty of fresh air. In this husbandwoman we find Murray's ideal of the single woman who lives the good life for human beings. Though never married and far advanced in her years, the "farmeress" exhibited neither "peevishness" nor "discontent." This woman was no "old maid." She educated herself, revered herself, made clear and direct contributions to her community, and enjoyed local, perhaps even international, fame.[37]

Murray's second example was provided by "Widow Birmingham," a female entrepreneur overseas whose husband died when her children were small. She put her sons out for military training, and educated her daughters for business. Widow Birmingham ran a "capital-trading house" as a family business. Murray heard of her reputation through Boston merchants and sea captains with whom she negotiated the disposal of large and valuable cargoes. According to them, Widow Birmingham and her daughters were the best in the business. "Upright in their dealings, and unwearied in their application, these ladies possess a right to prosperity; and we trust that their circumstances are as easy, as their conduct is meritorious."[38] Widow Birmingham is another example of an unmarried woman who acts on her own authority. She is engaged in the rational activity of commerce. Allowed this kind of human freedom, these women are virtuous: "upright," "unwearied," "meritorious," and deservingly prosperous. They exhibited none of the distortions of rationality, speech, or action that appeared as vices in the domesticated and oppressed fair sex. In a sense, they married the world.

Clearly, when Murray conceptualized women and fame, her vision was cosmopolitan. And so it was when she envisioned her own fame. Murray's desire for fame is represented in her writings as both a political principle and a personal ambition. Her essays reiterate the point that the desire for fame is a virtue, the "master spring of every great achievement."[39] Ambition came from a desire for praise. One had to do good deeds to please the public; such was the essence of patriotic sacrifice. It was desire for fame and approval from one's family and community that ultimately led a man to brave the perils of the soldier. Like other Federalist sympathizers, Murray believed that ambition need not be merely an extension of vanity; it could be a virtue if it came from the need for approbation from others.

Here, of course, Murray distinguished herself from Mercy Warren, who believed one ought to detach from the opinions of others and be neither "indifferent to the opinion of the world" nor "servilely courting its smiles." For Warren, ambition was selfishness that fueled corruption. Indeed, she believed that the Federalists were "interested and avaricious adventurers for place, who[,] intoxicated with the ideas of distinction and preferment . . . prostrated every worthy principle beneath the shrine of ambition."[40] Both women, however, considered themselves exceptionally talented, and both desired public notoriety. And both were sensitive to and tried to pre-empt the harsh criticisms they might receive as *women* writers. Both justified their abrogation of the domestic sphere by claiming to provide a domestic service, namely the education of children.

Like Warren, Murray feared that her work might be taken as evidence of vanity rather than talent; and in the feminine voice, she proclaimed that her "ruling passion" was merely *"to amuse."* But Murray had the audacity to admit a "fondness for literary fame."[41] Once Murray adopts the masculine persona of the Gleaner, in the first essay, "he" also begins by discussing his passion for fame. "Yes, I confess I love the paths of fame, / And ardent wish to glean a brightening name."[42] Here the audacity is freed and the apology drops out; "he" can say he is "seized with a violent desire to become a writer" and cannot overcome the "itch" for "scribbling." It is an "ungovernable mania" that drives his reason to make him a "candidate for applause."[43]

International recognition, support, and fame were the ultimate goals. The Gleaner wishes "that men of letters, and professors of the fine arts, would by mutual consent, form themselves into one great and illustrious commonwealth."[44] Murray envisioned a society in which struggling authors would submit their works to those who had already established their fame—Belknap, Pope, Addison—who would judge the newer works with the "strictest impartiality" to determine if the writers were fit to be admitted as members of the commonwealth. The society would then offer criticism and support so that the "smallest spark of genius, so far from being quenched by *cold neglect,* or extinguished by the *chilling blasts of criticism* should be furnished with those incitements, which are calculated to blow it into a flame."[45] Although not all writers could reach the heights of the giants, too many talented women were systematically denied opportunities and ridiculed. Talented women should be supported and encouraged to persevere. "[L]et not the mental energies be depressed; perseverance may do much; efforts gather strength by action, and emulation, lending wings to ambition, becomes an irresistible stimulus." Here the Gleaner urges that Sarah Wentworth Morton (Philenia) is a great writer but suffers from lack of encouragement. The lowly muse must not "resign" her powers on account of this "depression" of the "mental energies."[46]

Thus far we have seen that, reading selectively, Murray does indeed have the elements of a feminist theory. It includes a universalist conception of human nature, a critique of institutions and practices for failing to reflect equal human nature; and political prescriptions for progressive change, to make the Republic more legitimate. More specifically, Murray's concept of human nature encompasses sexual equality, where equality is defined in terms of the "sameness" of the soul, and thus, of rational capacity. Her critique of illegitimate institutions centers mainly on the patriarchal family, but extends outward to the bourgeois public sphere, in the printing house, the Puritan church, and implicitly, the university. Several practices involving females are deemed illegitimate, including the deprivation of education, objectification, and commodification in the marriage market. The unequal marriage contract is criticized as oppressively distorting female nature, and the prejudicial assumptions and actions against women writers are seen to rob women of their birthright to aspire for individual fame.

Murray's prescriptions follow logically from a vision of female emancipation. Girls must be encouraged in families to love themselves and prize their minds over their exteriors. They must be allowed an equal literary and scientific education, and be encouraged to aspire for whatever they can imagine. They should be given institutional and social support in their efforts to become economically self-sufficient and even famous. They will then be able to succeed in treating marriage as a true option, as men are able to do, and to survive without peril in the event of the death or disability of a marital partner. This, for Murray, is freedom and justice for all.

The First Fragmentation: Race, Class, and Human Nature

Interestingly, Murray does not apply her theory of equal human nature to race or class. Though the question of universal human nature and race had been raised well before the Revolutionary War, and hotly debated in the constitutional period in popular literature, Murray never appears to publicly address the question whether racial inequality reflects nature or culture.

We can, however, get a glimpse of her views on race through her private correspondence. Her letters, particularly to her brother Winthrop, slave owner and first territorial governor of Mississippi, reveal that at best she is complicitous with the institution of slavery.[47] In one of these letters, she reported fulfilling his request to buy "seventy pair of negro shoes" in Boston to ship to him, along with seeds and other items, with no apparent compunction that she was violating any kind of personal ethics by supporting the institution itself.[48] Nor did she express any inner turmoil in receiving her brother and his family, including his slaves, at her home in Boston. In light of how adamant she was about rejecting gender inequities and circumscribed roles for women, it is likely that if she had in fact been anti-racist, she would have written something that would have suggested the same.

It is difficult to tell whether Murray believed race to be a natural or cultural set of differences. In sharp contrast to her extraordinary efforts to challenge the apparent inferiority of white females, here she made no efforts to challenge the apparent inferiority of blacks, or to question their apparent lack of ambition to supercede enslavement. Just the opposite was true: When she heard reports from an acquaintance that the condition of the slaves on Winthrop's plantations surpassed that of many poorer whites in the United States, she felt "satisfaction." His statement that they "manifest[ed] no symptoms of discontent," and were "apparently tranquil, and even cheerful" was taken at face value.[49]

Important consequences flow from the nature/culture issue on race. If Murray believed that Africans were inferior by nature, then her universal view of the equality of the soul is actually particular to white males and females. Alternatively, if she believed that Africans were culturally inferior, it would seem logical for her to have shown at least some concern for their education and development, if not for their sakes, then for the good of the Republic. If the education of girls is necessary to make them rational wives and mothers, why isn't the education of slaves necessary to prevent the corruption of young white children into "miniature tyrants"?

Murray's concerns about the education of her brother Winthrop's children reveal her intermediate position as a member of the fair sex. Possessing neither the rights of citizenship nor a college education, Judith was still considered morally and intellectually competent to shape the education of her brother's children. Like other Enlightenment thinkers, Murray believed that moral character developed in childhood. Because children were so impressionable in the first eight to ten years of life, their education should be carefully constructed. Bad influences should be minimized. She asserts the cultural superiority of her whiteness as the bearer of civilized language, morals, and manners, particularly as they appear in relief against the backdrop of the uncivilized and ignorant black slave, the ever-present Other of the extended family.

In Murray's letters, blacks are characterized as uneducated, irrational, and dishonest. White children learned inferior "modes of speech and habit" from "cunning" and "duplicitous" slaves. With her own cultural and sexual superiority in the background, she advocated that her nephews and nieces converse as little as possible with blacks on their plantation:

> [T]he associating with . . . human beings, decidedly in a subordinate situation, either depresses the intellect, or originates an imperious manner of thinking, and of acting, which creating a tyrant in miniature, often renders the future man or woman unlovely and despotic. These remarks may perhaps be impertinent, but the affection which gave them birth will plead their apology.[50]

Murray's emphasis on cultural context and the fragility of rational development seem to suggest a consistency with her view of universal human nature. Given that debates on race and human nature were perhaps more prevalent than those on gender and human nature, it is conceivable that Murray would minimize racial differences in the same way that she minimized sexual differences. Indeed, if slaves are "human beings" in a "decidedly" subordinate situation, education and ideological critique could presumably emancipate such naturally equal beings, as in the case of oppressed white females. Interestingly, however, Murray maximizes racial difference.

In a sense, Murray displaces the problem of gender onto the problem of race. This displacement is evident in differences between European American and African American cultures that she finds troubling. Binaries such as rationality/superstition, proper grammar/vernacular, and virtue/vice are removed from the arena of gender and located in the clash between her white nephews and their black playmates or caregivers. For example, in a letter to her brother, she reports the tragedy of her nephew refusing to consider becoming a lawyer because of a superstition implanted in his mind by a slave: "if I be a lawyer, the black man will tear my soul from my body, and carry it to his dark hole, where he will keep it everlasting by burning!" His head had been filled with "stories of hobgoblins . . . and bloody bones" as a result of being influenced by a "Negro girl" in charge of his friends on his journey to Nassau, where he had visited for several weeks. Murray also complains that Washington's knowledge of proper French had been supplanted by Creole French, which was spoken among the blacks with whom he associated. "We cannot expect he will emerge from the idle habits which from his long and most unfortunately protected voyage, have obtained much force: but we shall gradually win him to the way in which he should walk."[51]

As Murray takes up the project to reform her nephew(s), she mediates the dominant Anglo-American culture (including its emphasis on erudition in foreign language), while implicating herself as a privileged member of the fair sex. She maximizes her European American cultural superiority through racial difference, the "sex" of the "Negro girl" notwithstanding.

A similar maximization of difference occurs with respect to class. Murray's class bias basically reflects her identification with Federalist theory and politics. Like other Federalists of the mid- to late-1790s, Murray subscribed to a trustee view of government. In that view, one ought trust one's representatives to govern rather than instruct them how to govern. The trustee theory of the Federalists clashed with the delegate theory of representation held by the Democratic-Republicans. Disappointed in the failure of the federal government to represent their policy choices, they formed participatory societies. Merchants, craftsmen, small farmers, mechanics, and others thought to be of the "lower order" held that it was their right and duty as citizens to oversee and instruct their elected delegates. From the Federalist perspective, the United States adequately provided for real representation through the

Constitution; thus the "self-created" democratic societies that formed in coffeehouses in urban areas, as well as the rebellions that took place in western Pennsylvania and Kentucky, were considered a threat to liberty, order, and the Constitution itself.[52]

As Russell Hanson has noted, the word "democracy" hardly connoted good government in the 1790s or before.[53] For Murray, as well as Washington, Hamilton, Adams, Jay, and Madison, it suggested a leveling of ability and talent for mob rule. While all human beings were endowed with the same basic rational capacity, they were not all equal in talent or ability. "The human being has varieties which may be almost pronounced endless. The degrees of intellect, if we may judge by effects, are very unequally proportioned."[54] Contrasting the "luminous genius" with the "unfortunate idiot," Murray argued that unvaried equality existed nowhere: not in nature or heaven, and certainly not in human nature. Consequently, subordination of intellectually inferior persons was efficient, right, and just. "There is no calculating the disorders which may result from relaxing the series of subordination," she wrote. Without subordination of lower ranks, disorder, chaos, and lack of productivity result.

Murray asks the reader to consider the following as a disastrous example of how democracy promotes anarchy. She is surrounded by a family of men and maid servants on a delightful morning. Upon rising, she sets out to get things done, but they see themselves as equals, and the entire division of labor breaks down:

> I supplicate Mary to direct her woman to prepare me an immediate breakfast; she, carelessly, pronounces me quite as eligible to that task myself. I apply to Abigail, who refers me to another, and another; and as *equality* admitteth no distinction, the probability is, that I am finally brought back again to Mary herself. Possibly, after many entreaties, the females may all combine; one bears a cup, another a saucer; a table is dragged from that apartment, and a tea-kettle from this; ignorant of each other's plans, and having no one to direct, the process is impeded and confused, and when at length the motley assemblage is completed and the refection presented, the spoiled tea, coffee, chocolate, and bread and butter, all evince the opposite hands employed in their manufacture.
>
> Well but to proceed. Breakfast over, I sally forth. I *advise* that the cattle be yoked, and that such a parcel of manure be conveyed to yonder sterile spot. Jonathan insists that the horse-cart is sufficient to drag it. Thomas is of his opinion. William sides with me, and we prepare for the

trial of strength; equally divided, our opposition bars our purpose; from words we proceed to blows; the females are alarmed; they take their sides; the plot thickens; appearances grow formidable; a doughty battle ensues; bloody noses are the consequences, and the day is sacrificed to discord.[55]

Day after day goes by with bickering and chaos, such that autumn arrives and the fields are uncultivated. Famine threatens, breeding fear, yet order cannot be imposed since "no member of the family hath authority to interpose the dictatorial document, and the commands of the fiend are perforce obeyed."[56]

Murray extends her metaphor of the disorderly household to the polity. When men assume they are equally able to govern, they destroy order:

As I have regarded power, in *unsteady* and *unskillful* hands, as a great evil, so I have called that man misguided, and an invader of the public peace, who advancing the doctrine of claims, hath inflated the fanciful and superficial with erroneous ideas of retaining prerogatives which, by their own free suffrages, they had voluntarily relinquished.

The commentary is obviously directed toward the Democratic-Republican proto party, whose participatory politics and delegate theory of representation threatened Murray and her Federalist cohort. Meetings of Democrats in coffeehouses and other public places to discuss the political decisions of their elected representatives threatened proper subordination:

He who violently or insidiously destroys the unquestionably necessary series of subordination, who produces the various classes of mankind as usurpers on those orders, which, in the scale of being, take rank above them, must inevitably throw a nation or a state into strong convulsions.[57]

Liberty ought not be confused with licentiousness. The proper citizen was not to instruct his representative how to act as a legislator, but to remain politically inactive except to cast his vote:

I am free to confess that I adopt in an unqualified sense, the sentiment which Homer hath put into the mouth of his Pylian sage: and at least until a *succeeding election*, I would say, "Be silent, friends, and think not here allowed/ that worst of tyrants, an usurping crowd."[58]

If we are to invoke the ancients as well, we might note that Murray's vision of politics is more Platonic than Aristotelian. Politics is viewed as a craft, in which only the few have true ability and expertise to govern. It is not an essentially human activity such that men can reach their full humanity only through active citizenship.

What I find so interesting is the way Murray naturalizes and maximizes differences in talent and ability to preserve class difference and minimize sexual difference. For example, she criticizes gentlemen acquaintances who routinely send their sons to college to avoid the "servile" occupations. They apparently should *not* be encouraged to aspire for anything in their purview. Murray attempts to deny class tensions by objecting to the designation "servile" and suggesting that the "mechanic" and other skilled laborers actually possess "real dignity of character."[59] Once steered in that direction, however, it is obvious that such working men would rank among the class that Murray would silence between elections:

> It is true, I cannot regard a pure unmixed democracy as that precise form of government, which is, in all its parts, the most friendly to the best interests of mankind. I cannot think that the art of legislation is within the knowledge of every man.

Those whose minds were filled with agricultural or commercial pursuits, whose education and subsequent occupation had been principally directed to a particular business or profession, would lack sufficient leisure to investigate and attend to the great art of government.[60]

Similarly, Murray's desire for fame inevitably leads her to think in cosmopolitan terms for herself that she cannot accept for others, particularly those of less educated classes. She jumps on the Federalist bandwagon to deride foreign influence on the Democratic-Republicans, who are obviously inspired by the principles of the French Revolution, and who favor France in the war between France and England. Those "misguided sons of liberty" are told to embrace their independence and nationalism: "Disdain to wear the badge of foreign influence—cultivate an exchange of good offices with every nation who will accept your consistent and dignified advances, but do not pusillanimously court their favour." Yet Murray saw nothing pusillanimous about American writers courting the favor of English authors. She did not consider Anglophilic identification a threat to order, independence, or American nationalism.

The Second Fragmentation: Liberal Feminism and Fair Sex Ideology

Murray's inconsistencies regarding universal human nature and the prescriptions for education that flow from it spill over into her thinking on gender as well. Murray reverses, denies, or submerges every radical claim about human nature, sexual equality, self-love, ambition, independence, and fame. Ultimately she reproduces the public man/private woman binary that her examples of ideal women had transcended. Murray reproduces fair sex ideology in all of her fictional works. "The Story of Margaretta," and the plays *Virtue Triumphant* and *Traveller Returned*, involve plots of women and romance which are resolved when the virtuous heroine marries well, or when wayward husbands or wives are brought back to domestic virtue. In all of them, marriage is the *summum bonum* of women's lives. None of the women are happily single, financially self-sufficient through their own efforts, or famous for their work.

Even Murray's radical "feminist" essays contain denials and reversals. The reversals are evident when Murray turns from her critique of patriarchy to proposals for reform. Every radical proposal is later reversed or denied. Radicalism and reversal take place *within* single essays. Writing as Constantia, she confronts men directly for their abuses of power. "Yes, you lordly, you haughty sex, our souls are by nature equal to yours." Murray articulates the problem to be one of systemic abuse: narcissistic male "ignoramuses" pervert reason in order to "rob" women of power: "Strange how blind self love renders you men; were you not wholly absorbed in a partial admiration of your own abilities, you would long since have acknowledged the force of what I am now going to urge."[61] In the "Equality of the Sexes" essay, Constantia claims that the domestication of girls distorts their minds, leaving them little to discuss but gossip and fashion. The needle and the kitchen "leave the intelligent principle vacant." More is clearly needed to stimulate a mind equal to man's. And yet at the end of the essay, when addressing men, Murray promises that if females are properly educated, they will do these and other domestic tasks with greater efficiency and enthusiasm. Women have the time for education, and education will render them "worthy of rational beings." They will be better conversationalists, and less likely to "blast" the reputation of others. Those who have no servants will be more efficient household managers:

Oh, ye arbiters of our fate! We confess that the superiority is indubitably yours; you are by nature formed for our protectors; we pretend not to vie with you in bodily strength; . . . shield us then, we beseech you, from all external evils, and in return *we* shall transact *your* affairs. Yes, *your* for are you not equally interested in those matters with ourselves? Is not the elegancy of neatness as agreeable to your sight as to ours; is not the well-favored viand equally delightful to your taste? And doth not your sense of hearing suffer as much from the discordant sounds prevalent in an ill regulated family, produced by the voices of children and many et ceteras?[62]

Constantia cannot decide if domesticity is a curse or a virtue, the cause of women's subordination or the source of her redemption. She cannot, it seems, break away from the logic of separate spheres. Men are here aligned with the "world," as women's protectors; women are shielded in the home, as household managers. Physical strength, previously deemed irrelevant for rational beings engaged in rational pursuits, is now a qualifying factor for life in the world; now it disqualifies women as equals, rendering them weak and in need of protection from men. The body now requires that women be household managers rather than independent women of commerce, politics, agriculture, or war.

Writing in the masculine persona of "the Gleaner" did not free Murray from these inconsistencies.[63] In "Observations on Female Abilities," the Gleaner also retreats from the logical implications of exposing a canon of famous women. After proving by historical examples that women have done everything men have done as well or better, including military battle, "he" denies that he means to suggest women ought to aspire for *actual* equality.

Gleaner essay number 88 congratulates the fair sex for the "happy revolution" made in their favor. The reference is to the development of female academies in the 1790s. "He" sets out to "improve" upon the opinions of Wollstonecraft and contend for equality in the *quantity* as well as the *quality* of mind. The Gleaner urges the younger generation of women to refute the popular sentiment that female education will threaten the fulfillment of their domestic duties. Rather, those duties are now "necessary occupations, that must ever be considered as proper to the department and comprised in the duties of a judiciously instructed and elegant woman."

The Gleaner promises that all of the conservative virtues of fair sex ideology will be maintained and improved upon with the advancement of female learning. He reiterates Constantia's promises of greater efficiency in housework, greater industry, and less preoccupation with fashion. He also promises that the rational woman will be less vain, devoid of "prepossessing ideas" originating in the bosom of a beautiful exterior. Education will cultivate women's humility, when they discover the largeness of the world and how little they actually know. They will practice "mild benignity," "modesty," and "every sexual grace." Their "rancorous passions" will give way to "mild temperatures of the soul." They will assume "unembarrassed" manners and "unaffected" personalities.[64]

Their rationality will lead them to make systematic deductions, their conclusions based on evidence and fact rather than speculation and fancy. Their refined thinking will make them better friends to their life partners. And more. Their knowledge will never lead them to demand respect: "They will not be assuming; the characteristic trait will still remain; and retiring sweetness will insure them that consideration and respect, which they do not presume to demand." There will be no semblance of pedantry, and they will never outshine their husbands intellectually: "They will *question* rather than *assert*; and they will make their communications on a supposition, that the point in discussion has rather *escaped the memory* of those with whom they converse, *than that it was never imprinted there*." "He" assures men that educating women will not disrupt the separation of spheres, but will merely add sophistication and rationalization to their domesticity.[65]

The Gleaner fully annihilates every radical argument that Constantia so bravely voiced. In his persona, Murray promises that women will now distort their own minds and speech to preserve marital hierarchy and harmony. Murray's utopia of ambitious, famed, and economically independent women is destroyed, as is her foundation, the free mind of an equal, immortal soul. The metaphor of marriage as death, of "domestication" as inhumane treatment of female human beings, is also gone. In their places we find "the family of reason," an "enchanting society" where communicative rationality is effectively perverted to instrumental rationality between husbands and wives, through the willful subordination of women. The desire for fame in the world is now offset by an impassioned vision of "companionable and serious" wives and mothers who boast "competency."

> Surely the wide globe cannot produce a scene more truly interesting. See! the virtues are embodied—the domestic duties appear in their place, and

they are all fulfilled—morality is systematized by religion, and sublimed by devotion—every movement is the offspring of elegance, and their manners have received the highest polish. A reciprocation of good offices, and a mutual desire to please, uniformly distinguishes the individuals of this enchanting society—their conversation, refined and elevated, partakes the fire of genius. . . . Such is the family of reason—of reason cultivated and adorned by literature.[66]

The Gleaner reassures women that the basic structure of gender relations will not change. "'Would you, good Mr. Gleaner, station us in the compting house?' No, my fair country-women, except circumstances unavoidably pointed the way." The Gleaner does not wish to "unsex" his fair readers. Females should be educated in case their husbands die and leave them without resources. Thus, the essays establishing a canon of women who demonstrated actual equality were only an *exercise*: "I do but hold up to your view, the *capability* of your Sex . . . as that it may, if occasion requires, assist in establishing you above that kind of dependence, against which the free-born mind so naturally revolts." Retreating from the arguments for individual social equality, the Gleaner now quotes approvingly the words of an unnamed male author who assigned to women the superiority of the "feelings of the heart."

The pleasures of women must arise from their virtues. It is by the cradle of their children, and in viewing the smiles of their daughters, or the sports of their sons, that mothers find their happiness. Where are the powerful emotions of nature? Where is the sentiment, at once sublime and pathetic, that carries every feeling to excess? Is it to be found in the frosty indifference, and the sour severity of some fathers? No—but in the warm and affectionate bosom of a *mother*. It is she, who, by an impulse throws herself across the flames to save a sleeping infant—It is she, who, with dishevelled locks, pale and distracted, embraces with transport, the body of a dead child, pressing its cold lips to hers, as if she would reanimate, by her tears and her caresses, the insensible clay. These great expressions of nature—these heart-rending emotions, which fill us at once with wonder, compassion and terror, always have belonged, and always will belong, only to Women. They possess, in those moments, an inexpressible something, which carries them beyond themselves; and they seem to discover to us new souls, above the standard of humanity.[67]

Taking the essays "On the Equality of the Sexes" and "Observations of Female Abilities" from *The Gleaner* as one piece, as the author asks us to do, we are left dangling in the indeterminacy of contradiction. Is the soul eternal and universal, or is it mortal and gendered? Does it find itself authentically through the body in which it is housed, or is it only trapped there by convention? Are women equal to men, or are they different? Are they morally superior, "above the standards of humanity?" Then why must they subordinate themselves in daily conversations with men?

Murray's compromise of a "better domesticity" for women certainly reproduces the sexual contract of the patriarchal family, in which the husband figures as its head and the wife as his economic and intellectual dependent. The compromise does afford white women something, however. Educated, they become rational mothers and wives, imposing their rationality on children, who figure as subordinate "others."

Consider Murray's essay "On the Domestic Education of Children" (May 1790), published only a month after part two of her "Equality" essay. Constantia paints a picture of the new rational family with the mother who knows herself as a modern subject primarily through the authority she exercises over children. "Martesia" is an exemplary mother who has eliminated the violent coercion of the rod and instead employs reason to rule her family. Her family is "a well-regulated commonwealth," where virtue prevails. Martesia distributes posts of honor among her children according to merit. As an authority figure, her rule is never to lose control or show any "irregular passion" in the presence of her children. They never see her "ruffled." To increase her authority with them, she implants in their minds the "most elevated opinion of her understanding"; and she conceives that they cannot be too early impressed with an idea of her possessing superior abilities. As a result, they rarely question her judgment.

Martesia teaches her children to emulate the virtues necessary to sustain republican society: sentiments of humanity and benevolence; obligations to each other as required by God; and dependence on and respect for elders, including servants, "for her view is to choke, if possible the first buddings of unbecoming pride." She tells them "well-chosen tales" with morals calculated to promote virtue and excite commiseration. Her rewards are precisely tailored to the merit of any child's good deeds. Martesia finds love, respect, and satisfaction in her family. The greatest felicity they can possibly experience is simply to be in her presence.

The foundations of Murray's feminist theory are compromised, if not destroyed, by female essentialism. Once the soul is gendered, domesticity again becomes naturalized, and the justification for female education must fit within the logic of separate spheres. Her advocacy of education to provide women economic and psychological independence is compromised by the more moderate justification of female academies as institutions that would make women accept their allotted places in domesticity with more efficiency, enthusiasm, and rational sophistication. The best the fair sex can do in the Age of Enlightenment is to become literate housewives and mothers, and possibly provide for themselves in the case of abandonment or death of their husbands. Thus, what began as a confrontation with white men for equal subjectivity and social equality is inevitably transformed to a reproduction of separate spheres, in which woman is essentially different from man; but like man, she has an "Other" over whom to enforce moral judgments. Women finally arrive as modern subjects, in their capacities as mothers, through the alterity of children.

Concluding Remarks: Gleaning Meanings from Fragmentation

Murray's logic is strained by tensions between the universal and the particular. In selected texts, sex is a social construction placed on universal and equal souls. In these texts, the inferior intellects of females are seen to be constructed as such by an oppressive culture, not by nature. When Murray discusses class and race, however, apparent intellectual inferiority is taken as the natural order of things. No efforts are made to deconstruct putatively inferior intellects of blacks or working-class whites, or to encourage ambition, the birthright of the naturally equal rational soul in the Federalist polity.[68] Her logic is also loose when considering the soul of the category "woman." Even if we limit the category by race and class, as she does, we are left with the contradiction of woman as equal to man, versus woman as the fair sex intermediary.

To address the first contradiction on race, class, and universal human nature, we might well conclude that Murray's political purposes were limited to the promotion of equal educational opportunity for white males and females, and perhaps even equal economic opportunities. Use of the universal to minimize the differences between a particular set of people seems to reflect a strategy of expedience, where Murray is basically serving her own interests behind the cloak of philosophy. Although many challenged the idea that racial inferiority stemmed from nature, few would challenge the idea that Europeans and their white descendants were the most civilized persons on the globe. Thus, Murray was able to leave unchallenged questions of racial oppression that logically flowed from the assumption of a universal human nature.[69] It is also evident that Murray had much to lose and seemingly little to gain by suggesting that an "equality of the races" demanded emancipation, or at the very least education, for the slaves.

Murray's position on class hierarchy is confused. Her concept of class is economic, intellectual, and political: Those who lack education, leisure, and property should subordinate themselves to others who possess those things. Murray would only disrupt this hierarchy for women, as they are placed in the lower class arbitrarily, that is, with no opportunity to advance or become famous. And yet she is clearly not concerned about poor women's education and social advancement. Her concept of sexual equality really makes sense only within the upper class, with women who would have mirrored Murray herself. Even within the upper class, she never suggests that leisured, intelligent women should be able to participate in politics directly. Single or married, rich or poor, educated or illiterate, all women are viewed as political subordinates to the properly masculine state. In short, Murray privileges herself as a subject by subjecting already present others, the black, the savage, and the uneducated mob.

But how are we to reconcile her inconsistencies and reversals on the category "woman"? For she can only assert herself as a subject in the male world of publishing when she is claiming equality with white men. Here I return to my original question. Does Murray resort to the *sexual* difference of fair sex ideology as an exoteric strategy or because she identifies with domination and willingly submits herself?

Surely the threat of persecution was real. Murray could not fit neatly within any of the categories defining women in her day. To live within the limits of fair sex orthodoxy would have entailed the death of her soul. To throw aside that orthodoxy would have entailed ostracism and alienation. Murray had witnessed the ostracism of Mary Wollstonecraft, ignobly labeled the "philosophical wanton" and "female illuminati." Though Murray firmly denounced democratic societies and the "rights of man," she could not escape criticism for identifying with much of Wollstonecraft's feminist politics and principles.[70]

But the suggestion that Murray's conservatism on the category woman was mainly part of a an exoteric strategy presents problems of its own. It requires the assumption of a fixed and stable identity, "the real Judith Sargent Murray," behind a performance. Accepting this assumption might be easier if there was a difference in the political content between her private and published writings. But the same sorts of inconsistencies appear in her letters, making the choice of a single, coherent Judith Sargent Murray require a reading far too selective.[71]

It may be more fruitful to consider Murray as a woman in contradiction, living, thinking, and writing in the cracks, between the boundaries of the Enlightened "individual," and the other-directed wife and mother of fair sex ideology. The between-spaces provide a freedom for her to evade ostracism and restriction by those categories of being. She appears to desire to break free from sexual oppression, in her political theorizing and in her attempt to achieve fame and earn an income as an author. But for Murray to assert herself as a subject in her own right consistently might have led [mainly male] readers and publishers to denigrate her work and abandon her. Such was her rationale behind the male persona of the Gleaner. Murray could not afford to risk this alienation psychologically or materially. She needed the money from sales of *The Gleaner* to support herself and her family, as her husband was no longer able to do so.

To reduce the risks of alienation, Murray exhibited a kind of masochism. She chose to reproduce sexual difference and sexual submission. Jessica Benjamin's psychoanalytic work has suggested that the masochistic woman endures the pain of torture and objectification because she desires recognition of her self by the master. Murray, of course, desired recognition and fame from the masculine power holders—Federalists and male literary artists—in Anglo-American culture. The search for this recognition would have come with a price, however. For the masochist, "intense pain causes the violent rupture of the self, a profound experience of fragmentation and chaos." The loss of self-coherence becomes a kind of sacrifice that actually creates the master's power, the coherence of patriarchy, and masculine privilege, in which she can take refuge.[72] She sells her volumes, makes a handsome sum, and attains "fame" through her almost perfect identification with federalism. The price of admission to this more powerful self is fragmentation—the splitting of the self by a few, very deep, consistently held inconsistencies.

7

Conclusion

Woman has no political existence. . . . she is only counted, like the slaves of the South, to swell the number of lawmakers who form decrees for her government, with little reference to her benefit.
                                                    —Sarah Grimke, 1838[1]

If rights are founded on the nature of our moral being, then the mere circumstance of sex does not give to man higher rights and responsibilities, than to woman.
                                                    —Angelina Grimke, 1838[2]

I do not wish to be understood to say that all men are hard, self-ish, and brutal, . . . but I refer to those characteristics . . . that distinguish what is called the stronger sex. For example, the love of acquisition and conquest, the very pioneers of civilization . . . are powers of destruction when used to subjugate one man to another or to sacrifice nations to ambition. Here that great conservator of woman's love, if permitted to assert itself . . . would hold all these destructive forces in check.
                                                    —Elizabeth Cady Stanton, 1869[3]

If the civilization of the age calls for an extension of suffrage, surely a government of the most virtuous, educated men and women would better represent the whole, and protect the interests of all than could the representation of either sex alone. . . . Will the foreign element, the dregs of China, Germany, Ireland, and Africa supply this needed force, or the nobler types of American womanhood who have taught our presidents, senators, and congressmen the rudiments of all they know?
                                                    —Elizabeth Cady Stanton, 1869[4]

White women in the United States have always had a precarious identification with white men, as well as with racial and ethnic minorities.

At times they have maximized both identifications, viewing themselves as the moral equals of white men, yet unjustly oppressed, like the slave or disfranchised Other. This dual identification works as a strategy to criticize hierarchical relations that unjustly privilege white men and oppress women and minorities. Sarah and Angelina Grimke's observations exemplify this strategy. Their identification of the white woman in marriage and coverture with the enslaved black is used to criticize patriarchy as well as racism.

In other moments, white women have maximized differences between themselves and marginalized Others to assert superiority, and justify their own political ends. They disavow their likeness to other oppressed groups, underscoring their racial identification with white men. This racial identification then becomes the springboard for a narrowly conceived "equality," which preserves sexual and racial differences. The quotes from Elizabeth Cady Stanton, which distinguish women from the "stronger sex" and *white women* from the "foreign element" preserve gender and racial differences, as well as the hierarchy on which they are based. Stanton and other nineteenth-century woman suffragists, including Susan B. Anthony and Carrie Catt, all used the play of differences between men and women, and whites and non-whites (or foreigners), to assert a privileged place for white American women within racial patriarchy. White women deserved the suffrage, they argued, as tender, sympathetic, and peace-loving *females* who alone could counter the destructive forces of *men*. White women also deserved the vote as educated, civilized *whites* whose moral worth was higher than that of the uncivilized, uneducated dark or immigrants.

The idea of radical equality that the Grimke sisters embraced in the struggle for women's rights did not originate with them. Such ideas were present in others, including Abigail Adams, during the Revolution. Neither did the idea of white women as civilizing intermediaries between harsh, acquisitive, white men and uneducated foreigners originate in the woman suffrage movement. Both strategies for female liberation can be traced back to the Revolutionary and founding era. As we have seen, the mediating position of white women as the protectors of Anglo-American civilization, as well as the "weaker" sex, was firmly established through fair sex discourses in the post-revolutionary period. As the dominant set of discourses on gender, fair sex ideology provided the discursive universe from which the woman suffrage movement developed, especially at the conclusion of the Civil

War, when black men became enfranchised through the Fifteenth Amendment. Thus, the beginnings of American feminism, and feminist racism, may be traced to the Revolutionary and founding period of American politics.

The American Revolution brought modernity to educated white women. The idea of natural equality and God-given rights inspired Warren, Adams, and Murray to participate as rational human beings in discursive situations. Each expected she could make normative political claims in the great debates of the age, just as white men were doing. In the radical consciousness of the Revolution, each of these women also envisioned a utopia in which white women played important roles in politics, in and outside of their homes. Mercy Warren and Abigail Adams even envisioned the extension of natural rights to nonwhite inhabitants. And yet, as we have seen, all three women eventually signed on to the basic terms of white supremacy and modern patriarchy.

The awareness that gender inequality was socially constructed did not lead Warren, Adams, and Murray to treat racial and ethnic inequalities as equally unjust. Although Warren and Adams made efforts to include nonwhites in the category of rational human nature, their underlying class and race-bound views of "civilization" undercut such efforts. The recognition that hierarchical differences among demographic groups was largely a product of education and environment did not lead them to prescribe the same educational remedy for nonwhites that they prescribed for white women. All three signed on to the racial contract, and eventually consented to the sexual contract.

A summary of evidence on the three women and their positioning with respect to the racial and sexual contracts appears in the appendix. The table also includes evidence on their consent to class hierarchy, because class privileges reinforced these women's risk-aversive behaviors with respect to race and gender struggles.

Three general conclusions are warranted from the evidence. First, each woman consented to racial hierarchy more easily than she consented to gender hierarchy.

Mercy Warren considered "women" the rational equals of "men" by nature, but she did not consider African Americans the rational equals of Anglo-Americans. She could no more imagine a black yeoman farmer than she could a Native American philosopher queen. The joke that she repeated on racial mixing, highlighting the "purity" of white Yankees, against the backward Southerners who mixed with blacks, only underscored her view of black inferiority. And her praise of Phillis Wheatley's poetry was set in the context of the lack of civilization in Namibia, Wheatley's reputed homeland. Warren's use of "slavery" to make the case for white Americans against British tyrants, and later, for the Antifederalists against the Federalists, was usurpative. She completely ignored the implications of natural rights arguments on racial slavery, the only slavery that actually existed in her midst, illegitimately seizing the power that the word "slavery" carried. These examples, along with her failure to acknowledge black resistance in the Boston Massacre and the American Revolution in her *History,* displayed the misrepresentation, evasion, and self-deception indicative of consent to the racial contract.

Abigail Adams continued to criticize and resist the subordination of women, but not slavery, after her husband ridiculed her ideas of radical equality. She had no compunction about taking advantage of racial discrimination in wages and racial slavery. She paid less for black labor during the Revolution, and then exploited slave labor during her husband's terms in the executive office. During this time she also viewed Native Americans as odd savages, and accepted wars of conquest with the Natives as a matter of course.

Judith Sargent Murray, the most adamant advocate of women's natural rights, was explicitly racist. To the extent that she was financially aided by her brother Winthrop, she enjoyed the benefits of his plantation. In addition, Murray's statements about the negative influence of slaves on her nephews showed her concern for racial purity, as well as a complete disregard for the injustice of slavery, or slaves' right to education. Thus, it is difficult not to conclude that all three women consciously and/or unconsciously accepted racial and ethnic hierarchy as "natural," despite some efforts to extend the logic of enlightenment rationality universally.

Second, despite the progression of "feminist" thinking from Warren to Murray, or the oldest to the youngest woman, all three appear to have ultimately accepted gender hierarchy. While Mercy Warren argued for the inclusion of women in the category of rational human nature, and did envision women as political philosophers, historians, and moral authorities in families, she never actually challenged the exclusion of women from political and individual rights, or the gendered spheres of modern republicanism. And, when the Federalists nationalized politics, her own vision of woman citizenship, based on small-scale state politics, rendered her powerless as a woman. Adams and Murray, who made the boldest claims for gender equality and the erosion of gendered spheres, reversed, withdrew, or recanted those views, adopting fair sex ideology in their place. Thus, the utopian gender ideals of all three were defeated in the founding era.

Third, the three women's acceptance of white supremacy and its privileges, including class privileges, may have influenced their acceptance of *gender* hierarchy. Interest and logic combined to facilitate acceptance of their mediating roles prescribed by fair sex ideology. Their class privileges, reinforced by race, would likely have been risked through radical and consistent resistance to gender hierarchy. For example, to claim with consistency that *all* women were equal to *all* men would have disrupted the racial and class privileges that they enjoyed by putting nonwhite women on par with themselves. The acceptance of whiteness, and European—especially, Anglo-Saxon—origins as markers of civilization and good breeding, gave most white women a privileged position in the hierarchy of racial patriarchy. This was evident particularly in the willingness of white patriarchs to consent to education and literacy for white women in the post-revolutionary period.

It seems logical that the adoption of fair sex discourse must have ingrained in those who repeated it the idea that differences in race and sex mitigated claims for equality among human nature. In other words, it is possible that white women's acceptance of rational difference based on *race* logically opened the door for them to accept rational difference based on *sex*. In any case, repetition of fair sex discourses would have indicated that they did not take the adage "all men are created equal" literally, or if they did, they certainly did not find it in their interest to press the point. Warren, Adams, and Murray chose to protect their race and class privileges within modern patriarchy rather than risk them for a radical equality that would have eliminated racial as well as gender differences.

Fair sex ideology facilitated this process. Discourses on the fair sex merged race and sex hierarchy, and their usage signaled acceptance of both the racial and sexual contracts. Many of the same virtues and characteristics that were thought to distinguish the "nature" of women from that of men, such as tenderness, sympathy, modesty, propriety, delicacy, and a greater propensity toward "civilized" manners, were also thought to distinguish white women from nonwhites of both sexes.

By accepting racial privileges, as well as gender subordination, they and other white women of their generation acted in a risk-averse manner that assured them at least some benefits. Most important, fair sex ideology ushered white women into modernity. It forged an identity for white women as an exclusive group, just as white men were an exclusive group. It empowered white women with a limited moral authority that allowed them to become "somebody" through the subordination of "Others." These others included nonwhites, foreigners, and children. Although white women were not citizens of the early Republic, they certainly had a privileged position. By mediating the racial, ethnic, class, and gender hierarchies of racial patriarchy, they became modern subjects.

Epilogue

It is fashionable for politicians and political strategists to refer to the Founding Fathers to justify their own political agendas. These agendas often include a subtle reification of the values and hierarchies that were in place in the late eighteenth century. I wrote *The Fair Sex* to uncover these hierarchies and to present the political thought of three Anglo-American women in that context. In the process, I discovered parallels between cultural struggles of the early national period and those of our own, and was thereby led to reconsider several current issues in light of the theory of racial patriarchy.

Recent issues that have involved race and gender struggles simultaneously resonate with the theory of racial patriarchy. Of course any serious attempt to integrate the theory of racial patriarchy with current or recent political struggles would require thorough investigation that is beyond the scope of this book. Thus, the following ideas are not essential to any arguments made in preceding chapters, and should be read only as reasonable speculations.

The policy area of affirmative action has involved struggles over the continuing existence of racial patriarchy. Social scientists have documented that attitudes about affirmative action portray division among the citizens by race and sex. Blacks are categorically more likely to favor it than whites; women are more likely to favor it than men, especially in the white community. Supporters have generally justified affirmative action as a small step in the right direction toward renegotiation of the racial and sexual contracts. Reasons for the growing opposition to and elimination of affirmative action programs include white fears of reverse discrimination as well as the loss of Anglo-American cultural values, including Western rationality.

For the past two decades, conservatives have succeeded in their efforts to dub affirmative action policies "quotas" that result in "reverse discrimination." They conveniently disregard historical de jure and de facto quotas of one or zero for racial minorities and females. Instead, they focus simplistically on present day "color-blindness," which requires neither detailed historical knowledge nor a disruption of racial patriarchy. This policy stance appeals to whites, especially white men, because it costs them nothing. Not surprisingly, support for affirmative action policies is waning, and several state universities have eliminated race, ethnicity, and gender criteria in admissions.

In this decline, the African American movement for economic "reparations" has gained momentum. Aside from the myriad complexities that would arise in identifying beneficiaries, the reparations movement sparks controversy because it is racially divisive on its face. A negative focus on self-interested movements among blacks as racially divisive, however, distracts attention from those practices among whites that make black separatist strategies seem logical.

The categories of the recent census and the reporting that has flowed from it exemplify such divisive practices. Orlando Patterson has argued that the division of the category "white" into "non-Hispanic" and "Hispanic," as well as the treatment of the Hispanic category as a racial group is a kind of double dipping that promotes white supremacy.[1] In the 2000 census, the 48 percent of Hispanics who designated themselves white were separated from other whites by exclusion through the category "non-Hispanic white." Hispanics may be viewed either as a separate race or a cultural group within the white race.

Categorizing in this manner has enabled political scientists, politicians, and journalists to report estimates that "whites" will be a minority race at mid-century. But these estimates are actually referring to the *subset* of Anglo- or European American whites, who will account for 52 percent of the total population in 2050, while the broader category of whites will account for almost 75 percent.[2] If it is true that second-generation Hispanics are assimilating faster than immigrants of the nineteenth and early twentieth centuries, as Patterson has suggested, then the more realistic scenario presents a very strong and growing "white" population indeed.

Racial patriarchy may be strengthened through this kind of slippage. On one hand, white and nonwhite Hispanics are able to claim the benefits of affirmative action. On the other hand, hiring white Hispanics can fulfill claims of diversity without disrupting white supremacy. Additionally, reports of a declining white population incite fears of an impending minority status among European Americans, which in turn stimulate opposition to affirmative action and its current beneficiaries. Fears of the loss of cultural dominance unify European Americans across gender lines, so that white women revert to their traditional, mediating roles in racial patriarchy. This seems to have happened in California. White women favored Proposition 209, which banned racial, ethnic, and gender preferences for hiring and contracting by state and local governments, and admissions in state universities.[3] White women placed primacy in race, identifying with privileges shared with white men rather than discrimination shared with nonwhite women.

From a black perspective the potential losses of these political dynamics are all too familiar. The dual racial identity within the category Hispanic is reminiscent of school desegregation plans, especially in Texas, that desegregated white schools by admitting Hispanics as nonwhites, and black schools by admitting Hispanics as whites. The increasing tendency of Hispanics to identify with whites intensifies the stigmas attached to the residual category "nonwhites." Not only will blacks be disadvantaged by racial discrimination, but they will also be forced to contend with a growing number of Hispanics who can play both angles, claiming the benefits of both affirmative action and white supremacy. At the same time, the more that Anglo-Americans perceive themselves to be in danger of minority status, the more likely Anglo-American women will put primacy in their racial identities. In this context, it is no surprise that African Americans are mobilizing an exclusive reparations movement tightly bound by race.

Another issue involving race and gender that resulted in a racial divide was the 1995 O. J. Simpson criminal trial.[4] The Simpson case also demonstrates political struggles over primacy. Whether the case was primarily about race, class, or gender depends on one's perspective, which may in turn depend on one's own positioning in racial patriarchy as it is today. Whites in general considered O. J. guilty of murdering his ex-wife, Nicole, as well as her friend Ron Goldman. White feminists charged that the case represented only the most famous example of the sort of spouse abuse that occurs every day in the United States, and all over the world. Other whites focused more narrowly on Simpson's "guilt" without regard to the problem of the tainted evidence or the "fruit from the poisonous tree."

Newspapers indicated that the "not guilty" verdict was celebrated in most black communities. Gender was not at issue for most black women, including the nine who sat on the jury. Most black women identified with the injustices toward black men, not the murdered white wife, even though domestic violence occurs in black families as frequently as it does in white ones.

The Simpson criminal trial took place only a few years after the police beating of Rodney King, and the ensuing criminal trial. In that case, the four white police officers who were videotaped beating and kicking black motorist Rodney King were acquitted. The verdict was followed by race riots. Blacks were and continue to be outraged by racial profiling, police brutality, and unequal sentencing in the criminal justice system.[5] In this context, the O. J. verdict was welcome. It proved to African Americans that with a good attorney, a wealthy black man could get off, just as a wealthy white man could. Thus, they celebrated the momentary renegotiation of the racial contract, and the extension of patriarchy to a famous black man of the upper economic class.

White Americans were quick to sympathize with Nicole Brown Simpson. Some identified with her as an abused wife and lamented the jury's protection of the most brutal vestige of the sexual contract. I suspect other whites may have felt outraged primarily for reasons having to do with fair sex ideology and the failure of white supremacy: the issue of racial purity, or the legitimacy of black men's marrying the fair sex, and the momentary failure of the system to convict a black man. In any case, I have never seen white American men and women unify with equal intensity against domestic violence that takes place in households of famous or ordinary *white* people.

Fair sex ideology and hierarchies of racial patriarchy may also lie beneath divisive attitudes toward the black, sister tennis champions, Venus and Serena Williams. I have personally heard whites in several different casual conversations refer to the sisters as "men." But most blacks I know are proud of Venus and Serena as heroines in their community. Those who designate the sisters "men" justify their statements by noting that Venus and Serena are over six feet tall, have great muscle definition, and can serve at speeds comparable to and even exceeding those of many male professional players.

Those who dub the sisters "men" also disparage them for lacking the morals, manners, and sociability appropriate in elite tennis circles. I suspect that the masculine designation stems from vestiges of fair sex ideology, and the threat that is still posed when women, white or black, ignore its norms. The Williams sisters do not appear to display virtues of modesty, softness, deference to white men, mild benignity, or sympathy, but then neither do many white female players who somehow escape reproach for being unfeminine.[6] The major difference seems to be that Venus and Serena do not befriend the white tennis establishment. At least in public, they defer only to a black patriarch: their father, their coach. They disregard fair sex ideology and the hierarchy of racial patriarchy, and they win.

The clearest and most visible example of today's rendition of fair sex ideology is probably provided by "family values" discourses. In recent years, prominent conservatives including Newt Gingrich, William Bennett, and Ralph Reed have campaigned for "family values" and turned to the American founders for support. Many of these same conservatives have championed "English only" laws. Taken together, these cultural priorities seem to encourage traditional Anglo-American norms, such as the public/private split, heterosexual marriages, reproduction, and the gendering of virtue, especially for white women.

The campaign for English-only legislation seems to stem from a discomfort with multiculturalism, especially challenges from Hispanics, the fastest growing demographic group in the United States today. Taken with the parallel struggle to eliminate the welfare state, it is possible that a double standard is in play. "Good," bourgeois women, most of whom are white, should ideally concentrate solely on their families, while "good" poor women, who are disproportionately black and brown, should work outside the home to support theirs. In other words, domesticity is good for the nation as long as one is dependent on a family patriarch, not the state. For many reasons, this scenario is still much more common for white families than it is for nonwhite ones.

Insofar as family-values discourses reassert fair sex ideology, the theory of racial patriarchy may also be useful to interpret the Clinton-Lewinsky scandal. Many white liberals, including feminists, found themselves defenseless against the conservatives' assault on President Clinton's impropriety and lack of family values. At first, liberals tried to defend the president by reasserting the old public/private split, underscoring the privacy of sexuality. White feminists were suspended between conservatives and liberals by their obligation to criticize Mr. Clinton's behavior as sexual harassment, on one hand, and their general support for the president's stances on gender issues, on the other.

Interestingly, the Black Congressional Caucus came up with the strongest defense of the president, which included a challenge to the dominance of Anglo-American family values. Although black leaders acknowledged the tragedy of the president's infidelity, they viewed it as a human error rather than a fatal flaw. The vice of sexual infidelity took a back seat to other moral issues far more pressing in black communities, to which President Clinton had arguably been faithful. These included his diplomatic visits to African nations, and his record of addressing racial gaps in employment, wealth, and government representation, which were now being eclipsed by a single-minded, prurient focus on his sexuality.

President Clinton came out of the scandal with his highest approval rating, but this approval did not indicate the death of family-values ideology. George W. Bush, the official winner of the closest presidential race in U.S. history, campaigned partially on his deference to family values, which would restore "dignity" to the White House, and "civility" to Washington.[7] Even Al Gore felt it necessary to incorporate family values in his campaign. He distanced himself from President Clinton, and at the Democratic National Convention, greeted his wife with a demonstrative French kiss as if to portray the vitality of his monogamous relations.

I do not mean to suggest that black Americans completely eschew family-values ideology. Indeed, there is a parallel family-values movement in many black churches, and especially within the separatist Nation of Islam led by Louis Farrakhan. Although the "Million Man March" undoubtedly took on meanings independent of Mr. Farrakhan's preachings, there is little doubt that his message of black male responsibility included an endorsement of the sexual contract within black families.[8] Farrakhan and his organization limited participation in the march to black men, and instructed black women to serve supportive roles in their homes. Although black men's struggle to achieve patriarchy in their communities is understandable given the history of racial patriarchy, black women did not fill the role of the "sex" blindly. The momentary domestication and exclusion of black women created controversy, resulting in the subsequent "Million Family March," and "Million Mom" marches throughout the nation.

I have touched on a few recent examples that I consider suggestive of the continuing existence of racial patriarchy. Exactly how it is structured and functions today is a subject for further research. In any case, I hope I have provoked readers to think about it.

Appendix

	MERCY WARREN	ABIGAIL ADAMS	JUDITH MURRAY
RESISTANCE TO THE SEXUAL CONTRACT	Argued for equality of intellect between the sexes	Criticized law of coverture	Published critique of sexism in religion
	Idealized communicative rationality between the sexes in families	Applied the doctrine of natural rights to women	Published critique of forced domesticity, and marriage as a woman's end in life
	Vision of the philosopher queen	Rejected virtual representation for women; advocated suffrage	Published critique of female objectification
	Published writings as a dissenter in political debates of the age	Advocated female education	Argued for female education and ambition
		Arranged for Nabby's classical studies	Advocated economic self-sufficiency for all women
			Reconstructed a canon of women in world history
			Encouraged limitless female aspirations
			Praised the "single life" for women

	MERCY WARREN	ABIGAIL ADAMS	JUDITH MURRAY
RESISTANCE TO CLASS HIERARCHY	Criticized Federalists for creating a new class system based on money, power, and ambition Advocated "delegate" theory of representation and an *active* citizenry		
RESISTANCE TO RACIAL CONTRACT	Suggested that Natives had natural rights Praised work of Phillis Wheatley	Argued natural rights for enslaved: anti-slavery stance during Revolution	
CONSENT TO SEXUAL CONTRACT	No real challenge to gendered spheres or law of coverture Didn't support Abigail Adams on her idea of claiming women's rights Justified writing her *History* with fair sex ideology	Adopted fair sex ideology after reading Fordyce Enjoyed or settled for vicarious citizenship through elite husband Reversed on suffrage and female representation rights, reasserting separate spheres	Adopted fair sex ideology: reasserting biological sexual differences Promised continued female subordination if women were educated (instrumental rationality) Marriage and domesticity as goal for all female heroines in her fictional writings

	MERCY WARREN	ABIGAIL ADAMS	JUDITH MURRAY
CONSENT TO CLASS HIERARCHY	Assumed property ownership to be a valid qualification for citizenship (yeoman farmer ideal) Viewed ambition and individualism an outrage	Viewed Shays's rebels and Antifederalists as licentious mob Viewed debtors as morally inferior to herself Preferred class hierarchy in England over unruliness of Americans Used husband's class position to subvert gender limits	Advocated passive citizenry between elections (trustee theory) Advocated appropriateness of subordinate servant class Identified manual laborers with intellectual and political inferiority
CONSENT TO RACIAL CONTRACT	Viewed Blacks and Natives as uncivilized barbarians and savages Failed to extend doctrine of natural rights to enslaved Identified blacks with body, whites with reason (e.g., Boston Massacre) Joked about racial "impurity" of Southern whites Ignored black contributions to the Revolution in her *History* Usurped concept of slavery to inspire white Americans to fight British, Federalists	Capitalized on wage discrimination with black laborer on the farm Sought cheaper black and enslaved help as wife of Vice President and as First Lady Unconcerned about education for nonwhites Considered Natives only as savages Viewed war with Natives as inevitable and normal (never entertained natural rights of Natives)	No attempt to apply arguments on equality across racial lines Complicity with slavery (brother's plantation) Racial privileging based on "uncivilized" influence of slaves on nephews Did not extend arguments for education to enslaved, black, or other oppressed groups Assumption of black inferiority

Notes

NOTES TO CHAPTER 1

1. See Rogers Smith, *Civic Ideals;* Gary B. Nash, *Race and Revolution;* Mark E. Kann, *A Republic of Men.*

2. Prominent examples include: Bernard Bailyn, *The Ideological Origins;* Gordon Wood, *The Creation of the American Republic,* 606–615; and *The Radicalism of the American Revolution,* 229–270; J. G. A. Pocock, *The Machiavellian Moment,* 522; Russell L. Hanson, *The Democratic Imagination in America,* 72; John Patrick Diggins, *The Lost Soul of American Politics.*

3. On patriarchy, see Joan Hoff, *Law, Gender, and Injustice;* and Joan Hoff-Wilson, "The Illusion of Change." On republican motherhood, see especially Linda Kerber, *Women of the Republic;* and Mary Beth Norton, *Liberty's Daughters.* Norton claimed there that republican motherhood ideology gave white men and women social equality. Despite her greater appreciation for continuing legal inequities, Linda Kerber has argued that republican motherhood ideology conferred a kind of "citizenship" to women. See Kerber's "The Paradox of Women's Citizenship." Her most recent book, *Toward an Intellectual History of Women,* has reduced that claim to one of "deferential citizenship," but the status is still celebrated as an advancement for white women.

4. Carole Pateman, *The Sexual Contract.*

5. Nancy Cott, *Public Vows.*

6. Jurgen Habermas, *The Theory of Communicative Action;* Diana Coole, "Habermas and the Question of Alterity," in *Habermas and the Unfinished Project of Modernity: Critical Essays on the Philosophical Discourses of Modernity,* eds. Maurizio Passerin d'Entreves and Seyla Benhabib (Cambridge, MA: MIT Press, 1997), 221–44.

7. Norton, *Liberty's Daughters,* 298.

8. Kerber, *Women of the Republic,* 283–85.

9. Jan Lewis, "The Republican Wife," especially at 698–99.

10. Mary Kelley, "Reading Women/Women Reading."

11. Jan Lewis, "'Of Every Age Sex & Condition': The Representation of Women in the Constitution," *Journal of the Early Republic* 15 (Fall 1995): 359–87, quote at 361.

12. Kimberlé Crenshaw, "Demarginalizing the Intersection of Race and Sex: A Black Feminist Critique of Antidiscrimination Doctrine, Feminist Theory, and Antiracist Politics (1989)," in *Feminist Legal Theory: Readings in Law and Gender*, eds. Katharine T. Bartlett and Rosanne Kennedy (Boulder: Westview Press, 1991), 57–80.

13. Jacqueline Jones, "Race, Sex, and Self-Evident Truths: The Status of Slave Women during the Era of the American Revolution," in *Women in the Age of the American Revolution*, eds. Ronald Hoffmand and Peter J. Albert (Richmond: University Press of Virginia, 1989). Carroll Smith-Rosenberg, "Discovering the Subject of the 'Great Constitutional Discussion.'"

14. Winthrop Jordan, *White over Black*; Kathleen Brown, *Good Wives, Nasty Wenches*; Nash, *Race and Revolution*.

15. Charles Mills, *The Racial Contract*; Paul Gilroy, *The Black Atlantic*.

16. Jones, "Race, Sex, and Self-Evident Truths," at 298.

NOTES TO CHAPTER 2

1. Plato, The Republic, Book III.

2. Pateman, *The Sexual Contract*.

3. For general references, see Susan Moller Okin, *Women in Western Political Thought* (Princeton, NJ: Princeton University Press, 1979); Martha Lee Osborne, *Women in Western Thought* (New York: Random House, 1979); Mary Lyndon Shanley and Carole Pateman, eds., *Feminist Interpretations and Political Theory* (University Park: Pennsylvania State University Press, 1991); Linda J. Nicholson, *Gender and History: The Limits of Social Theory in the Age of the Family* (New York: Columbia University Press, 1986); Nancy Hartsock, *Money, Sex, and Power: Toward a Feminist Historical Materialism* (New York: Longman, 1983).

4. Terrell Carver, "'Public Man' and the Critique of Masculinities," *Political Theory* 24:4 (673–86), quote at 675.

5. David Hume may have been exceptional in this regard, recognizing that conventions of the "public interest" were the foundations of the laws of chastity which governed female education and behavior. See Vicki Sapp, "The Philosopher's Seduction"; Christine Battersby, "An Enquiry Concerning the Humean Woman," *Philosophy* 56 (1981): 303–12.

6. James Otis, "The Rights of the British Colonists," 418–70, 423.

7. John Adams to Abigail Adams, 14 April 1776, *Adams Family Correspondence*, L. H. Butterfield et al., eds., 1: 382.

8. John Adams to Abigail Adams, 14 April 1776; John Adams to James Sullivan, 26 May 1776; quoted in Hoff, *Law, Gender, and Injustice*, 60–63.

9. Thomas Jefferson to George Washington, 4 December 1788, in *The Pa-*

pers of Thomas Jefferson 14, Julian P. Boyd, ed., (Princeton: Princeton University Press, 1958), 330.

10. Rosemarie Zaggari, "The Rights of Man and Woman"; Hoff, *Law, Gender, and Injustice*; Ruth Bloch, "The Gendered Meanings of Virtue."

11. Mills, *The Racial Contract*, 67–72.

12. Ibid., 67.

13. John Locke, *Second Treatise*, ch. 5, "Of Property," and ch. 16, "On Conquest"; and Jennifer Welchman, "Locke on Slavery."

14. Of course, it has also been persuasively argued that Greece was actually civilized by Afro-Asiatics sometime around 2000 B.C. See Martin Bernal, *Black Athena: The Afroasiatic Roots of Classical Civilization, Vol. One* (Rutgers: Rutgers University Press, 1987); for opposing views, see Mary Lefkowitz and Guy Maclean Rogers, eds., *Black Athena Revisited* (Chapel Hill: University of North Carolina Press, 1996).

15. See Mills, 70; and Emmanuel Eze, "The Color of Reason"; Earl W. Count, ed., *This Is Race*.

16. Jordan, *White Over Black,* at 253; Adam Smith, *The Wealth of Nations*, 729.

17. Otis, "Rights of the British Colonists," at 424, 439.

18. Ibid., 444, 447, 435–46.

19. Nash, *Race and Revolution*.

20. "On the Slave Trade," *Massachusetts Magazine* (October 1789): 615–618.

21. See Shannon Lanier, *Jefferson's Children: The Story of One American Family* (New York: Random House, 2000); and Joseph J. Ellis, *American Sphinx: The Character of Thomas Jefferson* (New York: Random House, 2000).

22. Excerpt from Thomas Jefferson's *Notes on the State of Virginia*, reprinted in the *Massachusetts Magazine* (September 1789): 567–68.

23. "Address to the Heart on American Slavery," *American Museum* (June 1787): 540–44.

24. Hume, "Of National Characters," quoted in Jordan, *White over Black*, 253.

25. See also Thomas Jefferson, *Notes on the State of Virginia*; Jonathan Boucher, *A View of the Causes and Consequences of the American Revolution*; Richard Nisbet, *Slavery Not Forbidden by Scripture*; Benjamin Rush, *Address on Slavery of the Negroes* (1773); and Arthur Lee, *An Essay in Vindication of the Continental Colonies of America, from a Censure of Mr. Adam Smith, in His Theory of Moral Sentiments. With Some Reflections on Slavery in General* (London, 1764). As Jordan reports, even Benjamin Franklin, who later became the president of the Quaker abolitionist society in Philadelphia, had expressed in 1751 his disdain for blacks as a soiling of America.

26. "On the Causes and Variety of Complexion and Figure in the Human Species," *American Museum* (Philadelphia) (August 1789), at 124; (September 1789), at 184, and (April 1790), at 198.

27. See Gary Nash, *Red, White, and Black*; Oren Lyons, et al., *Exiled in the Land of the Free*; Carole Shammas, "Anglo-American Household Government"; Carroll Smith-Rosenberg, "Discovering the Subject of the 'Great Constitutional Discussion.'" On gender relations within the Iroquois nations, see Nancy Shoemaker, "The Rise or Fall of Iroquois Women"; Judith K. Brown, "Economic Organization and the Position of Women Among the Iroquois"; Gretchen Green, "Molly Brant, Catharine Brant, and Their Daughters."

28. See Pauline Schloesser, "The Fair Sex."

29. Kann, *Republic of Men*; on the duty of a wife to inculcate virtues in and reform her husband, see Lewis, "The Republican Wife."

30. *Commentaries on the Laws of England (1765–1769)*, quoted in The *Law of Sex Discrimination*, eds. Ralph Lindgren and Nadine Taub, 6–7.

31. Zaggari, "The Rights of Man and Woman," esp. 216.

32. Hoff, *Law, Gender, and Injustice*, at 84–85.

33. Kerber, *Women of the Republic*; Hoff, *Law, Gender, and Injustice*; Toby Ditz, "Ownership and Obligation," quote at 257. Elizabeth Crane, "Dependence in the Era of Independence." See also Marylynn Salmon, "Life, Liberty, and Dower"; and *Women and the Law of Property*.

34. Arthur Zilversmit, *The First Emancipation*; Graham Russell Hodges, *Slavery and Freedom in the Rural North*, 135. Other methods for attaining freedom included running away; negotiating a private manumission with one's master; purchase by a relative; receiving freedom as a reward for military service during the Revolution; as a reward for exposing other slaves' plans of rebellion; for discovery of a medical cure; or for service of one's master in his or her last will and testament. See Oscar Reiss, *Blacks in Colonial America*, 24.

35. David H. Fowler, *Northern Attitudes Towards Interracial Marriage*, 52–54 and 62–65; Elizabeth Rauh Bethel, *The Roots of African-American Identity*, 44.

36. Angela Davis, *Women, Race, and Class*; Barbara Omalade, *The Rising Song of African American Women* (New York: Routledge, 1994); Patricia Hill Collins, *Black Feminist Thought*; Deborah Gray White, *Arn't I a Woman? Female Slaves in the Plantation South* (New York: W. W. Norton, 1985). For a view of the intricacy of gender relations among slaves, see Elizabeth Fox-Genovese, *Within the Plantation Household: Black and White Women of the Old South* (Chapel Hill: University of North Carolina Press, 1988).

37. On economic and agricultural changes that invigorated demand in the domestic slave trade, see Jordan, *White Over Black*, 320–21; Steven Deyle, "The Irony of Liberty"; James Oliver Horton and Lois E. Horton, *In Hope of Liberty*, at 82.

38. Hodges, *Slavery and Freedom*, 125; Bethel, *Roots*, 37–38.

39. See for example, Davis, *Women, Race, and Class*; and Collins, *Black Feminist Thought*.

40. Wood, *Radicalism*.

41. Bethel, *Roots*; Wood, *Radicalism*, 169, 229–34; Gary Nash, *Forging Freedom*, 214; Reiss, *Blacks*.

42. Shane White, *Somewhat More Independent*, 156–66; Horton and Horton, *In Hope of Liberty*, 110.

43. Nash, *Forging Freedom*, 147–49.

44. Hoff-Wilson, "Illusion"; Susan Branson, "Women and the Family Economy in the Early Republic: The Case of Elizabeth Meredith," *Journal of the Early Republic* 16 (Spring 1996): 47–71. Consider also the daughters of Abigail Adams and Judith Sargent Murray. While Abigail Smith Adams kept up a correspondence to apprise her husband of political and personal information, and to support herself and her family by managing the farm and importing European goods for resale in Massachusetts, her daughter Abigail was never engaged in productive agricultural or paid labor. Judith Sargent Murray, who earned an income from her published writings, had a daughter Julia in 1790, who married a plantation owner and had no direct contact with the market economy.

45. Benjamin Quarles, *The Negro in the American Revolution* (Chapel Hill: University of North Caroline Press, 1996).

46. Sidney Kaplan and Emma Nogrady Kaplan, *The Black Presence in the Era of the American Revolution*; on The Parting Ways, see Bethel, *Roots*, 34–42; Horton and Horton, *In Hope of Liberty*, 78–79.

47. Joan R. Gundersen, "Independence"; Wayne Bodle, "Jane Bartram's 'Application': Her Struggle for Survival, Stability, and Self-Determination in Revolutionary Pennsylvania," *The Pennsylvania Magazine of History and Biography* 115, no. 2 (April 1991): 185–220; and Kerber, "Paradox."

48. See Shane White, "'It Was a Proud Day,'" and *Somewhat More Independent*; also Bethel, *Roots*, 6–7.

49. Hoff-Wilson, "Illusion"; Gundersen, "Independence"; Judith Apter Klinghoffer and Lois Elkis, "'The Petticoat Electors.'" On the expansion of white male suffrage, see James Kettner, *The Development of American Citizenship*; and Wood, *Radicalism*.

50. The District of Columbia disfranchised blacks when it was incorporated, in 1802. Ohio disfranchised blacks in 1803, and New Jersey disfranchised all blacks and all women in 1807. The disfranchisement of other territories and states occurred as follows: Louisiana (1812), Indiana (1816), Alabama (1819), Missouri (1821), North Carolina (1835), Arkansas (1836), Michigan (1835), Pennsylvania (1838), Texas and Florida (1845), Iowa (1846), Wisconsin (1848), California (1850); Minnesota (1858), Oregon (1859), Kansas

(1861), West Virginia (1863), and Nevada (1864). Charles Wesley, "Negro Suffrage in the Period of Constitution-Making, esp. 153–56.

51. See also Leon F. Litwack, "The Federal Government and the Free Negro"; Kettner, *Development*; and Kerber, "Paradox."

52. Lorraine Smith Pangle and Thomas Pangle, *The Learning of Liberty*.

53. For general sources, see Kerber, *Women of the Republic*, ch. 7; Norton, *Liberty's Daughters*, ch. 9. On literacy, see Kenneth A. Lockridge, *Literacy in Colonial New England*, 38–39; Joel Perlmann and Dennis Shirley, "When Did New England Women Acquire Literacy?"; Gloria L. Main, "An Inquiry into When and Why Women Learned to Write in Colonial New England," *Journal of Social History* 24:3 (Spring 1991): 50–67; and Joel Perlmann, Silvana R. Siddali, and Keith Whitescarver, "Literacy, Schooling, and Teaching."

54. Ruth Wallis Herndon, "Research Note."

55. Karen C. Chambers Dalton, "'The Alphabet is an Abolitionist': Literacy and African Americans in the Emancipation Era," *The Massachusetts Review* (Winter 1991): 545–80; Marsha Watson, "A Classic Case: Phillis Wheatley and Her Poetry."

56. Linda K. Kerber, "Daughters of Columbia," quote from Mason on 47–48; Mary Kelley, "Reading Women"; and Margaret A. Nash, "Rethinking Republican Motherhood."

57. Kelley, "Reading Women," at 403; Kerber, "Daughters," 58; Smith-Rosenberg, *Disorderly Conduct*.

58. Jordan, *White over Black*; Orlando Patterson, *Slavery and Social Death: A Comparative Study* (Cambridge: Harvard University Press, 1982); Edmund Morgan, *American Slavery, American Freedom: The Ordeal of Colonial Virginia* (New York: W. W. Norton, 1975); Brown, *Good Wives, Nasty Wenches*.

59. Jurgen Habermas, *The Structural Transformation of the Public Sphere*.

60. See Sandra M. Gilbert and Susan Gubar, *The Norton Anthology of Literature by Women*.

61. Nancy Cott, *The Bonds of Womanhood*. See also Smith-Rosenberg, *Disorderly Conduct*, especially the chapter on "The Female World of Love and Ritual." Quote from Catherine A. Brekus, *Strangers and Pilgrims*, at 57.

NOTES TO CHAPTER 3

1. Rosemarie Zaggari has argued that the origins of republican motherhood come from the Scottish Enlightenment, and are not new to America. She locates the demand for [white] women to "improve and refine the manners of men" with the Scottish conception of "civilization" and "progress," making the point that the whole concept of republican motherhood is transatlantic. My

analysis would agree with her findings. But I am more interested in investigating the racial and ethnic politics of the binary civilization/barbarism, which is present in the works of Hume, Smith, and other authors Zaggari cites. This binary is left unexamined by the republican motherhood trope, which celebrates white women's moral authority and uncritically accepts its racial boundaries. Zaggari, "Morals, Manners, and the Republican Mother."

2. Jordan, *White over Black*, 7.

3. See Richard Ames, "The Pleasures of Love and Marriage" (1691); C. Cotton, "Sonnet. Goe, false one, now I see the cheat," and "Woman. Pinadrick Ode," in *Poems on Several Occasions* (1689); K. Phillips, "The Earl of Orrery to Mrs. Phillips," in Poems (1667); Locke, Essay on Human Understanding (1690). Fair Sex ideology explodes in the eighteenth century. See M. Chudleigh, "Ah! Wretched Israel! All they Beauty's fled!," in *Essays on Several Subjects* (1710); Gould, "To the Memory of Mrs. Mary Peachley," and "To my Lady Abingdon," in *The Works* (1709); C. Montagu, "An EPISTLE to the Right Honourable CHARLES Earl of Dorset and Middlesex, Occasion'd by His Majesty's Victory in IRELAND," in *Poetical Works* (1716). Other eighteenth-century authors whose poetry contains the words "fair sex" include those by Pennecuik, Pattison, Oldisworth, Nicol, M. Montagu, M. Masters, Lovibond, Alexander Pope, James Fordyce, Robertson, Stevenson, Ward, S. Wesley, J. Williams, and James Wilson. For an analysis of fair sex discourse in the writings of David Hume, see Sapp, "The Philosopher's Seduction."

4. See Chadwyck-Healey, *The English Poetry Full-Text Database*, especially Richard Ames, "The Pleasures of Love and Marriage," (1691) at 13; Robert Gould, "To my Lady Abingdon," from *The Works* (1709) in *The English Poetry Database*, at 119. By contrast, the poem "Woman. Pinadrick Ode" (1689) by Charles Cotton suggests a woman's virtue is a function of chastity unrelated to whiteness. "And who has Vertue once, can never see/ Any thing of Deformity/ Let her Complexion swart, or Tawny be,/ A Twilight Olive, or a Mid-night Ebony./ She that is Chast, is always fair,/ No matter for her Hue,/ And though for form she were a Star,/ She's ugly, if untrue;/ True Beauty always lies within,/ Much deeper, than the outer skin,/. . . ." (from Poems on Several Occasions, *English Poetry Database*, at 289. It is interesting to compare the virtues of the English fair sex with those of the figure Snow White (Schneewitten) in the German folktale written by the Grimms in 1812. Snow White is the "fairest" maiden of them all. She has skin as white as snow, lips as red as blood, and hair as black as ebony. Her beauty is coupled with domestic virtues. For she is told by the dwarves, all male, that all of her needs will be provided by them, so long as she cooks, cleans, knits, and sews for them while they are away at work in the mines. Although her stepmother is the primary evil character, both Snow White and her stepmother are stained by vice. Vanity leads the Queen to want to kill Snow White. It also leads Snow White to disobey the

dwarves, by letting in a stranger and accepting luxuries such as poisonous lace, a comb, and an apple. See *The Complete Fairy Tales of the Brothers Grimm*, translated with an introduction by Jack Zipes (New York: Bantam Books, 1987), 196–204.

5. Ames, "Pleasures of Love and Marriage," p. 1, 3; long quote from 6–7.

6. Ibid., 9.

7. Ibid., 9–10.

8. Norton, *Liberty's Daughters*; Kerber, *Women of the Republic*; Barbara Clark Smith, "Food Rioters and the American Revolution," *William and Mary Quarterly*, 3rd ser., 51, no. 1 (January 1994) 3–38.

9. See Pocock, *Machiavellian Moment*, chs. 14, 15; Smith-Rosenberg, "Discovering," esp. 847; Smith, *Civic Ideals*, 72–77.

10. David Szatmary describes the credit crisis from the perspective of the farmers in *Shays's Rebellion*.

11. James Warren to John Adams, 30 April and 22 October 1786, *Warren-Adams Letters*: 271–73; John Adams to James Warren, 4 July 1786, *Warren-Adams Letters*: 276–77; quote from John Adams to James Warren, (January 9, 1787), 280.

12. "The Politician. No. VI," *Massachusetts Magazine* (Boston), November 1789: 765; (*Massachusetts Magazine* hereafter cited as MM).

13. Wood, *Creation*.

14. See Wood, *Creation*, esp. ch. 12, "The Worthy against the Licentious"; quote from Rev. Thomas Reese, "Essay on the Influence of Religion in Civil Society," *American Museum* (Philadelphia), May 1791: 265. See also "On Politeness," *Ladies Magazine* (Philadelphia), April 1793: 230; (*Ladies Magazine* hereafter cited as LM).

15. George Brock, quoted in Szatmary, *Shays's Rebellion*, at 57.

16. Camillus, "Observations on the late insurrection in Massachusetts . . . Letter I," *American Museum* (October 1787): 315–318, 316. Quoted in Smith-Rosenberg, "Discovering," 854.

17. 'Philo,' "No. I," MM (October 1789): 557–58.

18. "Letter from a Brother to a Sister," *Lady's Magazine and Repository of Entertaining Knowledge* (Philadelphia), November 1792: 260; (*Lady's Magazine and Repository of Entertaining Knowledge* hereafter cited as LMREK). "General Remarks on Women," MM (January 1794): 20–21. On the comparison of the more liberal American gender system to that of despotic Eastern harems, see "On the Treatment of the Fair Sex," *The Lady's Magazine and Musical Repository* (New York), April 1801: 214–215; and "Short Account of the Women of Egypt," *American Museum* (June 1790): 319; "On Temper as it Respects the Married State," LMREK (December 1792): 33, 35.

19. "General Remarks on Women," 20–21; "Letter from a Brother to a Sister," 260; "Letter to a very good-natured lady who is married to a very ill-natured man," *American Museum* (October 1789): 316; "On Conjugal Affection," MM (June 1794): 344.

20. "On Matrimonial Obedience," LM (July 1792): 64, 66.

21. "School for Husbands and Wives," *American Museum* (October 1789): 312–13; "On Conjugal Affection," 344.

22. Shane White, "'It Was a Proud Day'"; "On Female Accomplishments Most Agreeable to a Husband," MM (January 1794): 39.

23. Rev. James Fordyce, *Sermons to Young Women*, Vol. 1, Sermon 3, 107–108. "On Female Accomplishments Agreeable to a Husband," 39; "On Female Manners," MM (April 1795): 42–43.

24. "General Remarks on Women," 21. "The Ladies' Friend," LMREK (August 1792): 126; "The Economy of Female Life," MM (April 1793): 204.

25. "The Pleasures of Female Conversation," *Lady and Gentleman's Magazine* (November 1796): 223.

26. "On the Happy Influence of Female Society," *American Museum* (June 1787): 62.

27. "On Temper as it Respects the Married State," LMREK (December 1792): 35; "Letter to a very good-natured lady," 316.

28. Norton, *Liberty's Daughters*, at 163, 170, 194; Kerber, *Women of the Republic*, at 78–84.

29. Thomas Jefferson to Angelica Schuyler Church, 21 September 1788, in *The Papers of Thomas Jefferson*, 13, Boyd, ed. at 623. Jurgen Habermas, *The Philosophical Discourses of Modernity* (Cambridge: Polity Press, 1987), and *Structural Transformation*, 32–51.

30. Hamilton, "Report on Manufactures," in *The Papers of Alexander Hamilton*, eds. Harold C. Syrett and Jacob E. Cooke (New York: Columbia University Press, 1966), 253. Noah Webster, from *On the Education of Youth in America*, 69.

31. "On Temper as it Respects the Married State," 35.

32. Joan Tronto, *Moral Boundaries: A Political Argument for the Ethic of Care* (New York: Routledge, 1993); and Zaggari, "Morals"; "The Essayist No. 8. 'Sympathy,'" MM (November 1793): 681–82.

33. "Address to the Heart on American Slavery," *American Museum* (June 1787): 540–544.

34. "'Julia,' The African: A Sketch," *The Lady's Magazine and Musical Repository* (April 1801): 217–18; "Selico: An African Tale," (May 1793): 284–291.

35. See Carol Gilligan, *In a Different Voice*; and "Reply to Critics," in *Ethic of Care*, ed. Mary Jeanne Larrabee (New York: Routledge), 207–14.

36. "Family Disagreements the Frequent Cause of Immoral Conduct," *American Museum* (January 1787): 64.

37. "On Conjugal Affection," 343; "On Temper as it Respects the Married State," 34; "On Female Accomplishments Most Agreeable to a Husband," 37–38.

38. "On Female Accomplishments Most Agreeable to a Husband," 39.

39. "Philo No. II," MM (October 1789): 648; "Moral Disquisition for the MM: The General Observer No. 36" (February 1797): 93.

40. "Philo No. II," 648; "On Female Authorship," LM (January 1793): 71.

41. "On Female Authorship," 68–69.

42. "Letter from a Brother to a Sister," 260. 'Ignotus,' "To 'A Friend of the Fair Sex,'" *Philadelphia Repository and Weekly Register* (March 14, 1801): 5.

43. "On the Happiness of Domestic Life," *American Museum* (February 1787): 156.

44. Ruth Bloch, "American Feminine Ideals"; Kerber, *Women of the Republic*; Lewis, "Republican Wife."

45. "Dissertation on Industry," MM (August 1790): 491; "Scheme for Increasing the Power of the Fair Sex," LM 22.

46. "Female Influence," *New York Magazine* (May 1795): 297–305.

47. Kerber, "Daughters"; 'O.,' "Plan for the Emancipation of the Fair Sex," *The Lady's Magazine and Musical Repository* (New York), January–June, 1802: 43–44. Quotes from Rush and Webster are from *Essays on Education in the Early Republic*, ed. Frederick Rudolph (Cambridge: Belknap Press of Harvard University Press, 1965); Rush, "Thoughts upon Female Education," at 39; Webster, "On the Education of Youth," at 71.

48. Rush, "Thoughts," 27.

49. Ibid., 37–38.

50. Webster, "On the Education of Youth," 71, 71n.

51. Bloch, "Gendered Meanings"; Hoff, *Law, Gender, and Injustice*, esp. pp. 50–55, "From Virtuous Men to Virtuous Women."

52. Thomas Paine, "An Occasional Letter on the Female Sex."

53. Ibid., 362.

54. Ibid., 363–64.

55. "Various Traits of the Africans," MM (November 1793): 683, and "Interview with the Women of Mount Etna," MM (March 1793): 131. "Of Complexion and Figure," *American Museum* (August 1789): 129–130.

56. "Character of the Creoles of St. Domingo," *American Museum* (December 1789): 467–69.

57. "Account of a Singular Custom at Metilin, with some conjectures on the antiquity of its origin. By the Right Hon. James Earl, President of the Royal Irish Academy," LMREK (August 1792): 125.

58. "Account of a Singular Custom at Metilin," and "Thoughts on Bashful-

ness," LMREK (August 1792): 125–126. See also "An Account of the Mode of Courtship and Marriage amongst the Malays of Quedah," LMREK (January 1793): 67.

59. Klinghoffer and Elkis, "Petticoat Electors," quote at 190–91.

NOTES TO CHAPTER 4

1. Mercy Otis Warren (MOW) to Catherine Macaulay, 29 December 1774, Mercy Otis Warren Papers; *History of the Rise, Progress and Termination of the American Revolution*, xlii; "Observations on the New Constitution"; see also her poem, "The Genius of America weeping the absurd Follies of the Day.—October 10, 1778, 'O Tempora, O Mores!'" in Benjamin Franklin V, ed., *The Plays and Poems of Mercy Otis Warren*, 246–51.

2. Pocock, *Machiavellian Moment*, 77; Warren, *History*, xviii. Mercy Warren's letters are preserved in the Mercy Warren "Letterbook," Mercy Otis Warren Papers. Warren's plays "The Adulateur" (1773), "The Defeat"(1773), "The Group" (1775), and her book *Poems Dramatic and Miscellaneous* (1790), which contains the plays "Sack of Rome" and "Ladies of Castille," are reprinted in Franklin V, ed., *Plays and Poems*. Franklin also includes *The Blockheads* (1776) and *The Motley Assembly* (1779) as Warren's, though others doubt her authorship of these works. More of Warren's poems are reprinted in Edmund M. Hayes, ed., "The Private Poems of Mercy Otis Warren." Warren's *History of the Rise, Progress, and Termination of the American Revolution, Interspersed with Biographical, Political and Moral Observations* (Boston: Manning and Loring, 1805) has been republished by Lester Cohen, ed. (Indianapolis: Liberty Classics, 1988) in two volumes. See also Warren, "Observations." Quote from Warren's *History*, at 641.

3. Harry Stout, *The New England Soul*, 7.

4. Warren, *History*, 631.

5. MOW to Abigail Adams, February 1774. Mercy Otis Warren Papers.

6. Hanson, *Democratic Imagination*, at 60.

7. Warren's *History*, 3.

8. Ibid.

9. On the Socratic view of the soul, see Plato, *The Republic*, Book IV, at 115; and Warren, *History*, 3–15.

10. MOW to son Winslow Warren, in Edmund Hayes, ed., "Mercy Otis Warren versus Lord Chesterfield," at 620.

11. MOW to Betsey Otis, no date, Mercy Otis Warren Papers.

12. Warren's *History*, at 630, and "Observations," at 275.

13. Warren's *History*, at 13, 28–29; James Otis [1764], "Rights of the British Colonists."

14. Warren's "Observations," at 274.

15. Herbert Storing, *What the Anti-Federalists Were For: The Political Thought of the Opponents of the Constitution* (Chicago: University of Chicago Press, 1981), 17, n14; Warren, "Observations," at 274, and MOW to Hannah Lincoln, 1774 Lb, 35.

16. Szatmary, *Shays's Rebellion*, 1–18, 131.

17. Warren, *History*, 50; letter to Hannah Lincoln, no month, 1774, Mercy Otis Warren Papers.

18. The reference is to Socrates' view of the "healthy" city in contrast with the "sick" one. See Plato, *The Republic*, Book II, at 48; and for Aristotle's concept of polity, or the "middle constitution," see *The Politics*, Book IV, ch. xi.

19. Warren, *History*, 649.

20. Szatmary, *Shays's Rebellion*, 6.

21. Warren, "Observations," 273; *History*, 14. The parallels between Warren and J. J. Rousseau are striking. Both feared the corruption of modernization and commerce; both harkened back to the simplicity of "nascent society" as a foundation for true republicanism. Yet nowhere does Warren make reference to Jean-Jacques Rousseau or his works.

22. Warren, *History*, 3–5, 15, 644–45; MOW to Catharine Macaulay, August 1775, Mercy Otis Warren Papers.

23. Warren, *History*, 8; "Observations," 274.

24. MOW to [no name], 23 February 1783, Mercy Otis Warren Papers.

25. *History*, 98; Norton, *Liberty's Daughters*; Kerber, *Women of the Republic*; Lewis, "The Republican Wife."

26. Mercy Otis Warren, *Poems Dramatic and Miscellaneous* [1790], in Franklin V, ed., *The Plays and Poems of Mercy Otis Warren*, 163–64, 170.

27. MOW to Abigail Adams, February 1774; letter to Sally Sever, 20 July 1784, Mercy Otis Warren Papers.

28. MOW to Lady Hesilrige, no month 1773, Mercy Otis Warren Papers.

29. MOW to son James Warren, June 1776; to son Winslow Warren, 1 December 1779, and 25 March 1780: to James Warren, June 1776; and to Winslow Warren, 4 December 1779. Mercy Otis Warren Papers.

30. MOW to Catherine Macaulay, 2 August 1787. Mercy Otis Warren Papers; "Observations," 273; *History*, 115.

31. *The Warren-Adams Letters*, Vol. 2, 259, 315; (*Warren-Adams Letters* hereafter cited as WAL).

32. MOW to Abigail Adams 2nd, no month 1779, Mercy Otis Warren Papers.

33. MOW to son James, June 1776, Mercy Otis Warren Papers.

34. Pauline Schloesser, "Lamenting the Loss of a Woman-Centered Polity."

35. Pateman, *Sexual Contract*, 53–54, 96–102, 168–171. Some scholars have found feminist inspiration from social contract theories, but I have found none that have addressed and challenged Pateman's arguments on conjugal

right within the marriage contracts of the same. See for example Melissa Butler, "Early Liberal Roots of Feminism"; and Lynda Lange, "Rousseau and Modern Feminism," both in Shanley and Pateman, *Feminist Interpretations and Political Theory*. See also Thomas Pangle, *The Spirit of Modern Republicanism*, 230–43; Kerber, *Women of the Republic*, 17.

36. MOW to Betsey Otis, no date, Mercy Otis Warren Papers.

37. John Locke, *Two Treatises of Government*, 321; Pateman, *Sexual Contract*, 53; Linda Nicholson, *Gender and History: The Limits of Social Theory in the Age of the Family* (New York: Columbia University Press, 1986), 155.

38. Lange, "Rousseau and Modern Feminism," 102–105; Jean-Jacques Rousseau, *Emile: or On Education*, 365; Pateman, *Sexual Contract*, 99; and Rousseau [1764], 1979, 409.

39. MOW to Sally Sever, 20 July 1784, Mercy Otis Warren Papers.

40. MOW to Betsey Otis, no date, Mercy Otis Warren Papers.

41. MOW to Catherine Macaulay, 29 December 1774, Mercy Otis Warren Papers.

42. Hoff, *Law, Gender, and Injustice*.

43. John Adams to Mercy Otis Warren, 18 May 1775, WAL I, 49.

44. John Adams to Mercy Otis Warren, 15 March 1775, WAL I, 42, and 25 December, 1787, WAL II, 301. John Adams also ridiculed Mercy Warren after her *History* was published. Disappointed with her rendition of his character and contributions, he wrote that "history is not the Province of the ladies" (quoted in Norton, *Liberty's Daughters*, 123).

45. Jeffrey Richards, *Mercy Otis Warren*, 61.

46. Warren, *Poems Dramatic and Miscellaneous*, 249, 197; and "Observations," 272.

47. MOW to Rebecca Otis, no month 1776; letter to Sally Sever, 20 July 1784, Mercy Otis Warren Papers.

48. MOW to Abigail Adams, February 1774, Mercy Otis Warren Papers.

49. Warren, "An Address to the Inhabitants of the United States," in *History*, xli–xliii.

50. MOW to Hannah Lincoln, 3 September 1774, Mercy Otis Warren Papers.

51. Warren, *History*, 25 (emphasis added).

52. Otis, "Rights," 423.

53. Warren was not unique in this move; as Gordon Wood has documented, other American political writers also described their fears in terms of slavery and bondage. See Wood, *Radicalism*, at 172–73.

54. Warren, *History*, 110–111.

55. Ibid., at 14.

56. Ibid., at 180.

57. See Kaplan and Kaplan, *Black Presence*, at 6–8; Warren, *History*, at 52–53.

58. Warren, "Observations," 271–72.

59. Ibid., 275.

60. Warren, *History*, 639–40, 679; "Observations," 272–274.

61. See Douglass Adair, *Fame and the Founding Father*, 8.

62. The *Federalist*, 51; John P. Diggins, *The Lost Soul of American Politics*, 85–99; Wood, *Creation*, 612–13; Richard K. Matthews, *If Men Were Angels*, 159, 183.

63. Matthews, 159, 183; Hanson, *Democratic Imagination*, 76; *The Federalist*, 49.

64. Matthews, *If Men Were Angels*, 153; Pangle, *Spirit*, 72–73; Wood, *Creation*, 609. Later, as a response to Antifederalist pressure, freedom of conscience, association, and press would be added to the list in the 1791 *Bill of Rights*.

65. Hanson, *Democratic Imagination*; Pangle, *Spirit*, 94–95.

66. Pangle and Pangle, *Learning of Liberty*, 76–77, 103, 118, 132–33. See also Bloch, "Gendered Meanings"; and Lewis, "The Republican Wife."

67. Warren, "Observations," 272–73.

68. Warren, *History*, 283–84.

69. Ibid., 287.

70. Ibid.

71. Lester Cohen, "Mercy Otis Warren."

72. Warren, "Observations," 272.

73. MOW letter "To a Young Lady presenting a volume of Mrs. Chapone's works," no month 1790, Mercy Otis Warren Papers.

NOTES TO CHAPTER 5

1. My understanding of political pragmatism is aided by Charles Anderson's *Pragmatic Liberalism*.

2. John Adams (JA) to Abigail Adams (AA), 1 July 1774, L. H. Butterfield et al. eds., *Adams Family Correspondence*, (hereafter cited as AFC), 1:136.

3. AA to Mercy Otis Warren (MOW), 13 April 1776, AFC 1:377; AA to JA, 11 April 1776, AFC 1:375.

4. James Warren to JA, 27 April 1777, WAL 1:319–20. See also JA to AA, 15 May 1777, AFC 2:238.

5. AA to JA, 22 August 1777, AFC 2:323–24; Norton, *Liberty's Daughters*, 216–17.

6. Ibid.

7. See AA to JA, 17 April 1777, AFC 2:212; and 15 May 1777, AFC 2:238; 23 June 1777, AFC 2:270, and 10 July 1777, AFC 2:279.

8. AA to JA, 9 July 1778, AFC 3:61; AA to JA, 16 January 1780, 3:259; AA

to JA, 23 March 1782, AFC 4:301 (n.b., editor's note 4); Ingraham and Bromfield to AA, 1 July 1782, AFC 4:339.

9. JA to AA, 28 April 1776, AFC 1:400.

10. AA to James Lovell, 13 December 1779, AFC 3:249.

11. A good correspondence takes place between AA and John Thaxter from December 1779 through December 1783.

12. AA to James Lovell, 4 January 1779, AFC 3:148; JA to AA, 28 April 1776, AFC 1:400; JA to Mary Palmer, 5 July 1776, AFC 2:34. See also MOW to AA, 19 January 1779, AFC 3:152; 15 March 1779, AFC 3:190; and 6 July 1779, 3:209. For information about James Warren's public career, see *The Warren-Adams Letters.*

13. AA first writes Lovell 4 January 1779; letters heat up in the months after. See AA to JL, 18–26 June 1779, AFC 3:206; 13 February 1780, AFC 3:273–74; and JL to AA, 9 March 1779, AFC 3:186; and 9 August 1779, AFC 3:219; and 6 January 1780, AFC 3:256.

14. JA to AA, 9 July 1774, AFC 1:135.

15. AA to JA, 22 September 1774, AFC 1: 161–62.

16. AA to JA, 31 March 1776, AFC 1:369.

17. Edith Gelles, *Portia: The World of Abigail Adams*, 1–23.

18. Linda Grant DePauw, "The American Revolution and the Rights of Women," 203; Hoff, *Law, Gender, and Injustice*, 39, 59; and Charles Akers, *Abigail Adams*, 43–44.

19. AA to JA, 31 March 1776, AFC 1:370.

20. JA to AA, 14 April 1776, AFC 1:382.

21. AA to MOW, 27 April 1776, AFC 1:396–98.

22. Ibid.

23. JA to James Sullivan, 26 May 1776, *Letters of Delegates to Congress* (Washington, DC: Government Printing Office, 1979), 4:72–75, quoted in Hoff, *Law, Gender, and Justice*, at 61–62.

24. Ibid., and JA to AA, 14 April 1776, AFC 1:382.

25. There is no record of a response, supportive or critical, from Mrs. Warren to this letter. But there is evidence that Mrs. Warren was thinking along different lines at the same period. Her letter to John Adams of April 1776 is primarily concerned with sustaining a backward-looking republicanism based on the spartan character development of citizens through the virtue of its leaders; Warren's republicanism did not voice the language of liberal rights, or criticize the restrictions of the franchise. See MOW to JA, April 1776, *Mercy Warren Letterbook* (Boston: Massachusetts Historical Society), 162–65.

26. AA to JA, 7 May 1776, AFC, 1:402.

27. JA to AA, 4 August 1776, Butterfield et al., eds., *The Book of Abigail and John*, 149–150; AA to JA, 14 August 1776, AFC 2:94. JA to Abigail Adams 2nd (Nabby), 18 April 1776, AFC 1:388.

28. AA to JA, 27 May 1776, AFC 1:416.

29. AA to JA, 14 August 1776, AFC 2:94.
30. Ibid.
31. JA to AA, 12 August 1776, AFC 2:110.
32. JA to AA, 11 August 1777, AFC 2:306.
33. JA to AA, 25 April 78, AFC 3:17.
34. Ibid.
35. AA to James Thaxter (JT), 15 February 1778, AFC 2:391,92.
36. JT to AA, 6 March 1778, AFC 2:400; AA to JT, 19 August 1778, AFC 3:78.
37. See Hayes, "Mercy Otis Warren," at 620; AA to MOW, 28 February 1780, 1 September 1780, AFC 3:289 and 402; AA to Nathaniel Willis, ante 4 January 1781, AFC 4:58–59.
38. AA to JA, 5 July 1780, AFC 3:372.
39. AA to JA, 25 December 1780, AFC 4:50.
40. Ibid.
41. See, for example, AA to Elbridge Gerry, 13 March 1780, AFC 3:297.
42. Abigail actually found out by accident, receiving a letter intended for Alice Shippen, "Mrs. A," mistakenly delivered to her. See AA to James Lovell, 30 June 1781, and AA to Alice Shippen, on the same date, AFC 4:164–68; quote at 165.
43. James Lovell to AA, 17 July 1781, AFC 4:181; AA to Lovell, 20 July–6 August 1781, AFC 4:184; and AA to Elbridge Gerry, 20 July 1781, AFC 4: 182–83.
44. Lovell to AA, 20 August 1781, AFC 4:195.
45. AA to Lovell, 12 September 1781, AFC 4:210.
46. AA to JA, 10 April 1782, AFC 4:306.
47. Ibid.
48. AA to JA, 17 June 1782, AFC 4:382.
49. AA to JT, 17 June 1782, AFC 4:331.
50. Ibid.
51. See Fordyce, *Sermons*, 1:108, 137, 140, 202, 272–73, 283.
52. AA to JT, 18 July 1782, AFC 4:349.
53. AA to JA, 17–25 March, 25 April, and 18 July 1782, AFC 4:295, 315, 345; JA to AA, 12 October 1782; and to James Warren, 16 October 1782, AFC 5:15–16.
54. AA to JA, 18 July 1782, AFC 4:346–47.
55. AA to Mary Smith Cranch (MC), 9 December 1784, AFC 6:15.
56. See Ryerson et al., eds., *Adams Family Correspondence*, vols. 5 and 6, "Introduction," 5: xxxii–xxxiii; AA to Lucy Cranch, 5 September 1784, AFC 5:438; AA to Mary Smith Cranch, 9 December 1784, AFC 5:16; and 15 April 1785, AFC 6:84.
57. JA to Thomas Jefferson (TJ), 22 May 1785, Lester J. Cappon, ed., *The*

Adams-Jefferson Letters, 1777–1804, 1:21. (*The Adams-Jefferson Letters* hereafter cited as AJL).

58. JA to TJ, 22 May 1785, AJL 1:21.

59. TJ to AA, 27 December 1785, AJL 1:110; see also TJ to AA, 9 August 1786, AJL 1:149.

60. AA to TJ, 29 January 1787, AJL 1:168.

61. Ibid.

62. Ibid.

63. See MOW to JA, 1 June 1784, 27 April 1785, September 1785; James Warren (JW) to JA, 4 September 1785, 6 October 1785, 30 April 1786, WAL2: 238–39, 252–55, 259–62; 262–64, 266–67, 271–73.

64. AA to TJ, 29 January 1787, AJL1:169; TJ to AA, 22 February 1787, AJL1:172.

65. AA to MC, 12 July 1789, Stewart Mitchell, ed., *New Letters of Abigail Adams*, 11–17. The Adamses may not have known that Mercy was the "Columbian Patriot," author of an Antifederalist pamphlet "Observations on the New Constitution and on the Federal and State Conventions." But they were right to connect her with its sentiments; the essay was attributed to Elbridge Gerry, hence Abigail's suspicion that Mercy and Gerry had a constant communication.

66. AA to MC, 9 August 1789, *New Letters*, 19–20.

67. Ibid.

68. AA to MC, 28 April 1790, 9 January 1791; 18 April 1791, 6 May 1791, 18 December 1791, *New Letters*, 48, 70, 72–73, 75.

69. Mrs. Adams reported favorably on the "Creek savages" who visited her daily in August 1790, but by February 1992, had supported the unpopular war with the Indians as necessary. See AA to MC 8 August 1791 and 5 February 1992, *New Letters*, 56, 77.

70. AA to NA, February 1793, quoted in Janet Whitney, *Abigail Adams*, 253.

71. See AA to MC, 3 June 1797, *New Letters*, 93, 94; and AA to MOW, 25 April 1798, WAL 2:337.

72. AA to MC, 5 May 1798, *New Letters*, 127.

73. Quoted in Whitney, *Abigail Adams*, 289.

74. John C. Miller, *The Federalist Era*, 233–34.

75. AA to TJ, 1 July 1804, AJL 1:273.

76. Ibid.

77. TJ to AA, 22 July 1804, AJL 1:275.

78. AA to TJ, 18 August 1804, AJL 1:276.

79. See also their earlier exchange over the injury and legality of Adams's midnight appointments in the federal government, just after John Adams lost the election. TJ to AA, 13 June 1804, AJL 1:269; and AA to TJ, 1 July 1804, AJL 1:272.

80. AA to TJ, 18 August 1804, AJL 1:277.

81. TJ to AA, 11 September 1804, AJL 1:278.

82. See Article II, Section 1, The U.S. Constitution: "Before he enter on the Execution of his Office, he shall take the . . . oath . . . : 'I do solemnly swear . . . that I will faithfully execute the Office of President of the United States, and will to the best of my Ability, preserve, protect and defend the Constitution of the United States."

83. TJ to AA, 11 September 1804, AJL 1:279. The Bill of Rights had not been incorporated to apply to state laws until the twentieth century; thus *states* were under no obligation to make laws restricting the freedom of speech, press, or association.

84. AA to TJ, 25 October 1804, AJL 1:280. It is important to note that this entire correspondence took place privately between Abigail Adams and Thomas Jefferson. John Adams noted on 19 November 1804 that "[t]he whole of this Correspondence was begun and conducted without my Knowledge or Suspicion." See AJL 1:282.

85. AA to MC, 15 November 1997, *New Letters*, 112.

86. AA to John Quincy Adams (JQA), 20 May 1796, quoted in Lynn Withey, *Dearest Friend*, 234; Whitney, *Abigail Adams*, 290.

87. AA to Elizabeth Smith Shaw Peabody, 19 July 1799, quoted in Norton, *Liberty's Daughters*, 250.

88. AA to JA, 7 May 1776, AFC 1:402.

NOTES TO CHAPTER 6

1. Vena Bernadette Field, *Constantia.*

2. See Kerber, *Women of the Republic,* and *Toward an Intellectual History of Women*; Nina Baym, "Introduction," *The Gleaner*; Pauline Schloesser, "A Feminist Interpretation of the American Founding," esp. ch. 6; Kirstin Wilcox, "The Scribblings of a Plain Man; Amelia Howe Kritzer, "Playing with Republican Motherhood"; Sharon M. Harris, Introduction to *Selected Writings*; Sheila Skemp, *Judith Sargent Murray.*

3. Murray, *The Gleaner.*

4. As Nancy Cott reports, in 1930, only 12 percent of U.S. women held jobs outside their homes; and these women were frequently criticized for disrupting and/or abandoning their 'real' vocations as wives and mothers. See Cott, *The Grounding of Modern Feminism.*

5. See Alison M. Jaggar, *Feminist Politics and Human Nature*; Zillah Eisenstein, *The Radical Future of Liberal Feminism.*

6. See Davis, *Women, Race, and Class*; Collins, *Black Feminist Thought*; Denise Riley, *Am I That Name*; Gloria T. Hull, Patricia Bell Scott, and Barbara Smith, eds., *All the Women Are White.*

7. Leo Strauss, *Persecution and the Art of Writing.*

8. Murray, "The Repository. No. 2."

9. See No. LXII, "Spirit Independent of Matter," *The Gleaner* (497); and "The Repository II," *Massachusetts Magazine* (October 1792), 614.

10. Locke, Second Treatise, ch. 2, 6:271; ch. 7, par. 82:321.

11. "Equality of the Sexes," March 1790, at 35.

12. See Mary Astell, *Reflections upon Marriage.*

13. Rousseau, *Emile*, 409.

14. Murray, "The Repository, No. XXV, *Massachusetts Magazine* (October 1794), 595.

15. Ibid., 225.

16. Ibid., 223.

17. Rousseau, *Emile.*

18. Murray, "Desultory Thoughts," at 251.

19. Murray, "On the Equality of the Sexes," at 223.

20. Murray, "Desultory Thoughts," at 252.

21. The same advice is repeated in "Industry, with the independence which it confers, celebrated and illustrated by facts," *Gleaner* XVII, 139.

22. Murray, "On the Equality of the Sexes," at 223.

23. Murray, "Industry," at 139.

24. *Gleaner*, 88, at 703.

25. Ibid., 705.

26. Ibid., 710.

27. *Gleaner*, 89, 711.

28. Ibid., 711–12.

29. *Gleaner*, 88, 706.

30. *Gleaner*, 89, 713.

31. *Gleaner*, 90, 716–17.

32. Ibid., 717.

33. Ibid., 719.

34. *Gleaner*, 88–91; See also Gilbert and Gubar, *Norton Anthology.*

35. *Gleaner*, 91, 727.

36. Ibid., 728.

37. Ibid., 728–29.

38. Ibid., 731.

39. *Gleaner*, 69, 538.

40. Warren, "Observations," 273.

41. *Gleaner*, at 13.

42. Ibid., at 15.

43. Ibid. Perhaps the masculine persona explains the shift; but we must also recognize the political context. Interestingly, Murray's audacity would challenge only the gendered corruption of federalism, not its otherwise healthy core.

By contrast, Warren's admission of the same or similar desire would have placed her into direct conflict with Antifederalist allies, and her neoclassical republican theory. In that political theory, "virtue" demanded that the self always be subordinated to the interests of the community. In keeping with that pre-modern conception of virtue, Warren apologized for writing and publishing. Gingerly, she sought approval from the "liberal-minded," "generous," and "virtuous" part of the community. See Murray, *Gleaner*, Preface to the Reader, 13. Warren, "An Address to the Inhabitants of the United States," in *History*, xliii.

44. "Probable utility of an amicable combination among the sons and daughters of literature," *Gleaner*, 69, at 537.

45. Ibid., 537–38.

46. "From the lyre of Philenia issues the most captivating strains; correct, and highly polished, her deathless page may stand without a rival; but, shall the lowly muse, for this resign those magic powers which give lustre to the eye of grief and sweetly whisper the soothing joys of mild tranquillity? Forbid it, every rich, enobling motive, which swells to emulation. No—rather let the action every glowing energy, each blest incitement, which may allure eminence, and adventurously assay the radiant path, in which the lovely vision, with beamy excellence, so splendidly succeeds." *Gleaner*, 69, at 538.

47. I am indebted to Sheila Skemp, whose paper "A View from Afar: Judith Sargent Murray and the Mississippi Frontier," alerted me as to where to find letters dealing with Murray's views on race. Paper presented at the Third Annual Natchez Conference, February 19, 1998.

48. Judith Sargent Murray to Winthrop Sargent, September 21, 1803, *Letterbook* 12, 879.

49. Judith Sargent Murray to Anna Sargent, October 12, 1799, *Letterbook* 11, 70.

50. Judith Sargent Murray to Winthrop Sargent, May 26, 1804, *Letterbook*, 931. Judith Sargent Murray to Winthrop Sargent, April 29, 1815, *Letterbook* 19, 97.

51. Judith Sargent Murray to Winthrop Sargent, October 5, 1812, *Letterbook* 17, 155–56.

52. On the trustee view of representation among Federalists, and the delegate view among Jeffersonian Democratic-Republicans, see Matthews, *If Men Were Angels*; and James Roger Sharp, *American Politics in the Early Republic: The New Nation in Crisis* (New Haven, CT: Yale University Press, 1993); Lance Banning, *The Jeffersonian Persuasion: Evolution of a Party Ideology* (Ithaca, NY: Cornell University Press, 1978); and Joyce Appleby, *Capitalism and a New Social Order*.

53. Russell Hanson, "'Commons, and 'Commonwealth' at the American Founding: Democratic Republicanism and the New American Hybrid," in *Conceptual Change and the Constitution*, edited by Terence Ball and J.G.A. Pocock, 165–93 (Lawrence: University Press of Kansas, 1988).

54. "Industry, with the Independence which it confers, celebrated and illustrated by facts," *Gleaner*, 27, at 215.

55. Ibid., 216–17.

56. Ibid.

57. *Gleaner*, 87, 696.

58. Ibid., "The acrimony of party spirit lamented—written December 1st, 1796," 695.

59. *Gleaner*, 17, at 134.

60. Ibid., 87, "The acrimony of party spirit lamented—written December 1st, 1796," 695.

61. "On the Equality of the Sexes," MM (April 1790): 224–25.

62. Ibid., 224.

63. Murray's use of the masculine persona (the "Gleaner") was originally intended to shield her from the prejudice of male readers whom she believed were hostile to female productions. Some have argued that the persona allowed Murray the freedom to discuss any topic, including politics, which was considered beyond the bounds of proper femininity. See Nina Baym's "Introduction" to Judith Sargent Murray, *The Gleaner*, i–xx; and Wilcox, "Scribblings."

64. "Observations on Female Abilities," *Gleaner*, 88, at 704.

65. Ibid.

66. Ibid., at 705.

67. Ibid., 91, at 731.

68. On Fame as a cornerstone concept of Federalist Political Theory, see Adair, "Fame and the Founding Fathers," 24; Hanson, *Democratic Imagination*; Diggins, *Lost Soul*.

69. As Carroll Smith-Rosenberg has noted, before and during the Revolution, British North Americans claimed not only a common political heritage and set of legal rights, but also a common "race" and color with their "imperial tyrant," the mother country. See "Discovering."

70. Michael Chandos Brown reports that another female author, Sally Sayward Barrell Wood, praised Murray's *Gleaner* for everything except its radicalism, and turned her own plot on the dangers of women becoming "enlightened." See Brown, "Mary Wollstonecraft," esp. 406–07; Wood, *Julia, and the Illuminated Baron. A Novel: Founded on Recent Facts, which have Transpired in the Course of the Late Revolution in Moral Principles in France. By a lady of Massachusetts* (Portsmouth, NH, 1800). Skemp reports as well that Murray defended Wollstonecraft after she had been attacked in the United States as a loose woman. See *Judith Sargent Murray*, 117–119.

71. See Skemp, "Conclusion," *Judith Sargent Murray*.

72. Jessica Benjamin, *The Bonds of Love*, quote on 61.

NOTES ON CHAPTER 7

1. Sarah Grimke, letter to Angelina Grimke, from *Letters on the Equality of the Sexes and the Condition of Woman. Addressed to Mary S. Parker, President of the Boston female Anti-slavery Society.* Boston, I. Knapp, 1838. Reprinted in Klosko and Klosko, *The Struggle for Women's Rights*, letter 12, quote at 90.

2. Angelina Grimke, Letters to Catherine E. Beecher, Letter 12, 1838, reprinted in Klosko and Klosko, quote at 95.

3. Elizabeth Cady Stanton, "Arguments in Favor of a Sixteenth Amendment," Speech to NAWSA, 1869, reprinted in Klosko and Klosko, at 123.

4. Ibid.

NOTES TO THE EPILOGUE

1. Orlando Patterson, "Race by the Numbers," *New York Times*, 8 May 2001.

2. Eric Schmitt, "Whites in Minority in Largest Cities, the Census Shows," *New York Times*, 30 April 2001.

3. Edward W. Lempinen, "A Fork in the Road for Race, Gender Relations," *San Francisco Chronicle*, 27 October 1996.

4. Sanford Cloud Jr., "Can we Talk? How to Promote Racial Unity," *Newsday*, 5 November 1995, Nassau edition; Richard Price and Jonathan T. Lovitt, "Poll: More Now believe O. J. is guilty," *USA Today*, 4 October 1996, final edition.

5. Martha T. Moore, "Overwhelmingly White Press Corps Is a Trial Silhouette," *USA Today*, 20 December 1996, final edition; Sharon Waxman, "At Long Last, O. J. Simpson under Oath; He Will Testify Today in Court but not on TV," *Washington Post*, 22 November 1996, final edition; Francis X. Clines, "Officer Charged in Killing That Roiled Cincinnati," *New York Times*, 8 May 2001.

6. Simon Barnes, "Venus Williams," *Times* (London), 2 April 2001.

7. Linda Feldmann, "Heirs of Christian Right Push Agenda Harder with GOP," *The Christian Science Monitor*, 18 February 1998; Robert L. Jackson, "Campaign 2000: Bush Asks the Christian Coalition for Support," *Los Angeles Times*, 1 October 2000.

8. Mary Alice Daniels, "Farrakhan Can't Claim Stature on One March," *Kansas City Star*, 4 November 1995, Johnson edition.

Bibliography

Adair, Douglass. "Fame and the Founding Fathers." In *Essays by Douglass Adair*, edited by H. Trevor Colbourn, 3–26. New York: W. W. Norton, 1974.

Adams, Charles, F., ed. *Correspondence between John Adams and Mercy Warren*. New York: Arno Press, 1972.

Akers, Charles W. *Abigail Adams, an American Woman*. Boston: Little, Brown, 1980.

Anderson, Charles W. *Pragmatic Liberalism*. Chicago: University of Chicago Press, 1990.

Anthony, Katharine. *First Lady of the Revolution: The Life of Mercy Otis Warren*. Port Washington, NY: Kennikat Press, 1972.

Appleby, Joyce. "Republicanism in Old and New Contexts." *William and Mary Quarterly* , 3rd ser., 1 (January 1986): 20–34.

———. *Capitalism and a New Social Order: The Republican Vision of the 1790s*. New York: New York University Press, 1984.

———. "The Social Origins of American Revolutionary Ideology." *Journal of American History* 64 (1978): 935–958.

Aristotle. *The Politics*. Trans. by T. A. Sinclair. New York: Penguin Classics, 1992.

Astell, Mary. *Reflections upon Marriage*. London: R. Wilken, 1706.

Bailyn, Bernard. *The Ideological Origins of the American Revolution*. Cambridge: Harvard University Press, 1967.

Ball, Terence, and J.G.A. Pocock, eds. *Conceptual Change and the Constitution*. Lawrence: University Press of Kansas, 1988.

Banning, Lance. "Jeffersonian Ideology Revisited: Liberal and Classical Ideas in the New American Republic." *William and Mary Quarterly*, 3rd ser., 43 (January 1986): 3–19.

———. "Some Second Thoughts on Virtue and the Course of Revolutionary Thinking." In *Conceptual Change and the Constitution*, edited by Terence Ball and J. G. A. Pocock, 194–212. Lawrence: The University Press of Kansas, 1988.

Baym, Nina. Introduction to *The Gleaner: A Miscellany*, by Constantia [Judith Sargent Murray]. Schenectady, NY: Union College Press, 1992.

Benjamin, Jessica. *The Bonds of Love: Psychoanalysis, Feminism, and the Problem of Domination*. New York: Pantheon, 1988.

Bennett, William J. *The Devaluing of America: The Fight for Our Culture and Our children.* Colorado Springs: Focus on the Family Publishing, 1994.

Bethel, Elizabeth Rauh. *The Roots of African-American Identity: Memory and History in Antebellum Free Communities.* New York: St. Martin's Press, 1997.

Bloch, Ruth H. "American Feminine Ideals in Transition: The Rise of the Moral Mother, 1785–1815." *Feminist Studies* 4 (June 1978): 101–26.

———. "The Gendered Meanings of Virtue in Revolutionary America." *Signs* 13 (Autumn 1987): 37–58.

Bonsignore, John J., Ethan Katsh, Peter d'Errico, Ronald M. Pipkin, Stephen Arons, and Janet Rifkin, eds. *Before the Law: An Introduction to the Legal Process.* Boston: Houghton Mifflin, 1989.

Boucher, Jonathan. *A View of Causes and Consequences of the American Revolution; in Thirteen Discourses, Preached in North American between the Years 1763 and 1775; with an Historical Preface.* London, 1797.

Brekus, Catherine A. *Strangers and Pilgrims: Female Preaching in America, 1740–1845.* Chapel Hill: University of North Carolina Press, 1998.

Brown, Judith K. "Economic Organization and the Position of Women Among the Iroquois." *Ethnohistory* 17 (Summer-Fall 1970): 151–67.

Brown, Kathleen M. *Good Wives, Nasty Wenches, and Anxious Patriarchs: Gender, Race, and Power in Colonial Virginia.* Chapel Hill: University of North Carolina Press, 1996.

Brown, Michael Chandos. "Mary Wollstonecraft, or the Female Illuminati: The Campaign Against Women and 'Modern Philosophy' in the Early Republic." *Journal of the Early Republic* 15 (Fall 1995): 389–424.

Butler, Melissa. "Early Liberal Roots of Feminism: John Locke and the Attack on Patriarchy." In *Feminist Interpretations and Political Theory*, edited by Carole Pateman and Mary Lyndon Shanley. University Park: Pennsylvania State University Press, 1991. First published in *The American Political Science Review* 72 (1978): 135–50.

Butterfield, L. H., Marc Friedlaender, and Mary-Jo Kline, eds. *The Book of Abigail and John: Selected Letters of the Adams Family, 1762–1784.* Cambridge: Harvard University Press, 1776.

Butterfield, L. H., Wendell D. Garrett, and Marjorie E. Sprague, eds. *Adams Family Correspondence.* Cambridge: Harvard University Press, 1963.

Cappon, Lester J., ed. *The Adams-Jefferson Letters: The Complete Correspondence between Thomas Jefferson and Abigail and John Adams.* 2 vols. Chapel Hill: The University of North Carolina Press, 1959.

Carey, Matthew, ed. *The American Museum,* or *Universal Magazine.* Philadelphia, 1787–1789.

Chadwyck-Healey, Ltd. *The English Poetry Full-Text Database,* 1995. Alexandria, VA, and Cambridge, England. Accessed by author at the Wilson Library, University of Minnesota, Twin Cities, 1998.

Chambers Dalton, Karen C. "'The Alphabet Is an Abolitionist': Literacy and African Americans in the Emancipation Era." *The Massachusetts Review* (Winter 1991): 545–80.

Cohen, Lester H. "Explaining the Revolution: Ideology and Ethics in Mercy Otis Warren's Historical Theory." *William and Mary Quarterly*, 3rd ser., 37 (1980): 200–18.

———. "Mercy Otis Warren: The Politics of Language and the Aesthetics of Self." *American Quarterly* 5 (Winter 1983): 481–98.

Collins, Patricia Hill. *Black Feminist Thought: Knowledge, Consciousness, and the Politics of Empowerment.* Cambridge, MA: Unwin Hyman, 1990.

Constantia [Judith Sargent Murray]. "Desultory Thoughts upon the Utility of Encouraging a Degree of Self-Complacency, Especially in Female Bosoms." *The Gentleman and Lady's Town and Country Magazine* (October 1784): 251–53.

———. "On the Equality of the Sexes." *The Massachusetts Magazine* (March and April 1790): 132–35 and 223–26.

———. "On the Domestic Education of Children." *Massachusetts Magazine* (May 1790): 275–77.

———. "The Repository, No. 2." *Massachusetts Magazine* (October 1792): 614–15.

———. "The Repository, No. 25." *The Massachusetts Magazine* (October 1794): 595.

———. *The Gleaner: A Miscellany.* Boston: I. Thomas and E. T. Andrews, 1798. Reprinted with an introduction by Nina Baym. Schenectady, NY: Union College Press, 1992.

Cott, Nancy F. *Public Vows: A History of Marriage and the Nation.* Cambridge: Harvard University Press, 2000.

———. "Divorce and the Changing Status of Women in Eighteenth-Century Massachusetts." *William and Mary Quarterly*, 3rd ser., 33 (October 1976): 586–614.

———. *The Bonds of Womanhood: "Woman's Sphere" in New England, 1780–1835.* New Haven, CT: Yale University Press, 1977.

———. *The Grounding of Modern Feminism.* New Haven, CT: Yale University Press, 1987.

Count, Earl, ed. *This Is Race: An Anthology Selected from the International Literature on the Races of Man.* New York: Henry Schuman, 1950.

Crane, Elizabeth. "Dependence in the Era of Independence." In *The American Revolution: Its Character and Limits*, edited by Jack P. Greene. New York: New York University Press, 1987.

Davis, Angela. *Women, Race, and Class.* New York: Vintage, 1984.

De Pauw, Linda Grant. "The American Revolution and the Rights of Women: The Feminist Theory of Abigail Adams." In *The Legacy of the American Revolu-*

tion. Edited by Larry Gerlach et al., 199–219. Logan: Utah State University Press, 1978.

———. "Women in Combat: The Revolutionary War Experience." *Armed Forces and Society,* 7 (Winter 1981): 209–26.

Deyle, Steven. "The Irony of Liberty: Origins of the Domestic Slave Trade." *Journal of the Early Republic* 12 (Spring 1992): 37–62.

Diggins, John Patrick. *The Lost Soul of American Politics: Virtue, Self-Interest, and the Foundations of Liberalism.* Chicago: University of Chicago Press, 1984.

Ditz, Toby. "Ownership and Obligation: Inheritance and Patriarchal Households in Connecticut, 1750–1820." *William and Mary Quarterly,* 3rd ser., 47 (April 1990): 235–65.

Dowd, Gregory Evans. "Declarations of Dependence: War and Inequality in Revolutionary New Jersey, 1776–1815." *New Jersey History* 103 (1985): 47–67.

Eisenstein, Zillah. *The Radical Future of Liberal Feminism.* New York: Longman, 1981.

Eze, Emmanuel. "The Color of Reason: The Idea of 'Race' in Kant's Anthropology." In *Anthropology and the German Enlightenment: Perspectives on Humanity,* edited by Katherine Faull, 196–237. Lewisburg, PA: Bucknell University Press, 1995.

Ferguson, Ann L. "The Plays of Judith Sargent Murray." Master's Thesis, Indiana University, 1982.

Field, Vena Bernadette. *Constantia: A Study of the Life and Works of Judith Sargent Murray, 1751–1820.* Orono, ME: University Press, 1931.

Filmer, Sir Robert. *Patriarcha and Other Political Works of Sir Robert Filmer.* Edited with an Introduction by Peter Laslett. Oxford: Basil Blackwell, 1949.

Fleming, Marie. *Emancipation and Illusion.* University Park: Pennsylvania State University Press, 1997.

Fordyce, James, D.D. *Sermons to Young Women,* 2 vols. London: A. Millar and T. Cadell in the Strand, J. Dodsley in Pall-Mall, and J. Payne in Pater-Noster Row, 1766. Text-fiche.

Foucault, Michel. *Power/Knowledge: Selected Interviews and Other Writings, 1972–1977.* Edited by Colin Gordin. New York: Pantheon, 1980.

Fowler, David H. *Northern Attitudes Towards Interracial Marriage: Legislation and Public Opinion in the Middle Atlantic States of the Old Northwest, 1780–1930.* New York: Garland, 1987.

Franklin, Benjamin V. *The Plays and Poems of Mercy Otis Warren: Facsimile Reproductions Compiled and with an Introduction by Benjamin Franklin V.* Delmar, NY: Scholars' Facsimiles and Reprints, 1980.

Friedman, Lawrence, and Arthur H. Shaffer. "Mercy Otis Warren and the Politics of Historical Nationalism." *The New England Quarterly* 48 (1975): 194–215.

Gelles, Edith. *Portia: The World of Abigail Adams.* Bloomington: Indiana University Press, 1992.

The Gentleman and Lady's Town and Country Magazine, or Repository of Instruction and Entertainment. Printed by Weedon and Barnett. Boston, 1784–85.

Gilbert, Sandra and Susan Gubar. *The Madwoman in the Attic.* New Haven, CT: Yale University Press, 1984.

———. *The Norton Anthology of Literature by Women: The Traditions in English.* New York: W. W. Norton, 1996.

Gilligan, Carol. *In a Different Voice: Psychological Theory and Women's Development.* Cambridge: Harvard University Press, 1982.

Gilroy, Paul. *The Black Atlantic: Modernity and Double-Consciousness.* Cambridge: Harvard University Press, 1993.

Gingrich, Newt. *To Renew America.* New York: HarperCollins, 1995.

Green, Gretchen. "Molly Brant, Catharine Brant, and Their Daughters: A Study in Colonial Acculturation." *Ontario History* 81 (September 1989): 235–50.

Gundersen, Joan R. "Independence, Citizenship, and the American Revolution." *Signs* 13 (Autumn 1987): 59–77.

Habermas, Jurgen. *The Theory of Communicative Action, Vol.1: Reason and the Rationalization of Society.* Trans. by Thomas McCarthy. Boston: Beacon Press, 1984.

———. *The Structural Transformation of the Public Sphere: An Inquiry into a Category of Bourgeois Society.* Trans. by Thomas Burger. Cambridge, MA: MIT Press, 1991.

Hamilton, Alexander, James Madison, and John Jay. *The Federalist.* New York: Modern Library, 1941.

Hanson, Russell L. *The Democratic Imagination in America: Conversations with Our Past.* Princeton, NJ: Princeton University Press, 1985.

Harris, Sharon M. Introduction to *Selected Writings of Judith Sargent Murray.* Ed. by Sharon M. Harris. New York: Oxford University Press, 1995.

Hartz, Louis. *The Liberal Tradition in America.* New York: Harcourt, Brace, Jovanovich, 1955.

Hayes, Edmund. "The Private Poems of Mercy Otis Warren." *The New England Quarterly* 54 (1981): 199–224.

———, ed. "Mercy Otis Warren versus Lord Chesterfield (1779)." *William and Mary Quarterly* 3rd Ser., 40 (October 1983): 616–21.

Herndon, Ruth Wallis. "Research Note: Literacy Among New England's Transient Poor, 1750–1800." *Journal of Social History* 29 (Summer 1996): 963–65.

Hewitt, Nancy A. "Beyond the Search for Sisterhood: American Women's History in the 1980s." *Social History* 10 (October 1985): 299–321.

Hodges, Graham Russell. *Slavery and Freedom in the Rural North: African Americans in Monmouth County, New Jersey, 1665–1865.* Madison, WI: Madison House, 1997.

Hoff, Joan. *Law, Gender, and Injustice: A Legal History of U.S. Women.* New York: New York University Press, 1991.

Hoffmann, Ronald, and Peter J. Albert. *Women in the Age of the American Revolution.* Charlottesville: University Press of Virginia, 1989.

Hoff-Wilson, Joan. "The Illusion of Change: Women and the American Revolution." In *The American Revolution: Explorations in the History of American Radicalism*, edited by Alfred Young, 383–445. DeKalb: Northern Illinois University Press, 1976.

Horton, James Oliver, and Lois E. Horton. *In Hope of Liberty: Culture, Community, and Protest Among Northern Free Blacks, 1700–1860.* New York: Oxford University Press, 1997.

Hull, Gloria T., Patricia Bell Scott, and Barbara Smith, eds. *All the Women Are White, All the Blacks Are Men, But Some of Us Are Brave.* New York: The Feminist Press, 1982.

Hurston, Zora Neale. "How It Feels to Be Colored Me." In *I Love Myself When I Am Laughing*, edited by Alice Walker. New York: The Feminist Press, 1979.

Hutcheson, Maud Macdonald. "Mercy Warren, 1728–1814." *William and Mary Quarterly*, 3rd Ser. 10 (July 1953): 378–402.

Jaggar, Alison M. *Feminist Politics and Human Nature.* Totowa, NJ: Rowman and Littlefield, 1983.

Jefferson, Thomas. *The Papers of Thomas Jefferson.* Ed. by Julian P. Boyd. Princeton, NJ: Princeton University Press, 1958.

———. *Notes on the State of Virginia.* In *The Portable Jefferson*, edited by Merrill D. Peterson. New York: Penguin, 1975.

Jordan, Winthrop. *White over Black: American Attitudes Toward the Negro, 1550–1812.* Chapel Hill: University of North Carolina Press, 1968.

Kann, Mark. *A Republic of Men: Gender and Patriarchal Politics in the Early Republic.* New York: New York University Press, 1998.

Kaplan, Sidney, and Emma Nogrady Kaplan. *The Black Presence in the Era of the American Revolution.* Amherst: University of Massachusetts Press, 1989.

Kelley, Mary. "Reading Women/Women Reading: The Making of Learned Women in Antebellum America." *Journal of American History* 82 (September 1996): 401–24.

Kelly, Joan. *Women, History, and Theory: The Essays of Joan Kelly.* Chicago: University of Chicago Press, 1984.

Kerber, Linda K. "Daughters of Columbia: Educating Women for the Republic, 1787–1804." In *The Hofsteadter Aegis*, edited by Stanley Elkins and Eric McKitrick, 36–59. New York: Knopf, 1974.

———. "The Republican Ideology of the Revolutionary Generation." *American Quarterly* 37 (1985): 474–95.

———. *Women of the Republic: Intellect and Ideology in Revolutionary America.* New York: W. W. Norton, 1986.

———. "Separate Spheres, Female Worlds, Woman's Place: The Rhetoric of Women's History." *Journal of American History* 75 (June 1988): 9–39.

———. "The Paradox of Women's Citizenship in the Early Republic: The Case of *Martin vs. Massachusetts*, 1805." *American Historical Review* 97 (April 1992): 349–78.

———. *Toward an Intellectual History of Women: Essays by Linda K. Kerber.* Chapel Hill: University of North Carolina Press, 1997.

Kettner, James. *The Development of American Citizenship, 1608–1870.* Chapel Hill: University of North Carolina Press, 1978.

Klinghoffer, Judith Apter, and Lois Elkis. "'The Petticoat Electors': Women's Suffrage in New Jersey, 1776–1807." *Journal of the Early Republic* 12 (Summer 1992): 159–93.

Klosko, George, and Margaret G. Klosko, eds. *The Struggle for Women's Rights: Theoretical and Historical Sources.* Upper Saddle River, NJ: Prentice Hall, 1999.

Kramnick, Isaac. *Republicanism and Bourgeois Radicalism: Political Ideology in Late Eighteenth-Century England and America.* Ithaca, NY: Cornell University Press, 1990.

Kritzer, Amelia Howe. "Playing with Republican Motherhood: Self-Representation in Plays by Susanna Haswell Rowson and Judith Sargent Murray." *Early American Literature* 31 (Fall 1996): 150–66.

The Lady and Gentleman's Pocket Magazine of Literary and Polite Amusement. Printed by J. Tiebout for J. Lyon and Company. New York, 1796.

The Lady's Magazine and Musical Repository. Printed by G. and R. Waite for N. Bell. New York, 1801–1802.

The Ladies Magazine. W. Gibbons, proprietor. Philadelphia, 1792–93.

Lange, Lynda. "Rousseau and Modern Feminism." In *Feminist Interpretations and Political Theory*, edited by Carole Pateman and Mary Lyndon Shanley. University Park: Pennsylvania State University Press, 1991. Originally published in *Social Theory and Practice* 7 (1981): 245–77.

Levin, Phyllis Lee. *Abigail Adams: A Biography.* New York: St. Martin's Press, 1987.

Lewis, Jan. "The Republican Wife: Virtue and Seduction in the Early Republic." *William and Mary Quarterly*, 3rd ser., 44 (October 1987): 689–721.

Lindgren, J. Ralph and Nadine Taub. *The Law of Sex Discrimination.* St. Paul, MN: West Publishing, 1988.

Litwack, Leon, "The Federal Government and the Free Negro, 1790–1860." *Journal of Negro History* 63 (October 1958): 261–78.

Locke, John. *Two Treatises of Government.* Ed. by Peter Laslett. Student ed. New York: Cambridge University Press, 1988.

Lockridge, Kenneth. *Literacy in Colonial New England: An Enquiry into the Social Context of Literacy in the Early Modern West.* New York: W. W. Norton, 1974.

Lyons, Oren, et al., 1992. *Exiled in the Land of the Free: Democracy, Indian Nations, and the U.S. Constitution.* Santa Fe: Clear Light Publishing.

Massachusetts Magazine. Printed by I. Thomas and E. T. Andrews. Boston, 1792–1794.

Matthews, Richard K. *If Men Were Angels: James Madison and the Heartless Empire of Reason.* Lawrence: University Press of Kansas, 1995.

Miller, John Chester. *The Federalist Era, 1789–1801.* New York: Harper and Brothers, 1960.

———. *The Wolf by the Ears.* New York: The Free Press, 1977.

Mills, Charles W. *The Racial Contract.* Ithaca, NY: Cornell University Press, 1997.

Milton, John. *Paradise Lost.* In *The Norton Anthology of English Literature,* 6th ed. Ed. by M. H. Abrams, et al. New York: W. W. Norton, 1993.

Mitchell, Stewart, ed. *New Letters of Abigail Adams, 1788–1801.* Boston: Houghton Mifflin, 1947.

Murray, Judith Sargent. See Constantia, above.

———. Judith Sargent Murray Papers. Jackson: Mississippi Department of Archives and History.

Nash, Gary. *Red, White, and Black: The Peoples of Early America.* Englewood Cliffs, NJ: Prentice Hall, 1974.

———. *Forging Freedom: The Formation of Philadelphia's Black Community, 1720–1840.* Cambridge: Harvard University Press, 1988.

———. *Race and Revolution.* Madison, WI: Madison House, 1991.

Nash, Margaret A. "Rethinking Republican Motherhood: Benjamin Rush and the Young Ladies Academy of Philadelphia." *Journal of the Early Republic* 17 (Summer 1997): 171–91.

Nisbet, Richard. *Slavery Not Forbidden by Scripture.* Philadelphia, 1773.

The New York Magazine, or Literary Repository. Printed by Thomas and James Swords. New York, 1790–97.

Norton, Mary Beth. *Liberty's Daughters: The Revolutionary Experience of American Women, 1750–1800.* Boston: Little, Brown, 1980.

———. "The Evolution of White Women's Experience in Early America." *American Historical Review* 89 (June 1984): 65–91.

Olson, Mancur. *The Logic of Collective Action.* Cambridge: Harvard University Press, 1965.

Otis James. *The Rights of the British Colonists Asserted and Proved.* Boston: Edes and Gill, 1764. Reprint in *Pamphlets of the American Revolution, 1750–1776,* Vol. 1, edited by Bernard Bailyn and Jane N. Garrett, 419–70. Cambridge: Harvard University Press, 1965.

Paine, Thomas. "An Occasional Letter on the Female Sex." *Pennsylvania Magazine* (1 August 1775): 362–64. Text-fiche.

Palmer, Beverly Wilson. "Abigail Adams and the Apple of Europe." *New England Historical and Genealogical Register* 135 (April 1981): 109–120.

Pangle, Lorraine Smith, and Thomas Pangle. *The Learning of Liberty: the Educational Ideas of the American Founders*. Lawrence: University Press of Kansas, 1993.

Pangle, Thomas. *The Spirit of Modern Republicanism*. Chicago: University of Chicago Press, 1988.

Pateman, Carole. *The Sexual Contract*. Stanford, CA: Stanford University Press, 1988.

———. *The Disorder of Women: Democracy, Feminism, and Political Theory*. Stanford, CA: Stanford University Press, 1989.

———. "Equality, Difference, and Subordination: The Politics of Motherhood and Women's Citizenship." In *Beyond Equality and Difference*. Ed. by S. James and Gisela Bock. London: Routledge and Kegan Paul, 1992.

Pateman, Carole, and Mary Lyndon Shanley, eds. Feminist Interpretations and Political Theory. University Park: The Pennsylvania State University Press, 1991.

Pellegrini, Ann. *Performance Anxieties: Staging Psychoanalysis, Staging Race*. New York: Routledge, 1997.

Perlmann, Joel, and Dennis Shirley. "When Did New England Women Acquire Literacy?" *William and Mary Quarterly*, 3rd ser., 48 (January 1991): 50–67.

Perlmann, Joel, Silvana R. Sidddali, and Keith Whitescarver. "Literacy, Schooling, and Teaching among New England Women, 1730–1820." *History of Education Quarterly* 37 (Summer 1997): 117–39.

Plato. *The Republic*. Trans. by G.M.A. Grube. Indianapolis: Hackett, 1992.

Pocock, J. G. A. *The Machiavellian Moment: Florentine Political Thought and the Atlantic Republican Tradition*. Princeton, NJ: Princeton University Press, 1975.

Pope, Alexander. "Epistle 2, To a Lady: Of the Characters of Women." In *The Norton Anthology of English Literature*, 6th ed., Vol. 1, edited by M. H. Abrams, et al. New York: W. W. Norton, 1993.

Reiss, Hans, ed. *Kant: Political Writings*. New York: Cambridge University Press, 1991.

Reiss, Oscar. *Blacks in Colonial America*. Jefferson, NC: McFarland and Company, 1997.

Richards, Jeffrey. *Mercy Otis Warren*. New York: Twayne Publishers, 1995.

Riley, Denise. *"Am I That Name?" Feminism and the Category of 'Woman.'* Minneapolis: University of Minnesota Press, 1993.

Robbins, Caroline. *The Eighteenth-Century Commonwealthman: Studies in the Transmission, Development and Circumstance of English Liberal Thought from the Restoration of Charles II until the War with the Thirteen Colonies*. Cambridge: Harvard University Press, 1968.

Rousseau, Jean-Jacques. *Emile, or On Education*. Trans. by Allan Bloom. New York: Basic Books, 1979.

——. *Discourse on the Origin and Foundations of Inequality Among Men*. In *Rousseau's Political Writings*. Ed. Alan Ritter and Julia Conaway Bondanella. New York: W. W. Norton, 1988.

——. On Social Contract. In *Rousseau's Political Writings*, Ed. by Alan Ritter and Julia Conaway Bondanella. Trans. by Julia Conaway Bondanella. New York: W. W. Norton, 1988.

Rush, Benjamin. "Thoughts upon Female Education, Accommodated to the Present State of Society, Manners, and Government in the United States of America." Boston, 1787. Reprinted in *Essays on Education in the Early Republic*, edited by Frederick Rudolph, 1–24. Cambridge: The Belknap Press of Harvard University Press, 1965.

Ryerson, Richard Alan, Joanna M. Revelas, Celester Walker, Gregg L. Lint, and Humphrey J. Costello, eds. *Adams Family Correspondence*. 2 vols. Cambridge: Harvard University Press, 1993.

Salmon, Marylynn. "Life, Liberty, and Dower: The Legal Status of Women After the American Revolution." In *Women, War, and Revolution*. Ed. by Carol R. Berkin and Clara M. Lovett. New York: Holmes and Meier, 1980.

——. *Women and the Law of Property in Early America*. Chapel Hill: University of North Carolina Press, 1986.

Sandler, Todd, ed. *Collective Action*. Ann Arbor: University of Michigan Press, 1992.

Sapp, Vicki J. "The Philosopher's Seduction: Hume and the Fair Sex." *Philosophy and Literature* 19 (April 1995): 1–15.

Schloesser, Pauline. "Negotiating the Boundaries of Federalism and Feminism: The Political Thought of Judith Sargent Murray." Paper presented at the annual meeting of the Midwest Political Science Association, April 1993.

——. "From Woman Citizenship to Separate Spheres: The Changing Political Identities of Abigail Smith Adams." Paper presented at the annual meeting of the American Political Science Association, Washington, DC, September 1993.

——. "A Feminist Interpretation of the American Founding." Ph.D. dissertation, Indiana University–Bloomington, 1994.

——. "The Fair Sex: Civilizing Non-Citizens in Post-Revolutionary America." Paper presented at the annual meeting of the American Political Science Association, Boston, MA, September 1998.

——. "Lamenting the Loss of a Woman-Centered Polity: Mercy Warren's Critique of the U.S. Constitution." *Southeastern Political Review* 26 (September 1998): 545–69.

——. "Toward a Theory of Racial Patriarchy." Paper presented at the annual meeting of the Western Political Science Association, March 2000.

Schochet, Gordon. *Patriarchalism in Political Thought: The Authoritarian Fam-*

ily and Political Speculation and Attitudes Especially in Seventeenth-Century England. Oxford: Basil Blackwell, 1975.

Scott, Joan. *Gender and the Politics of History.* New York: Columbia University Press, 1988.

Shalhope, Robert. "Republicanism and Early American Historiography." *William and Mary Quarterly,* 3rd ser., 39 (April 1982): 334–56.

Shammas, Carole. "Anglo-American Household Government in Comparative Perspective." *William and Mary Quarterly,* 3rd ser., 52 (January 1995): 104–44.

Shoemaker, Nancy. "The Rise or Fall Iroquois Women." *Journal of Women's History* 2 (Winter 1999): 39–57.

Skemp, Sheila. *Judith Sargent Murray: A Brief Biography with Documents.* New York: Bedford Books, 1998.

Smith, Adam. *The Wealth of Nations.* 1776. Reprint, New York: Random House, 1937.

Smith, Rogers. *Civic Ideals: Conflicting Visions of Citizenship in U.S. History.* New Haven, CT: Yale University Press, 1997.

Smith-Rosenberg, Carroll. *Disorderly Conduct: Visions of Gender in Victorian America.* New York: Knopf, 1985.

———. "Discovering the Subject of the 'Great Constitutional Discussion.'" *Journal of American History* (December 1992): 841–73.

Storing, Herbert, ed. *The Antifederalist: Writings by the Opponents of the Constitution. Selections Chosen by Murray Dry.* Chicago: University of Chicago Press, 1985.

Stout, Harry. *The New England Soul.* New York: Oxford University Press, 1986.

Strauss, Leo. *Persecution and the Art of Writing.* Glencoe, IL: The Free Press, 1952.

Szatmary, David. *Shays's Rebellion: The Making of an Agrarian Insurrection.* Amherst: University of Massachusetts Press, 1980.

Tocqueville, Alexis. *Democracy in America.* Edited and abridged by Richard Heffner. New York: New American Library, 1956.

Ulrich, Laurel Thatcher. *Good Wives: Image and Reality in the Lives of Northern New England Women, 1650–1750.* New York: Oxford University Press, 1982.

Warren-Adams Letters, Being Chiefly a Correspondence Among John Adams, Samuel Adams, and James Warren. 2 vols. Boston: Massachusetts Historical Society, 1917.

Warren, Mercy Otis. *History of the Rise, Progress, and Termination of the American Revolution.* Boston, 1805. Reprint edited by Lester Cohen with Foreword and editorial additions. Indianapolis: Liberty Fund, 1988.

———. "Observations on the New Constitution, And on the Federal and State Conventions. By A Columbian Patriot, 1788." In *The Complete Antifederalist,*

Vol. 4, edited by Herbert F. Storing, 270–87. Chicago: University of Chicago Press, 1981.

Warren, Mercy Otis. The Mercy Otis Warren Papers. Massachusetts Historical Society. Boston, Massachusetts. Text-fiche.

Watson, Marsha. "A Classic Case: Phillis Wheatley and Her Poetry." *Early American Literature* 31 (May 1996): 103–27.

Weales, Gerald. "The Quality of Mercy, or Mrs. Warren's Profession." The Georgia Review 33, no. 4 (1979): 881–94.

Webster, Noah. "On the Education of Youth in America." Boston, 1790. Reprinted in *Essays on Education in the Early Republic*, edited by Frederick Rudolph, 41–78. Cambridge: Harvard University Press, 1965.

Welchman, Jennifer. "Locke on Slavery and Inalienable Rights." *Canadian Journal of Philosophy* 25 (1995): 67–81.

Wellman, Judith. "Women's Rights, Republicanism, and Revolutionary Rhetoric in Antebellum New York State." *New York History* (July 1988): 353–84.

Wesley, Charles. "Negro Suffrage in the Period of Constitution-Making, 1787–1865." *Journal of Negro History* 32 (April 1947): 143–68.

White, Shane. *Somewhat More Independent: The End of Slavery in New York City, 1770–1810*. Athens: University of Georgia Press, 1990.

———. "'It Was a Proud Day': African Americans, Festivals, and Parades in the North, 1741–1834." *Journal of American History* 81 (June 1994): 13–50.

Whitney, Janet. *Abigail Adams*. Boston: Little, Brown, 1947.

Wilcox, Kirstin. "The Scribblings of a Plain Man and the Temerity of a Woman: Gender and Genre in Judith Sargent Murray's *The Gleaner*." *Early American Literature* 30 (1995): 121–44.

Withey, Lynn. *Dearest Friend, A Life of Abigail Adams*. New York: Free Press, Macmillan, 1981.

Wood, Gordon S. *The Creation of the American Republic, 1776–1787*. New York: W. W. Norton, 1972.

———. *The Radicalism of the American Revolution*. New York: Vintage, 1993.

Young, Iris. *Justice and the Politics of Difference*. Princeton, NJ: Princeton University Press, 1989.

Zaggari, Rosemarie. "Morals, Manners, and the Republican Mother." *American Quarterly* 44 (June 1992): 192–215.

———. "The Rights of Man and Woman in Post-Revolutionary America," *William and Mary Quarterly*, 3rd ser., 55 (April 1998): 203–220.

Zilversmit, Arthur. *The First Emancipation: The Abolition of Slavery in the North*. Chicago: University of Chicago Press, 1967.

Index

About the Author

Pauline Schloesser received a Ph.D. from Indiana University in 1994, specializing in political theory, women's studies, and American politics. She has taught at Indiana University, DePauw University, and Iowa State University. Currently she serves as Associate Professor of Political Science at Texas Southern University.